UNPREPA
TO DIE

AMERICA'S GREATEST
MURDER BALLADS
AND THE TRUE CRIME STORIES
THAT INSPIRED THEM

First published in Great Britain in 2015
by Soundcheck Books LLP,
88 Northchurch Road, London, N1 3NY.

Copyright © Paul Slade 2015
ISBN: 978-0-9929480-7-8

A CIP record for this book is available from the British Library

Book design: Benn Linfield (www.bennlinfield.com)
Printed by: Bell & Bain Ltd, Glasgow

Front Cover Credits
Laura Foster: Karen Reynolds
Nick Cave: Stuart Wilson/Getty
Gillian Welch: furtwangl
Bob Dylan: Everett Collection Historical/Alamy
Louvin Brothers: Country Music Hall Of Fame/Getty

UNPREPARED TO DIE

AMERICA'S GREATEST
MURDER BALLADS
AND THE TRUE CRIME STORIES
THAT INSPIRED THEM

BY
PAUL SLADE

soundcheck books
the stories behind the sounds

For my parents.

"Almapa."

Contents

Introduction

*"Murder ballads are just part of the American repertoire.
It's human nature to obsess over the things that frighten us."*
Anna Domino, Snakefarm.

*"Once you get past the macabre side of things that sucks
some people in – 'It's a song about a guy that offed his family,
man!' – then you get into whatever the strange truth of the song is."*
Dave Alvin.

I blame Jon Langford.
It was his 2002 all-star compilation *The Executioner's Last Songs*
which first got me interested in murder ballads, and I've been obsessed
with the damn things ever since. Langford, a founder member of
1970s UK punk legends The Mekons, has been working with Chicago's
Bloodshot Records ever since moving to the city in 1991. Spurred
on by Steve Earle, he organised *The Executioner's Last Songs* project
to help fund a group calling for the abolition of the death penalty
in Illinois. The idea, he told me, was "to use death songs against the
death penalty" – and that meant including as many of America's
classic murder ballads as possible.

The list of artists Langford recruited for this magnificent album is a
who's who of Bloodshot's trademark "insurgent country" sound. The
disc includes Steve Earle's own version of "Tom Dooley"; "Knoxville
Girl" performed by The Handsome Family's Brett Sparks; Neko Case
singing "Poor Ellen Smith", and a dozen more tracks beside. I was hooked
from the day I bought it, and the more I listened to these songs, the
more fascinated I became by the questions they prompted. Was Earle's

terrifying Tom Dooley really the same man I'd heard The Kingston Trio warbling about back in the 1960s? What made the Knoxville Girl's companion fly so suddenly into that inexplicable rage? And why did so many of the guys in these songs seem incapable of distinguishing between true love and homicide?

Fast forward now to November 2003, and to the legendary San Francisco bookstore City Lights. I was mooching around in the basement's music section there one afternoon when I stumbled on a copy of Cecil Brown's book *Stagolee Shot Billy*, an investigation of the real 1895 St Louis killing which inspired Stagger Lee's ballad. Brown's book showed me that many of the crimes inspiring these songs were recent enough to research in the newspaper archives – a thought which had never occurred to me before. I'd been a jobbing journalist for over 20 years by that point, so I could see very clearly how he'd gone about putting the book together. Somewhere at the back of my brain, a rusty cog creaked into motion.

I began collecting other books on murder ballads too, some tackling just a single song, others aiming for an overview of the whole genre. The trouble was that most of these fell into one of two equally disappointing categories. On the one hand, there were the books produced by academics. These were carefully researched and reliable enough, but written in such a dry style that they drained all life from the subject. It's not easy to make a tale of chart-topping music and sadistic murder seem tedious, but these lads somehow managed it.

The second pile of books I was accumulating were written by rock journalists. You couldn't fault the lively style of these volumes, but the problem was you couldn't believe a word they said either. Almost all of them blithely mixed the facts about their chosen cases with any old bit of rumour or urban myth they happened to like the sound of. By abandoning any attempt to distinguish truth from fiction, they ensured they produced an entertaining read – but I wanted something that got its facts right too.

The wheels in my head were spinning faster now. If I couldn't find the books I wanted to read about murder ballads, then punk's DIY ethos dictated I must write them myself. I had enough passion for the subject to put in the necessary hours, I had the journalistic experience to combine proper research with a readable style, and – thanks to the internet – I had a platform to get all this stuff out there. If I wasn't the right guy to do this, then who was?

So I launched a website. PlanetSlade made its debut in 2009, with my murder ballads essays leading the site's content. The breakthrough had come when I realised that the way to write these essays was to intertwine the story of the murder itself with the story of its ballad's development and changing treatment down the years. Both elements – the true crime story and the song it inspired – had to be given equal weight, and allowed to converse with each other as the essay wound on.

I knew also that each piece must be allowed to stretch out to its natural length – something which pretty well ruled out pitching them as magazine articles. There was no point in researching a song's inspiration and history as fully as I'd begun to do if I then had to leave out half the most interesting material just to keep the length down. Each essay, I decided, would be a one-stop shop, offering all you needed to know about that particular song. The word count could look after itself.

Whenever the opportunity for a trip to the US arose, I used it to explore these songs' home cities. While others endured weeks on a sunny beach, I was visiting the murder scenes, searching through old paper court transcripts or interviewing local historians. PlanetSlade began to build a following on both sides of the Atlantic. I started to hear from all sorts of people who clearly found these songs just as fascinating as I did, and most were quick to say how much they liked my approach to covering them. The site's traffic figures climbed from a meagre 18,000 visits in its first year to nearly ten times that number in 2014. "This needs to be a book," I thought.

And now it is one. When you've completed the eight chapters here, my bet is that you'll have fallen just as firmly under these songs' spell as I did back in 2002. Soon, you'll find yourself compelled to start telling your friends all about them and – if my own experience is anything to go by – you'll get a fair few wary glances in reply. But don't blame me for that. Oh no.

Blame Jon Langford.

A great many people helped with the research and presentation of this book, and with the website that preceded it. I'm not going to name names as I'd be sure to forget someone, but I do want to thank all the authors, librarians, musicians, researchers, collectors, historians, publishers, editors, illustrators, readers, letter writers, radio producers, photographers, tour guides, DJs, journalists, drivers, songwriters, music fans, programmers, friends, bloggers and drinking companions who helped make both projects possible. You all know who you are, and if I can ever return the favour you have only to ask.

1 - Stagger Lee

*"William Lyons, 25, colored, a levee hand, living at 1410 Morgan Street,
was shot in the abdomen yesterday evening at 10 o'clock in the saloon of
Bill Curtis, at Eleventh and Morgan streets, by Lee Sheldon,
also colored. Both parties, it seems, had been drinking and
were feeling in exuberant spirits.*
*"Lyons and Sheldon were friends and were talking together.
The discussion drifted to politics, and an argument was started, the
conclusion of which was that Lyons snatched Sheldon's hat from his head.
The latter indignantly demanded its return. Lyons refused, and Sheldon
drew his revolver and shot Lyons in the abdomen [...] When his victim
fell to the floor Sheldon took his hat from the hand of the wounded man
and coolly walked away."*
St Louis Globe-Democrat, 26 December 1895.

There were four other murders that Christmas night in St Louis, but this was the one that counted.

Work songs, field chants and folktales describing how Lee "Stack Lee" Shelton killed Billy Lyons started to spring up almost immediately. The earliest written lyrics we have date back to 1903, and the first discs to 1923. There have been over 400 versions of Stack's story released on record since then, giving him a list of biographers which includes some of the biggest names in popular music. Duke Ellington, Fats Domino, Jerry Lee Lewis and James Brown have all recorded the song at one time or another, as have Wilson Pickett, The Clash, Bob Dylan, Dr John, Nick Cave and Amy Winehouse. Even Elvis Presley had a stab at it in a 1970 rehearsal session which later surfaced as a bootleg CD.

1

The new century's seen other media join in too. In 2006, Derek McCulloch and Shepherd Hendrix published a fat graphic novel telling Stagger Lee's story in careful detail. Movie versions have come from Samuel L Jackson, who gives a storming live rendition of the song in 2006's *Black Snake Moan*, and Eric Bibb, who uses it to comment on the action unfolding around his character in the following year's *Honeydripper*.

All these versions tell the same core story, but no two of them seem able to agree on the details. A man named Stack Lee – or Stagger Lee, or Stack O'Lee – goes to a bar called The Bucket of Blood – or sometimes The White Elephant – where he kills a man called Billy Lyons – or Billy Lion, or Billy DeLyon – for stealing – or winning, or spitting into – his Stetson hat. The story takes place in St Louis – or Memphis or New Orleans – in 1932 (Nick Cave), 1940 (The Grateful Dead) or just about any other year you care to name. Sometimes Stack kills the bartender first for disrespecting him and then moves on to Billy, who's done nothing to offend him at all. He's a sadistic killer in one version and a wronged innocent in the next. All these songs are about Lee Shelton – or "Sheldon" as the *Globe-Democrat* initially had it – but who was he?

To answer that question, let's start by looking at the city where he lived. St Louis had built its prosperity as a busy riverboat port, servicing the hundreds of steamers that sailed up and down the Mississippi between Minneapolis and New Orleans. This brought a constant traffic of gamblers, drifters and riverboat workers, all anxious to raise hell in St Louis for a day or two before continuing their journey. Itinerant railroad workers joined the party in the 1850s, as St Louis became a key conduit point for pioneers heading west. The end of the Civil War in 1865 brought a huge increase in St Louis's black population, as former slaves flooded up from the South for the new factory jobs and the greater liberty which a Northern city promised to provide.

Wages for all these new workers were low, but still gave them more disposable income than they'd ever had before, and they all needed somewhere to burn up their paycheck on a Saturday night. In 1874, the Mississippi was bridged at St Louis for the first time, opening the city's riverfront vice districts to the even rougher residents of East St Louis, just across the river. St Louis's population increased seven-fold between 1850 and 1900, reaching 575,238 as the new century began and making it the fourth largest city in America.

As all these new developments tumbled forwards, law and order struggled to keep pace. The city's Police Department was not fully established until 1846, and its first adequate courthouse not completed till 1862. Thirty years later, the novelist-to-be Theodore Dreiser worked as a *St Louis Globe-Democrat* reporter at the city's notorious Four Courts in Clark Street. This complex – which Dreiser knew during Lee Shelton's time – hosted not only courtrooms, but also the Police Department's offices, the gallows and the city morgue. It would be hard, Dreiser said, to find anywhere with a more dismal atmosphere. Here's how he described it:

> Harlots, criminals, murderers, buzzard lawyers, political judges, detectives, police agents and court officials generally – what a company! [...] The petty tyrannies that are always practiced by underlings and minor officials – how they always grated on me! The "grafting" of low, swinish brains! The tawdry pomp of ignorant officials! The cruelty and cunning of so-called agents of justice! [...] To me, it was a horrible place, a pest-hole of suffering and error and trickery. [1]

The Four Courts governed the nearby vice district of Deep Morgan, where black and white prostitutes alike worked around the clock. Even the humblest customers could find somewhere to get soused there, thanks to the many establishments selling "nickel shots" of rot-gut whiskey at just 5c a hit.

It was also an area where the normal segregation of the races was forgotten, allowing blacks and whites to intermingle and even have sex together. When business was slow in the main streets, the girls would try to drum up work by knocking on the windows of each bar they passed. This habit was much resented by the other prostitutes working inside the bars, and would sometime spark an entertaining catfight in the gutter outside.

St Louis's police force was all-white until 1901, and its dealings with the black residents and workers of Deep Morgan were not always convivial. As evidence of this, we have *Duncan & Brady*, the true story of a murdered cop, which inspired its own St Louis ballad. The killing took place at Charles Starkes' saloon, which stood within a block of Curtis's place, in October 1890. The two characters often swap roles in this ballad, but Leadbelly's version sticks to the facts by making James Brady the corrupt white cop and Harry Duncan the black barman who kills him:

> *Twinkle, twinkle, twinkle, little star,*
> *Up comes Brady in a 'lectric car,*
> *Got a mean look all 'round his eye,*
> *Gonna shoot somebody jus' to see them die,*
>
> *Duncan, Duncan was tending the bar,*
> *In walked Brady with a shining star,*
> *And Brady says, "Duncan you are under arrest",*
> *And Duncan shot a hole in Brady's breast.* [2]

Incidents like that help to explain how the St Louis of 1895 ended up as a city of only 500,000 people – about the size of Edinburgh or Albuquerque today – where five murders could take place in a single night. Translate that rate to London's modern population of about 8.5 million, and you'd have 85 corpses littering the streets by dawn.

Shelton and Lyons' home turf was the heart of Deep Morgan, between 8th and 15th streets, bordered by Washington Avenue and what's now Dr Martin Luther King Drive. James Dawson, a beat cop who patrolled this neighbourhood in the 1890s, described it like this:

> It was by no means a desirable location for even half decent people to live in, and was the hang out of a low order of bawds, colored and white, and also many crap shooters. Lee and Lyons [were both well known] by reason of their attention and activity in that very doubtful avocation. Their environments and avocation was bad indeed and their morals, if possible, were worse. [3]

Smack in the middle of this district were two of the town's most notorious bars. Curtis's joint stood on the corner of 11th and Morgan, while Henry Bridgewater's saloon was just a block away on 11th and Lucas. The two establishments were bitter rivals, and not only because they vied for the same business: Bridgewater was a prominent black Republican, while Bill Curtis's saloon seems to have served as a meeting place for Democrat activists. Both bars had a bad reputation. The *St Louis Post-Dispatch* counted Curtis's among the "worst dens in the city", calling its clientele "the lower class of river men and other darkies of the same social status". Not to be outdone, the *St Louis Globe-Democrat* labeled Bridgewater's "a den of vice". [4]

Lyons had good reason to think of Curtis's as enemy territory. He was Bridgewater's brother-in-law, and had been involved in brawls at the Morgan Street saloon before – sometimes ones he'd started himself. In fact, Dawson was clear that Lyons was generally a more violent man than Shelton:

> The principal and only difference between the two men was in their temper and disposition to fight. If I recall correctly from memory, Lee was no fighter. [...] Lyons when under the influence of liquor, which occurred occasionally, was quarrelsome and at times dangerous.

He goes on to recall an incident at Curtis's a few years before Lyons' murder. The drunken Lyons had got into a fight with William Curtis, the saloon's owner, and started waving a vicious long-bladed knife around. When Dawson arrived to see what was going on, he found all the other customers had fled, leaving Curtis and his attacker alone in the bar. Curtis was cowering behind a billiard table while Lyons continued to brandish the knife. "I seized Lyons by the throat and, with the assistance of Curtis, I disarmed him and arrested him," Dawson recalled. "I was obliged by reason of his violence to place the handle of the knife in my teeth and brought him to the station three blocks distant, finally throwing him to the floor of the then captain's office."

Cecil Brown, author of 2003's *Stagolee Shot Billy*, was able to obtain some private notes taken at Lyons' inquest, and reproduces some extracts from them in his book. The testimony recorded in these notes tells us that, on Christmas Day 1895, Lyons left Bridgewater's Saloon with his friend Henry Crump and that the two men walked to Curtis's together. Lyons paused at the entrance to borrow a knife from Crump, and then they went in. He bought himself a drink at the bar, turned round, and saw Shelton walking in.

Shelton was a local carriage driver who sometimes moonlighted as a barkeep at Curtis's. He also helped run a "lid club" called The Modern Horseshoe for Deep Morgan's black clientele. Clubs like these were so-named because they used a legitimate bar out front to keep a lid on the illegal gambling and prostitution operating in their back rooms. Whether Shelton actually ran his own stable of girls at The Modern Horseshoe is a matter of some debate, but he would certainly have been ideally placed to do so.

As a streetwise young man, just 30 years old when he shot Lyons, working in the heart of St Louis's most notorious vice district, he could hardly have escaped the trade altogether. Even if we discount the club, his job as a carriage driver meant he was well-placed to guide St Louis's gentleman visitors to whichever brothel or bar paid him best for steering business their way. No doubt his role at Curtis's offered entrepreneurial opportunities of its own, and a chance to scare up customers for all his other enterprises too.

Shelton's prison records show he was 5ft 7½ ins tall with a crossed left eye and a light enough skin to suggest mixed parentage. He seems to have been dressed in full pimp regalia that night including – perhaps – the fashionable John B. Stetson hat which all the black dandies of Deep Morgan considered essential wear. These young men were known in the city as macquereaux, or "macks" for short, and we have a description of their typical clothing in John Huston's 1930 book *Frankie And Johnny*. "Mirrors were set in the toes," he writes. "The Gaiters matched the velvet trouser cuff, the vest and hat – the Stetson high roller, with nudes and racers inlaid with eyelets on the crown. The linens were of fine quality, with starched, embroidered bosoms and cuffs". [5]

As he entered the bar, Shelton cried out, "Who's treating?", and someone pointed him towards Lyons at the bar. He joined him there and the two men began drinking together in what onlookers thought was a friendly way. Everything was fine until, as the *Globe-Democrat* put it, "the discussion drifted to politics".

George McFaro, one of the 20-odd other customers at Curtis's that night, told coroner Walter Wait that he'd seen Shelton strike Lyons' derby hat, breaking its dome. At that point, McFaro said, they seemed to be just fooling around, but then Lyons grabbed Shelton's hat and announced he was going to keep it till Shelton handed over six bits [75c] to replace the ruined derby. Shelton refused, saying, "six bits would buy a box of those hats". When Lyons asked him why he'd hit the derby in the first place, Shelton made some unspecified gesture which I take to be a shrug of dismissal.

"They stood and talked awhile," McFaro continued. "Stack snatched out his pistol, and he said, 'If you don't give me my hat, I will blow your brains out." [...] When he pulled the pistol out, I walked out. I didn't stay any longer." [6]

Another witness told the inquest that Lyons responded to Shelton's threat by pulling out the knife he'd borrowed from Crump, and replying, "You cock-eyed son of a bitch, I'm going to make you kill me." And that's just what Shelton did, firing his Smith & Wesson .44 straight into Lyons' belly. Leslie Stevenson, another customer testifying at the inquest, described what happened next. Lyons managed to stay on his feet for a few seconds, he said, and then:

> He staggered against the side of the bar, leaned against the railing, holding the hat in his fingers like that, and it seemed he was getting weak, and he let the hat drop out of his hands. About that time, Shelton says, "Give me my hat, nigger". He says, "You got my hat," and he takes and picks it up and walks out into the brisk air. [6]

Crump retrieved his knife to make sure the police wouldn't be able to find it, then recruited another drinker called Arthur McCoy to help him carry Lyons' injured body outside for the journey to City Hospital. Discovering the bullet had lacerated Lyons' left kidney, doctors carried out a 2 a.m. operation to remove the damaged organ, but he continued to decline. "Lyons was in such an exhausted condition that he was unable to speak, though partially conscious," next day's *St Louis Globe-Democrat* reported. "He also suffered greatly from loss of blood." Lyons died at 4 a.m. on Boxing Day, his death certificate showing he was just 31 years old. [7]

By then, Shelton was already in custody. After the shooting, he'd walked calmly to a house he used on 6th Street, left his gun with a woman there for safekeeping, and then gone upstairs to sleep. The police tracked him there and arrested him about an hour before Lyons died. A few minutes later, they returned to the house and – almost as an afterthought – recovered the gun.

Shelton may have taken his "Stack Lee" nickname from a white man called Samuel Stacker Lee, whose father owned the famous Lee Steam Line of riverboats. This Stacker Lee joined the Confederate army at the age of 16, became a cavalryman, and fought Yankees for the next two years. He was still only 18 when the war ended in 1865, and returned to civilian life determined to have some fun. When his father, James Lee, started the Lee Line a year later, he gave his son one of the boats to captain and Stacker set about making up for lost time.

Travelling up and down the Mississippi between St Louis and New Orleans, he became well-known as a gambler, a hell-raiser and a ladies' man. He made a habit of fathering illegitimate children wherever his boat put in, often by black or mixed-race women. In his 1948 book *Memphis Down in Dixie*, Shields McIlwaine reports that Stacker's popularity meant there were "more colored kids named Stack Lee than there were sinners in hell". [8]

It's very unlikely that Shelton was really Stacker Lee's son, but he may well have adopted his nickname to hint at that possibility. Shelton's light skin, described by the prison authorities as a "mulatto complexion", would have made it easy for people to believe he had a white father. Who could blame him for hinting that his father was the glamorous son of a powerful, rich family? Even in their very first reports of Billy Lyons' death, in December 1895, the newspapers were referring to his killer as "Lee Shelton, alias 'Stag' Lee". By June 1896, he was well-known enough as "Stack Lee" for newspapers to rely on that nickname alone when writing headlines about him. "Stack Lee gives bond", or "Stack Lee's Trial" was all a headline needed to say for everyone to know exactly who was involved. [9]

The Lee Line also had a riverboat called the Stacker Lee, built in 1902 and named after the white cavalryman. It joined the fleet too late to influence Shelton's choice of nickname, but its regular trips between St Louis and Memphis may well have helped to spread his story's fame and spark new versions of the song – at least until it sank near Memphis in 1916. Other boats from the Lee Line inspired blues songs of their own, most notably Charley Patton's 1929 "Jim Lee Blues", but only the Stacker Lee came with a ready-made legend attached.

R agtime was St Louis's dominant music in the early 1890s, played by resident pianists at every bar and brothel in the city's black neighbourhoods. W. C. Handy, known today as the father of the blues, lived and worked in the city at that time, where he first heard the street music which inspired him to compose "St Louis Blues" a few years later. By 1895, ragtime was already taking a turn towards blues in Deep Morgan, while in the rival red light district of Chestnut Valley, just a few blocks south, jazzier stylings were starting to come through.

There are anecdotal accounts of a song about Lee Shelton's case being sung on the streets of St Louis as early as 1897. Our first concrete evidence dates from 21 August that year, when *The Kansas City Leavenworth Herald* announced an upcoming concert by a pianist called Charlie Lee, adding that he would "play Stack-a-Lee in variations". We know nothing about this version except its title, though the reference to variations suggests Lee would be playing it as a jazz instrumental. Clearly, it was a popular tune – and therefore worth singling out in the gig's publicity – which tells us again that a blues song of that name was already doing the rounds. Lee, like Handy or any other jobbing musician at that time, would have kept an ear out for topical local songs like this to ensure his own set stayed fresh.

As with New Orleans at the birth of jazz or Seattle in the grunge era, St Louis's vibrant musical scene ensured its own music spread nationwide – and carried songs about Lee Shelton right along with it. One of the first sets of lyrics we have was collected by John Lomax in 1910. He was given the verses by a Texas woman named Ella Scott Fisher, who described them as a work song sung by black labourers in Memphis while they loaded or unloaded river freighters on the Mississippi. They open like this:

'Twas a Christmas morning,
The hour was about ten,
When Stagalee shot Billy Lyons,
And landed in the Jefferson pen,
O Lordy, po' Stagalee,

Billy Lyons' old woman,
She was a terrible sinner,
She was home that Christmas mornin',
A-preparin' Billy's dinner,
O Lordy, po' Stagalee,

Messenger boy came to the winder,
Then he knocked on the door,
An' he said "Your ol' man's a-lyin' there,
Dead on the barroom floor",
O Lordy, po' Stagalee,

"Stagalee, O Stagalee,
What have you gone and done?
You've gone and shot my husband,
With a forty-four gatlin' gun",
O Lordy, po' Stagalee. [10]

Even this early in the song's history, we can see several of its key elements in place. There's the Christmas Day setting, the bar room location, both our protagonists correctly identified and a very specific calibre given for the murder weapon. We're in the right part of the country too, as the reference to Jefferson City's Missouri State Penitentiary makes clear. Most characteristically of all, it's clear that everyone's already firmly on Stack's side. He's given that "Po' Stagalee" line sympathising with him at the end of every verse, but no-one spares a thought for Billy at all. "[This is] the ballad as it was sung when the tale was news," Lomax writes. "It becomes immensely personal as you hear it, like a recital of something known or experienced by the singer."

Another early set of lyrics, this one published by *The Journal Of American Folklore* in 1911, confirms that Stack's Stetson hat had already won a place in the song. None of the 1895/6 newspaper reports I've seen specify what kind of hat he was wearing when the fight broke out – it's always just "his hat" – but here's the Stetson cemented into the lyrics just 15 years later. The verse in question also turns "Billy" into "bully", perhaps reflecting Lyons' own reputation as a brawler:

> *I got up one mornin', jes' 'bout four o'clock,*
> *Stagolee an' big bully done have one finish' fight,*
> *What 'bout? All 'bout dat raw-hide Stetson hat.* [11]

Ben Botkin doesn't say when the "Stagger Lee" lyrics quoted in his 1944 book *A Treasury Of American Folklore* were collected, but the fact that they give such a good estimate of Shelton's birth date suggests they were composed quite soon after Billy's death. The lyrics give Shelton's date of birth as 1861, against the real date of 1865, but even that discrepancy can be explained by the fact that their writer needed a date that more or less rhymed with "born" in his next line.

> *It was in the year of eighteen hundred and sixty-one,*
> *In St Louis on Market Street where Stackalee was born,*
> *Everybody's talkin' 'bout Stackalee.* [12]

Like many folklore versions of the song, Botkin's lyrics go on for 50 verses or more. But we can boil them down to a much more concise telling:

> *It was on one cold and frosty night,*
> *When Stackalee and Billy Lyons had one awful fight,*
> *Everybody's talkin' 'bout Stackalee,*
>
> *Stackalee got his gun, boy he got it fast!*
> *He shot poor Billy through and through; the bullet broke a lookin' glass,*
> *That bad man Stackalee,*

Stackalee shot Billy once, his body fell to the floor,
He cried out, "Oh, please, Stack, don't shoot me no more",
Oh tough man Stackalee,

"Have mercy," Billy groaned, "Oh, please spare my life,
I've got two little babies and an innocent wife",
Everybody's talkin' 'bout Stackalee,

Stack says, "God bless your children, damn your wife!
You stole my magic Stetson, I'm gonna steal your life",
Oh, oh, Lord, Lord, Lord,

Meanwhile the sergeant strapped on his big forty-five,
Says, "Now we'll bring in this bad man, dead or alive",
All about an old Stetson hat,

At midnight on that stormy night, there came an awful wail,
Billy Lyons and a graveyard ghost outside the city jail,
Everybody's talkin' 'bout Stackalee,

"Jailer, jailer," says Stack, "I can't sleep,
For around my bedside, poor Billy Lyons still creeps"
That bad man Stackalee,

And the other convicts whisper, "Whatcha know about that?
Gonna burn in hell forever over an old Stetson hat",
Oh tough man Stackalee.

By 1918, Stack's name had enough commercial clout for a blackface vaudeville duo to rename themselves "Stack & Lee". The first records to exploit his legend were instrumentals by white dance bands. Fred Waring's Pennsylvanians and Frank Westphal's Royal Novelty Orchestra released rival versions of a foxtrot called "Stack O'Lee Blues" in 1923, which sounds nothing like the tune we know today. Ma Rainey recorded a jazzy song called "Stack O'Lee Blues" in 1926, and Duke Ellington's Washingtonians added their own version of Westphal's instrumental the following year. [13]

Rainey may have called her song "Stack O'Lee Blues", but she makes no attempt to tell the story of Billy Lyons' killing. Instead, she borrows from "Frankie & Albert", another St Louis murder ballad of about the same vintage. Her Stack is certainly a villain but his sin, like Albert's, is treating his woman badly. "He was my man," Rainey groans. "But he done me wrong."

We had to wait until 1927 to get a record based on the real murder but then, rather like buses, three turned up at once. The bluesman Frank Hutchinson put out "Stackalee" in January that year and The Down Home Boys followed with their own "Original Stack O'Lee Blues" in May. Furry Lewis added "Billy Lyons And Stack O'Lee" five months later. Each has its points of interest, so let's tackle them one by one.

Hutchinson's version uses the same three-lines-per-verse structure as the Botkin lyrics above, closing with the same image of Billy's ghost haunting Stack in his cell. The long lines demand a breathless pace, which Hutchinson drives along with guitar and harmonica alone. Perhaps that combination of instruments is why Bob Dylan took it as his model when cutting "Stack A Lee" for his 1993 album *World Gone Wrong*.

Mississippi's Down Home Boys, also known as Little Harvey Hull and Long Cleve Reed, can't match Hutchinson's disc for sheer enjoyment, but they do manage to build a cheekily subversive element into the song. They cast Billy as a policeman – presumably a white policeman – who tries to arrest the black narrator on a trumped-up vagrancy charge. This was a common practice among southern cops at the time, who used such charges to scoop up innocent black men to boost the local prison farm's workforce at harvest time. This reference would not have escaped the song's original, all-black, audience.

It's also clear from The Down Home Boys' disc that Billy is a little afraid of Stack, and that Stack is confident enough to taunt this white authority figure to his face. When the cowardly, unjust, copper forces Stack to kill him, it seems like an entirely excusable crime, and we join Hull in an indulgent chuckle when Stack returns to his old roguish ways in the song's final verse. Like the Hutchinson and Lewis records, this take was released on a "race" label, aimed at an exclusively black audience and offering them a cathartic tale of a strong black man overcoming bigoted white authority. Stack had long been an anti-hero in the work songs and folktales telling his story, and most of the versions following The Down Home Boys' recording would take that line too.

Most, but not quite all. Furry Lewis is unusual – perhaps even unique – in giving the victim top billing in his "Billy Lyons And Stack O'Lee", and that priority reflects his attitude in the song too. He depicts Billy and Stack as two gamblers, and attributes the killing to Stack being a poor loser. His chorus chides Stack for such unsporting behaviour: "When you lose your money, learn to lose". As we'll see in a moment, the idea that Stack and Billy had been gambling when the fight happened rests on some pretty dubious foundations, but it's now an absolute fixture in the song. Over the 50 years following Lewis's recording, performers would gradually shift the blame for this gamblers' disagreement from Stack to Billy himself.

Mississippi John Hurt, who cut one of the most enduring recordings of the song in 1928, is just as determined as Lewis not to romanticise Stack's role. Augmented by some wonderfully pretty guitar playing, Hurt's delivery suggests a bone-weary sadness at the constant violence poor black communities like St Louis's would have had to endure from the crooks and thugs among them. He begins by berating the police for refusing to arrest Stack earlier and reminds us again and again just how cruel this bad man is. Stack may have felt Billy's theft of his Stetson obliged him to kill the man, but Hurt clearly thinks that's ridiculous.

He allows Stack a moment of dignity on the gallows – "head way up high" – but gives no sign of regretting his demise. When Beck came to cover Hurt's version of "Stack O'Lee" for a 2001 tribute album, he drove this point home by changing "They was all glad to see him die" to "We were all glad to see him die". On this reading, even the narrator of Stack's own song is glad to see the back of him.

Some people argue that this we/they discrepancy should be seen as evidence of unconscious racism. Only the white singers, it's claimed, are prepared to join in the rejoicing at a black man's death. McCulloch and Hendrix raise this point in their graphic novel, only to dismiss it almost instantly. White singers, they argue, re-make Stack in their own image as the song proceeds, and if their Stack is a white man, then how can the "we" be racist?

My own view is that the choice of pronoun depends less on the singer's race than on where he's decided to place himself in the song. A performer who wants to cast himself as a participant in the story becomes part of the crowd watching Stack's execution, and so uses "we". Someone preferring to remain a neutral narrator of the tale, watching it all from outside, would naturally opt for "they". It's also worth pointing out that the record of white singers' and black singers' pronoun use is far more jumbled than the racism theory suggests. And what are we to make of versions like the Beck one mentioned above, which uses "they killed him" and "we were glad" in two consecutive lines?

Shelton's casual attitude after the murder – he walked a few blocks to a house everyone knew he used and went upstairs to get some sleep – suggests he wasn't too worried about police pursuit. He may have assumed, with some reason, that the cops would take little interest in one black crap shooter killing another in that particular part of town. If so, he reckoned without Henry Bridgewater.

Bridgewater was one of the richest black men in St Louis, owning property there worth over $400,000 in today's money. He was also a prominent Republican at a time when black Americans' initial loyalty to that party was dropping away fast. The Civil War had brought an end to slavery in 1865, and the fact that this was achieved under the Republican President Abraham Lincoln was enough to ensure that most blacks voted Republican in their first few elections. Few of the party's promises to them had materialised, however, and by Lee Shelton's time the black vote was once again up for grabs.

Democrat activists responded by organising what they called "400 clubs" in St Louis's black bars – one of which was headed by Shelton at Curtis's. Three days after Shelton's arrest *The St Louis Star-Sayings* printed a letter from the club's financial secretary calling Shelton "our captain [...] our unfortunate member and brother". The *St Louis Post-Dispatch* of 17 March 1911, writing while Shelton was in jail, said he was "formerly a Negro politician".

As Shelton hustled for the Democrats, Bridgewater was hosting Republican meetings at his own bar. Saloon keepers like him were a crucial part of St Louis's political machine, just one step down from the ward bosses both parties relied on to bribe or intimidate voters. A saloon provided not only a venue for political meetings, but also a retail business to launder any cash the party's organisers might not want traced back to themselves and a ready supply of muscle when things got nasty. On polling day itself, many of the customers' votes could be bought for no more outlay than a few free drinks.

Bridgewater's Saloon was a more upmarket affair than Curtis's, often entertaining the black celebrities of the day, and able to attract a wealthier clientele. It was the neighbourhood's anarchic reputation which attracted these drinkers, though, and Bridgewater's remained rough enough for at least two murders to occur on the premises between 1890 and 1902. The picture at both these joints seems to be one of drunken gambling and whoring progressing on the ground floor, punctuated by the occasional fight, while hard-nosed political negotiations were conducted in an upstairs room.

Take all these facts together, and it starts to look like Bridgewater might have dispatched Lyons to Curtis's Saloon that night to broker some kind of deal between Deep Morgan's Republican and Democrat factions. That would explain why eyewitnesses thought Lyons and Shelton spoke in such a friendly way at first, and also why things turned ugly when they started discussing politics. Bridgewater was married to Lyons' sister Elizabeth, and may have decided that only a member of the family could be entrusted with this delicate task. He'd also have known that Lyons was more than capable of defending himself if there should be any trouble at Curtis's – or any trouble short of a bullet to the gut, anyway.

When the police arrested Shelton on Boxing Day, they took him to Chestnut Street police station and held him there. Next day, he was taken to the morgue at The Four Courts to be sworn in for the inquest. Waiting at the entrance was a crowd of about 300 blacks from what one paper called "the Henry Bridgewater faction", who taunted Shelton as he approached. The police escort had to summon reinforcements and fight their way through the crowd with batons in order to clear their prisoner's path to the door, as threats to lynch Shelton rang out all around.

Even with Shelton safely inside, the crowd refused to disperse. "Throughout the entire hearing, a large crowd of negroes was in attendance," reported the next day's *St Louis Globe-Democrat*. "As many of them as could pushed their way into the coroner's office, while the others crowded the hallway and congregated near the Eleventh street entrance". [14]

A rival St Louis paper, *The Star-Sayings*, added a paragraph to its own inquest report claiming that Shelton's quarrel with Lyons had its roots in a long-running grudge. "The feud which resulted in Shelton killing Lyons commenced five years ago," the paper said. "Harry Wilson, a noted negro character and friend of Shelton's, was shot and killed in Bridgewater's place [...] by Charley Brown, a step-brother of Lyons. Brown escaped conviction, and it is said that Shelton then swore he would avenge Wilson's death. It is said he had trouble with several of the Bridgewater crowd." [15]

The Star-Sayings attributes this only to an unnamed "informant" at the inquest, which is a little odd. The "Stagger Lee" scholar George Eberhart believes Bridgewater may have cooked up the theory as a way of suggesting Shelton was determined to kill Lyons long before the two men started arguing about their hats. Coroner Wait seemed rather sceptical about the whole idea, but the very fact that Bridgewater had ensured it reached the newspapers hurt Shelton's defence.

The mob outside the court remained in place when the inquest was over, agreeing to go home only after Wait had assured them Shelton would be referred to the Grand Jury pending charges of first-degree murder. He was taken first to a holding cell, and then to jail.

No-one knows how he managed it, but 24 hours after the inquest Shelton had already secured a top-flight lawyer to defend him. Nat Dryden was a brilliant Missouri attorney, who had secured the state's first-ever conviction of a white man for killing a black man – a conviction which, even more remarkably, had led to the white killer being executed. Dryden was also an alcoholic and an opium addict, but these habits did nothing to inhibit his courtroom performance as a fierce cross-examiner and a powerful orator. He'd proved himself capable of winning even the most unpromising murder cases, and he would not have come cheap.

Either Shelton was a wealthier man than his lifestyle suggests, or he had rich friends. On 3 January 1896, he paid $4,000 bail to get out of prison while he waited for the Grand Jury to decide if he should be indicted. That sum would be worth about $100,000 today. On 12 February, the Grand Jury ruled he should face first-degree murder charges, the bail money presumably went back to its owner, and Shelton was returned to jail to await his criminal trial. He was freed again on 25 June, when a St Louis pawnbroker called Morris Schmit provided another $3,000 in bail.

His murder trial's jury was finally sworn in on 13 July 1896, with Dryden defending Shelton and the prosecution team led by Orrick Bishop, the state's assistant circuit attorney. Bishop was every bit as formidable as Dryden, so everyone relished the prospect of these two great beasts clashing in public. "The trial promises to develop [into] a very pretty and interesting legal fight," The *St Louis Globe-Democrat* drooled.

It's that same *Globe-Democrat* piece, incidentally, which seems to have introduced the idea that Shelton and Lyons were gambling with dice when the fight broke out. "The man who is now on trial for his life was shooting craps with William Lyons," it claims. There's no mention of gambling in either the earlier newspaper reports or the inquest statements, however, so we have to take this assertion with a pinch of salt. Perhaps the reporter was genuinely confused, or could not resist embellishing his story with just one more colourful little detail. Whatever its beginnings, the gambling is now an immovable part of the song. In many versions, it's Billy's alleged cheating at craps that prompts Stack to shoot him.

Dryden was forced to accept his client had shot Lyons – there was no gainsaying the witness reports on that score – but argued strongly that this had been done in self-defence. The trial wrapped up on Friday 14 May, and next day the jury returned with a split verdict: seven votes for second-degree murder, two for manslaughter and three for acquittal. Judge Thomas Harvey dismissed them and ordered a retrial. A month later, *The Kansas City Leavenworth Herald* announced Charlie Lee's upcoming concert and the fact that he'd be including "Stack-a-Lee" in his set.

Unfortunately for Shelton, Nat Dryden went on an epic drinking spree before the new trial could be arranged, and died from its results on 26 August 1896. The knock-on effects of his unexpected death meant Shelton's retrial was not ready to begin till 11 May the following year. Dryden's old associate Charles Johnson replaced him as defence counsel, with Bishop once again heading the prosecution and Judge James Withrow on the bench.

The most dramatic incident at this second trial came when Bishop called Henry Crump, the friend who'd accompanied Lyons to Curtis's Saloon on the fatal night. The prosecution team had sat Crump down in private before the trial and persuaded him to sign a statement saying Lyons had never threatened Shelton with a weapon before the shooting. He told a different story in the witness box, however, saying there that Lyons *had* drawn his knife on Shelton before the trigger was pulled.

Bishop leapt to his feet, cutting his own witness short, and complaining this new testimony conflicted with the written statement Crump had already signed. Johnson, seeing this new version of events supported his client's plea of self-defence, pointed out that the written statement had not been produced under oath, and argued strongly that Crump's courtroom testimony must stand. Withrow was forced to clear the court while the two attorneys made their points. It was an angry and bad-tempered exchange, threatening at one point to break into a fist fight between two of the city's leading lawyers.

Withrow's ruling was that Crump had now proved himself to be such an unreliable witness that he should take no further part in the trial. The incident may have left just enough doubt in the jury's mind to save Shelton from the death penalty, but not from a hefty spell in prison. He was found guilty of second-degree murder and, on 7 October 1897, entered Jefferson Penitentiary to begin a 25-year sentence.

There was a steady flow of "Stagger Lee" covers in the 30 years following Mississippi John Hurt's recording, including versions by Woody Guthrie, Cab Calloway, Sidney Bechet, Memphis Slim, Fats Domino and Jerry Lee Lewis.

The British skiffle boom of the late 1950s brought a particularly strange take on the song from Chas McDevitt, who rewrote the story to have Stackolee steal the singer's Stetson hat and then flee. Forced to wear "a coon-skin cap instead", McDevitt was now out for revenge and determined to shoot Stackolee dead. Just in case that wasn't scary enough, he topped things off with a spot of the group's trademark whistling.

McDevitt failed to trouble the charts with that offering, but Stack's debut as a pop star was not far away. His big break came in February 1959, when Lloyd Price made the song a number one hit in America and reached number seven in the UK. Price, a black native of New Orleans, had a considerable musical pedigree. He'd written "Lawdy Miss Clawdy" in 1952 and scored his own number one R&B hit with the song five years before Elvis Presley covered it.

Price racked up four more US hits and then, in 1954, found himself drafted for the Korean War. He spent the next two years touring US bases in Korea and Japan entertaining the troops with his own army band. Looking for ideas to spice up the act, he remembered a 1950 version of "Stack-A-Lee" by a New Orleans singer called Archibald. Price took the seven core verses of Archibald's sprawling narrative, put together a routine based on the story they told and had soldiers act out the song while he sang it on stage.

Price got out of the army in 1956 and resumed his recording career. He got back in the US pop charts almost immediately with 1957's "Just Because", and then unleashed his own raucous version of "Stagger Lee" on the world. It's a runaway train of a record, fuelled by blaring horns and the backing singers' constant roars of encouragement. Drums thump like pistons beneath Price's powerful vocals and the raspingly abrasive sax solo which erupts every time he pauses for breath.

Even without the backing vocals constant refrain – "GO STAGGER LEE! GO STAGGER LEE!" – it's pretty clear where this version's sympathies lie. All Hurt's doubts about the killer's code of honour have vanished. In Price's account, Billy refuses to acknowledge Stack's winning throw at dice, and that makes him fair game. There's a moment of token sympathy for Billy – "that poor boy" – but Price soon gets back to cheering Stack on. Go, Stagger Lee! Shoot him again!

Price's version wasn't the first to mention the noise of a barking bulldog just as Billy gets shot – the image appears in Frank Hutchinson's lyrics too – but it's certainly the most famous. Some believe this sound represents Billy's soul as it's torn from his body in a violent death. Others point out that a popular revolver in the 1890s was nick-named "the bulldog" and claim it's therefore a handgun we hear barking in the song.

The British Bulldog – actually a Webley – was originally made for the British army in 1878, but was quickly copied by gun-makers all over the world. Its 2½ins barrel was short enough for the gun to be slipped in a coat pocket and carried around in secret. Charles Guiteau took advantage of this fact in 1881, when he used his own Bulldog to assassinate US President James Garfield.

The British army contract ensured these guns were distributed all over the world, so they would have reached St Louis in plenty of time for Shelton to use one in 1895. The American copies, made by Forehand & Wadsworth, sold for as little as $5. It's a pleasing co-incidence that the Bulldog took the same .44 or .45 calibre ammunition the song's rhyme scheme often requires Stack to use.

By making "Stagger Lee" a hit, Price introduced his story to the mass market white audience for the first time. Casual listeners in that group could easily have missed the Woody Guthrie or Jerry Lee Lewis versions of the song, but Price scored enough radio play to make his "Stagger Lee" inescapable. Everyone knew Stack and Billy's story now, and the beauty of Price's success was that it invited white folks in to join the fun.

For many, this was an intoxicating experience. They could relish the vicarious thrill of imagining themselves both freer and more frightening than they'd ever be in real life, while still enjoying the comforts which their safe, middle-class lives provided. A character like Stack can be very attractive to white suburban listeners, as the critic Bob Fiore pointed out in 2003 when discussing gangsta rap's typical protagonist. His description fits Stack to a "T":

> He lives a life of adventure, wealth, violence and indulgence, gets to murder people who annoy him, then obligingly reminds the audience of the relative security of their existence through his nasty and early demise. [...] To an audience that perceives itself constrained by new rules of decorum, he represents a kind of alpha-dog masculinity they can only dream of. [16]

That dream was thought far too dangerous for American TV viewers in the late 1950s, leading the presenter Dick Clark to insist Price cut a sanitised version of the song before he could appear on *American Bandstand*. In the bowdlerised lyrics, Stack and Billy argue rather than gamble, regret the harsh things they've said, and then part the best of friends.

Price's "Stagger Lee" remained in the US and UK charts for three months, making his arrangement the template for a host of new cover versions and drawing in artists from a couple of new genres to tackle the song. Until 1959, "Stagger Lee" had mostly belonged to folk and blues musicians, with just the occasional jazz or country outing thrown in. Price's hit prompted soul and reggae performers to join in too.

Ike & Tina Turner opened soul music's bidding in 1965 by placing Tina in a dance club where she watches Billy beating Stack to a pulp for kissing his (Billy's) wife. The song fades out before Stack has any opportunity to take revenge. James Brown funked things up with The Famous Flames' staccato horns in 1967, the same year Wilson Pickett galloped through his own version. Both Brown and Pickett stick closely to Price's plot.

Meanwhile, Jamaicans were listening to US R&B on the radio, adapting its storylines and rhythms for their own use. Prince Buster liked Price's tune enough to create a rude boy called "Stack-o-Lee" with his 1966 reggae version, prompting what was effectively an answer record the following year. The Rulers, an island rocksteady outfit, had already made a couple of records warning against the consequences of rude boys' delinquency, and saw Prince Buster's hit as an opportunity to drive this point home again. They open "Wrong 'Em Boyo" with a couple of lines from Price's song to remind us Billy cheated at dice, and then spend the rest of the number pointing out that this is really no way to behave. Crucially, their lyrics are just vague enough to leave you thinking both parties have been cheated in this altercation – Stack of his money, but Billy of his life.

When The Clash came to record their 1979 album *London Calling*, it was only natural that "Wrong 'Em Boyo" should come up as a candidate for one of their covers. Paul Simonon, the band's resident reggae expert, had ensured a copy of The Rulers' single found its way on to the jukebox at The Clash's Camden Town rehearsal rooms. Joe Strummer knew Price's version of "Stagger Lee" very well from his days performing it with his old pub rock band The 101ers.

The Clash turbo-charge The Rulers' hit into a piece of what the *NME's* Charles Shaar Murray called "tense, jumping ska", producing one of *London Calling's* stand-out tracks. Predictably enough, all the band's unique additions to this composite song tend to glamourise Stack at Billy's expense. First, they amend Price's opening verse to show Billy as the aggressor who kicks off all the violence by coming at Stack with a knife – the implication being that our hero was then forced to shoot Billy in simple self-defence. Their one addition to The Rulers' lyrics also places Stack as the wronged party in this whole affair. Billy's still the one who ends up dead, but now the song's scolding is aimed at him alone, and we emerge with a feeling that getting shot was his own stupid fault.

The Price version which both The Clash and The Rulers quote from takes Stack's side too, but never with the partisan ferocity The Clash bring to bear. "To live outside the law in Clash terms means being twice as honest as those who live within it," Murray concludes in his review. "[It] also means taking the consequences." Never slow to celebrate an outlaw, Strummer & Co use this cracking version of an old hit to give Stack his biggest vote of confidence so far.

Shelton had an eventful career in prison. Eberhart, who consulted the prison records held at the Missouri's State Archive, lists three occasions when Shelton was flogged there with a steel-tipped leather strap. On 9 March 1899, he was given five lashes for loafing in the yard, on 14 June the same year another eight for shooting craps and, on 16 July 1902, a further 10 for stealing a piece of ham from the prison kitchen. He also served a spell in solitary confinement, his offence on that occasion being that he'd snuck out of his cell one night to join a craps game. [3]

His Democrat friends outside the prison had not forgotten him, however, and continued to petition for his sentence to be reduced. By December 1899, the Bridgewater family was taking Shelton's chances of release seriously enough to fight back. Elizabeth Bridgewater, Lyons' sister, wrote to state governor Lawrence Stevens urging him to ensure Shelton served his full sentence. "As a sister, I beg you not to turn a man like him [loose] on the community at large," she wrote.

"If justice had been done, he would have been hung. Just think, he has not served half his term".

Judge Withrow, the man who'd sent Shelton to the penitentiary, weighed in on the other side of the argument, citing Henry Crump's testimony that Lyons had pulled a knife on Shelton in Curtis's saloon. "Lee Shelton has been incarcerated in the jail or penitentiary about six years for this offence," Withrow wrote in his 1901 letter to Stevens' successor Alexander Dockery. "It seems to me that an actual imprisonment of seven or eight years in this case would satisfy the ends of justice."

Henry Bridgewater died in 1904, and his family's protests started to drop away. A steady flow of support for Shelton's release continued, however, including one petition signed by ten Congressmen arguing that Lyons was a desperate character and that Shelton had acted only in self-defence. I've been able to trace only three of the names on that petition, but I'll bet it's no coincidence that they were all Democrats. Ed Butler, a prominent St Louis ward boss for the Democrats, organised his own petition too, on which William Curtis's name appeared as a signatory. Even Orrick Bishop and the chairman of the jury which had convicted Shelton eventually joined the campaign for his release.

All three of the state governors who held office during the first 12 years of Shelton's prison term – Lawrence Stevens, Alexander Dockery and Joseph Folk – were Democrats, but none felt able to set him free. Perhaps they feared it would look too blatant an act of party favouritism. Republican governor Herbert Hadley, who replaced Folk in January 1909, had no worries on that score, and my guess is it's that "Nixon in China" argument which finally allowed Shelton's supporters to prevail. He walked out of prison at the end of November 1909, having served 14 years – but he didn't stay out for long.

In January 1911, Shelton burgled a black man called Louis Akins, breaking his skull with a revolver before stealing $140 from the house. He was caught, sentenced to five years, and returned to prison on 7 May the same year. By then, he was 46 years old and suffering from tuberculosis. Hadley ordered his release on parole the following February – this time on health grounds – but Shelton was already too ill to be moved. He remained in the prison hospital, and died of consumption there on 11 March 1912.

Of course, if the songs and folktales are to be believed, matters didn't end there. Often, we follow him down to hell, where even Old Nick finds he's no match for Stack. Here's a few more verses from the song Ben Botkin collected:

> *Red devil was sayin', "You'd better hunt your hole,*
> *I've hurried here from hell just to get your soul",*
> *Everybody's talkin' 'bout Stackalee,*
>
> *Stackalee told him, "Yes, maybe you're right,*
> *But I'll give even you one hell of a fight",*
> *That bad man Stackalee,*
>
> *When they got into the scuffle, I heard the devil shout,*
> *"Come and get this bad man before he puts my fire out",*
> *Oh, tough man Stackalee,*
>
> *The next time I seed the devil he was scramblin up the wall,*
> *Yellin', "Come and get this bad man 'fore he mops up with us all",*
> *Everybody's talkin' 'bout Stackalee.* [12]

There's a strong tradition among New Orleans performers, made popular by Archibald's 1950 recording, which continues the story in this way as Stack descends into hell, terrifies the Devil and takes over his throne. Sometimes Billy ends up in hell too, allowing Stack to inflict still more punishment on him in the afterlife. This aspect of the story appears in the most unlikely places. Even the innocuous country crooner Tennessee Ernie Ford got in on the act with his 1951 "Stack-O-Lee", which has Satan fleeing in panic when he sees Stagger Lee approach. Stack casually plucks him up, places him out of the way on a convenient shelf, and proceeds to rule hell himself.

In other versions from this strand, we learn that Stack's Stetson was originally a gift from the Devil, and conferred magic powers of potency on its owner. There's no limit to the amount of baroque embellishment that this detail can inspire. One folklore tale collected by Botkin describes the Stetson as "an oxblood magic hat that folks claim he made from the raw hide of a man-eatin' panther that the devil had skinned alive".

It also tends to be the New Orleans strand which tells us that the women mourning Stack's death come "dressed in red". Both Archibald and Dr John use this line in their versions, for example. One theory is that this reflects an old African funeral custom, which dictated that mourning clothes should be the colour of blood. Another maintains that the line is imported from "Duncan & Brady".

The St Louis lawman James Brady is said to have been so strict that he banned local prostitutes from wearing the red dresses that advertised their trade. In that song, when the girls hear of his death they celebrate by digging out their red dresses again, and strutting round town in them to celebrate. When transferred to "Stagger Lee", this line's context suggests they've dressed in red as an act of solidarity with their favourite dead pimp. "Frankie & Johnny"'s Frankie Baker wears red in her ballad too, which early listeners may have recognised as signifying that she was in the same trade.

As "Stagger Lee" moved from one genre of recorded music to another, shifting persona as he went, there was one strand of his tale which remained firmly underground. No version of Stack's story sanctioned by the professional recording industry was ever going to be intense enough for those actually living in America's black ghettos to accept, so they produced their own "toasts" instead.

These were unaccompanied spoken-word accounts of Stack's life, chanted at the listener with percussive force and driving their points home through regular rhyming couplets. They were sexually explicit, usually told in the first person, and full of inventive swearing. Like the rappers who followed them, toasters could use these tales to portray themselves as charismatic, powerful gangsters who the white police held in awe. This attitude leaked into real life as well, as we can see from a 1908 Kansas City burglary case where the black defendant proudly told the court his name was "Stack Lee". The real Lee Shelton was still in jail at that time, but quite notorious enough for the 1908 offender to dress himself in a little borrowed glory. [17]

The first "Stagger Lee" toast was collected in 1911. For the next 50 years, it was taken for granted that the toasts were far too foul-mouthed to ever make a commercial recording. Isolated from every respectable genre of music, they retained their own unique take on Stack's story. The Stetson hat is mentioned only in passing and Billy slips into the background. Instead, Stack's primary victim is the barman at a place called The Bucket of Blood. Sometimes the barman deliberately serves Stack with rancid food. In other versions, he first refuses to recognise him, and then treats him with utter contempt. Then Stack shoots him.

The barman's name is never given, but it's pretty clear that he represents Henry Bridgewater, the saloon keeper responsible for getting Shelton arrested and jailed after the real murder. He's Lex Luthor to Stack's Superman, and that's the aspect of the story which the toasts set out to commemorate.

The Bucket of Blood, incidentally, was a real saloon/whorehouse in St Louis, operating in Lee Shelton's time. Whether it had any connection with Bridgewater I don't know, but someone obviously thought the name was too good to waste. Thirty years after Lyons' death, a St Louis bar on the corner of 22nd Street and Franklin Avenue earned the same nick-name, and for precisely the same reason. "It got a little too radical back there," the bluesman Henry Townsend recalled in his 1999 book *A Blues Life*. "Sooner or later it got the title 'Bucket of Blood'. People got to hurtin' one another, shootin' and killing, so then we stayed out of it. [...] One got hurt bad and one got killed, so that's why they called it the 'Bucket of Blood'." [18]

The first commercial recording of Stack's toast in anything like its uncut form appears on Snatch & The Poontangs' 1969 album *For Adults Only*. The Poontangs – an alias for R&B veteran Johnny Otis and his band – provide a whole album of uncensored street toasts, delivered with all the panache you'd expect from such road-hardened performers. There's a great deal of swearing, springing mostly from the fact that everyone in Stack's song seems to be a motherfucker.

Like most "Stagger Lee" toasts, The Poontangs' track can be traced back to verses which appear in Dennis Wepman's 1976 book *The Life: The Lore And Folk Poetry Of The Black Hustler*. Wepman includes a "Stagger Lee" toast performed by a black inmate called Big Stick at New York State's Auburn Prison in 1967. Roger Abrahams has a similar version in his 1964 book *Deep Down In The Jungle*, but it's anybody's guess when the words were first composed. These lines are from Big Stick's version:

He walked through rain and he walked through mud,
Till he came to a place called the Bucket of Blood,

He said "Mr Motherfucker you must know who I am",
Barkeep said "No and I don't give a good goddamn",

He said "Well bartender it's plain to see,
I'm that bad motherfucker named Stagger Lee",

Barkeep said "Yeah I heard your name down the way,
But I kick motherfucking asses like you every day",

Well those were the last words that the barkeep said,
'Cause Stack put four holes in his motherfucking head. [19]

Nick Cave fans will find this extract from Big Stick's story very familiar. When Cave and his band, The Bad Seeds, were recording their 1996 *Murder Ballads* album, Bad Seeds percussionist Jim Sclavunos brought a copy of Wepman's book into the studio. Cave discovered Big Stick's toast there, and had the band improvise a backing on the spot. Their brooding bassline, scratchy guitar and sudden, stabbing piano chords provide a perfect backdrop for Cave's supremely menacing vocals. He relishes every drop of cruelty the song provides, growling Big Stick's brutal words almost verbatim and drawing every ounce of value from their rhythmic punch. For the 5 mins 15 secs the song lasts, Cave seems both omnipotent and possessed. "I'M Stagger Lee!" he roars at one point. Who could doubt it?

Mick Harvey was The Bad Seeds' guitarist when they recorded "Stagger Lee" at London's Wessex Studios. He worked with Cave for 35 years, first in their school band The Boys Next Door, then in The Birthday Party and finally as a key member of The Bad Seeds, where he remained in place for the first quarter-century of that band's career. I called him at his Melbourne home to ask how The Bad Seeds reached their decision to record a whole album of murder ballads.

"Nick seemed to have a predilection for them," Harvey told me. "We'd done a version of 'Long Time Man', we'd done 'Hey Joe'. Even with The Birthday Party, there were songs like 'Deep In The Woods' and '6" Gold Blade': songs about Nick's fascination with some violent incident." [20]

The finished *Murder Ballads* CD would contain both "Stagger Lee" and "Henry Lee" from the canon of classic murder ballads, the latter being paired with "Knoxville Girl" when released as one of the album's singles. It also has a cover of Bob Dylan's "Death Is Not The End", plus seven of Cave and the band's own compositions in the same jugular vein. The most notable of this last group is the Kylie Minogue duet "Where The Wild Roses Grow", Cave's addition to country music's long chain of "dead-girl-in-the-river" ballads. Despite its dark content, this song gave the band an unexpected chart hit around the world.

For Harvey, it's the musical inspiration murder songs provide which give them their main appeal. "They're meaty subject matter to work with," he said. "I find heavy subject matter interesting because it lends itself to dark musical approaches, which is what I like: heavy, dark musical approaches. That's one thing that opens the musical possibilities to play the sort of things I find exciting and inspiring."

As they began thinking about their next project in 1995, The Bad Seeds already had "Song Of Joy" and "O'Malley's Bar" more or less completed. These were cut at the sessions for their previous album, 1994's *Let Love In*, but never found a home on that disc. "So we had these songs," Harvey said. "There was already a history of us recording murder ballads at different times, and it just became a bit of a talking point: 'Why don't we record an album of murder ballads?' It seemed like a fun extra project outside the normal run of Nick labouring to write a whole lot of songs that meant an enormous amount to him. It was something we could do that could be a bit looser and we could try different things with.

"That's the way it played out too. We just went into the studio and recorded a whole lot of stuff. Nick was looking through old books and sourcing all sorts of lyrics. Some of them he wrote himself, some he adapted from traditional songs. There was a whole mixture of stuff going on in where the lyrical stuff was coming from. It was like that with 'Stagger Lee' too. There was a book Nick had with all these lyrics, and that became his working version."

When the time came to record "Stagger Lee", the music began with Bad Seeds bassist Martyn Casey. "Nick had all the lyrics shaped pretty much by then," Harvey recalls. "Marty started up with a riff inspired by The Geto Boys and we all just joined in. I was playing this kind of percussive guitar, Jim came in with the drumbeat. I can't remember if the piano was on the basic track or not – it may have been – but it was very simple. It came together in an evening. We were pretty pleased with how it turned out. It was going to be a strong addition to the material on the album."

Both Cave and Harvey were aware of the song's long tradition when setting out to tackle it and both drew an extra measure of satisfaction from claiming a place in that long history. "It's been a very important song culturally," Harvey said. "It's one of those songs. That's kind of interesting in itself – it's nice to touch base with those things as you wobble through your world."

The song's since become a highlight of The Bad Seeds' live set, and remains so to this day. In their early days of playing it live, though, the band struggled to find an arrangement which did it justice. "It was quite difficult recreating it live, because it's driven by the story," Harvey said. "You can set up the basic groove, but then the music kind of goes nowhere – it just keeps churning round. On the recording, at least you can listen to the words and follow the story, but live it's a little harder to do that. Over time, it started getting more up-and-down dynamics in it. There'd be drop-down verses in it, and they happened fairly organically. But I think the early attempts to play it live probably weren't as exciting as it came to be later."

The band hit on the solution when they started making "Stagger Lee" their main encore, giving it a slot where it could stand slightly apart from the rest of the set. "It's a difficult one to just throw into the set, because it's so out of step with the other material," Harvey said. "Lyrically, it's quite an extreme song. I don't know we had many other songs that are quite that explicit – that pushed that far. They can be quite dark and strong and heavy, but this one is overtly foul-mouthed and rude. There's overt violence going on. It's such a *separate* kind of a song."

From Little Harvey Hull through Lloyd Price to The Clash and Nick Cave, every serious incarnation of "Stagger Lee" can be seen as a strong black man doing whatever it takes to make his way in an unjust white man's world. Rich or poor, aggressor or otherwise, he's always Fiore's "alpha dog" and always ready to extract a terrible revenge on anyone who fails to treat him that way. Stack may not be the healthiest of role models, but he's always been a potent symbol of black pride.

He's also the Godfather of every drug dealer and pimp populating gangsta rap tunes. Eithne Quinn makes this point in her 2005 book *Nuthin' But a 'g' Thang*, where she calls Stack "[one of] the most influential badman forebears of gangsta rap". She goes on to draw a direct comparison between his ballad's story and NWA's notorious 1988 track "Fuck Tha Police", which opens with a scene putting the white police themselves on trial for brutality. "The rebellious intent – pushing at the boundaries of what was permissible in its historical moment – matches that of 'Stackolee'," Quinn says. "Stackolee meets the LAPD, as it were". [21]

Thousands of young people in poor black neighbourhoods all over America are still trapped in "Stagger Lee's" violent world. Maybe that's why Bobby Seale, the Black Panther leader, decided to name his son Malik Nkrumah Staggerlee Seale. "He's named after his brother on the block, like all his brothers and sisters off the block," Seale explained in 1970. "Staggerlee is Malcolm X before he became politically conscious. Livin' in the hoodlum world." [22]

Draw a line from "Stagger Lee" through Seale's Panther buddies, and you come to gangsta rapper Tupac Shakur. In October 1993, Shakur came across two off-duty Georgia cops who he believed were harassing a black man by the side of the road. He got into a fight with them and ended up shooting them both, one in the leg, the other in the buttocks. Charges against him were dropped when it emerged that the cops had been drunk at the time, and carrying weapons stolen from an evidence locker.

Discussing this incident, the *NME* rhetorically asked why Shakur would sabotage his own lucrative career for what he called the thug life. "Fans of Tupac accuse the white community of missing the point," the paper's Randee Dawn replied. "They say Shakur is a black hero in the tradition of blues archetype Stagger Lee." From "Stagger Lee" through the Black Panthers to Tupac: the line of heritage seems clear enough. [23]

We're still waiting for the definitive gangsta rap take on Stack's own story, but that's not to say that rap has ignored him altogether. A St Petersburg combo called Billy's Band recently produced a rap cover of Nick Cave's "Stagger Lee". It's full of thunderous drums and rapped with a strong Russian accent. Putin's Russia can more than match the violence and corruption thrown up by St Louis in 1895, so perhaps this version is less of a cultural oddity than it seems.

We've come a long way from Mississippi John Hurt's sober and saddened account of Stack's violence back in 1928. Each successive generation that takes on the song has darkened it, stepped a little more keenly into the killer's shoes and cast aside another scrap of whatever pity remains for Billy. For Cave, though, it's the sheer sadism of versions like his that makes them so exhilarating. "What I like about it is that Stagger Lee's atrocious behaviour has nothing to do with anything but flat-out meanness," he told *Mojo* in 1996. "Just like Stagger Lee himself, there seems to be no limits to how evil this song can become." [24]

Way up high: 10 great versions of Stack's story.

"Stack O'Lee Blues", by Mississippi John Hurt (1928). One of three essential versions of the song – the others being Lloyd Price's and Nick Cave's. Hurt's guitar picking is gloriously pretty, his voice both sad and wise. He almost whispers the tale, making you lean in to avoid missing a single word.

"Stagger Lee", by Lloyd Price (1958). If you could press the essence of a damn good party on to 7" vinyl, it would sound like this. Pounding drums, blasting horns, a rasping sax and the backing singers' bellowed encouragement send Price's celebratory account into the stratosphere. A welcome reminder that R&B wasn't always a synonym for the blander end of soul.

"The Trial Of Stagger Lee", by Stella Johnson (1961). This chug-along sixties soul version is set in a courtroom packed with women. They're all anxious to believe Stack's claim that he didn't know the gun was loaded, chanting "Not Guilty" at the far more sceptical judge. Stagger Lee, we conclude, is just too much man for any woman to want to see him jailed

"Stagger Lee", by The Ventures (1963). The world's finest surf guitar act twang up Lloyd Price's tune to admirable effect on this long-neglected instrumental. Well worth the 36-year wait for Ace Records to exhume it on a 1999 compilation.

"Stagger Lee", by Elvis Presley (1970). Presley was rehearsing for a show in Culver City, California, when this fragment of the song was recorded. The sound quality on the inevitable bootleg recording is not great, but you can hear he's enjoying himself. "I got 300 little kids," he howls as the band loosens up behind him. "And a very horny wife."

"Stagolee's Victory", by The Savage Rose (1972). This Danish cult band pulls out all the stops for a full-on gospel treatment which makes

Stack a metaphor for every oppressed black man in America. There's the hint of a New Orleans funeral march in there, some splendidly macabre lyrics ("Stagolee ain't got no eyes") and a promise at the end that vengeance is coming. No wonder Bobby Seale's Black Panthers loved this band.

"Stagolee", by Dr Hook (1978). A disco-country take on the song by an international chart act sounds unlikely enough on its own, but the men behind "Sylvia's Mother" go a step further. This is one of the few versions to foreground Stack's magic hat, explaining how the Devil gave it to him and the powers of immortality it conveys.

"Stack-O-Lee", by Tom Morrell & The Time Warp Tophands (1994). Morrell and his western swing pals canter through Billy's slaughter, Stack's hanging and his take-over of hell with the aid of a saloon piano and a perky pedal steel guitar. Murder, execution, damnation and revolt have never sounded so jolly.

"Stagger Lee", by Nick Cave & The Bad Seeds (1996). Superbly sinister and powerful, this is far and away the song's single best recording of the past half-century. A stand-out track on the classic 1996 *Murder Ballads* album, it's been a mainstay of The Bad Seeds' live set ever since. Cave's personification of Stack on stage seems little short of possession.

"Poor Man's Stagger Lee", by Stagger Lee (2007). The eponymous singer warns a woman that the no-good waster she's with is nothing but "a poor man's Stagger Lee". Why can't she choose a hard-working good ol' boy like himself instead? A barbed-wire banjo accompaniment underscores his point, but we all know she isn't going to listen.

2 - Frankie & Johnny

*"Allen Britt, colored, was shot and badly wounded shortly after 2 o'clock
yesterday morning by Frankie Baker, also colored. The shooting occurred in
Britt's room at 212 Targee Street, and was the culmination of a quarrel.
The woman claimed that Britt had been paying attentions to another
woman. The bullet entered Britt's abdomen, penetrating the intestines.
The woman escaped after the shooting."*
St Louis Globe-Democrat, 16 October 1899.

Just 48 hours after Frankie Baker pulled that trigger, a ballad telling
her story was already being hawked on the city's street corners. Allen
wasn't even dead yet – he didn't finally succumb to his wounds until 19
October – but already the balladeers had him six feet under. The song's
been in constant circulation ever since.

The fact that Allen's murder took place just a few blocks from
where Stagger Lee had killed Billy Lyons four years before means the
two ballads have always tended to get tangled up with one another,
swapping fragments of their lyrics at will. It's no surprise that many of
Stag's musical biographers – including both Dylan and Presley – have
tackled Frankie's story too, but what is unique about her is the degree
of interest that Hollywood's always shown.

From Mae West's 1933 outing *She Done Him Wrong* to the 1991
vehicle for Al Pacino and Michelle Pfeiffer, Frankie has seldom been
off the silver screen. She's trod the theatre's boards pretty regularly
too, appearing in both John Huston's 1930 play about her crime and
Terrence McNally's *Frankie & Johnny In The Clair De Lune*, which was
given a London staging as recently as 2005. As we'll see, very few of
these productions have bothered themselves much with the facts, but

they have ensured that the two lovers' names remain firmly linked together in all our minds.

Frankie Baker was a young prostitute, aged about 24 when the killing took place, who lived and worked in the heart of St Louis's flourishing vice district. Richard Clay, a former neighbour, described her like this: "She was a beautiful, light brown girl, who liked to make money and spend it. She dressed very richly, sat for company in magenta lady's cloth, diamonds as big as hen's eggs in her ears. There was a long razor scar down the side of her face she got in her teens from a girl who was jealous of her. She only weighed about 115lbs, but she had the eye of one you couldn't monkey with. She was a queen sport." [1]

Allen Britt, who was about 17 when he died, shared Frankie's Targee Street rooms, and seems to have acted as her pimp. He was a talented piano player and known as a snappy dresser. He was also cheating on Frankie with an 18-year-old prostitute called Alice Pryar.

The film director John Huston, then a struggling writer, gives us Clay's comments in a footnote essay to his play, the text of which was published in 1930. "Frankie loved [Allen] all right," Clay recalled. "He was wise for his years but not old enough to be level with any woman. Frankie was ready money. She bought him everything he wanted and kept his pockets full. Then while she was waiting on company he would be out playing around."

Clay, who had sat with Allen while he died in City Hospital, also gave Huston his own account of what happened on the fatal night. He said Frankie had surprised Allen with Alice at the Phoenix Hotel, calling him out into the street for a furious public row. Allen, Clay said, had refused to go home with Frankie, so she'd stormed off back to Targee Street alone. Allen turned up there about dawn, admitted he'd spent the night with Alice, and threatened to leave Frankie for good. According to Clay, Frankie had then begun crying and started out the door to find Alice. Allen threatened to kill her if she took another step and that's when the fight broke out.

Frankie gave her own version of events when testifying in court. She said she'd known Allen was at a party with Alice on the Saturday night but was determined not to let that bother her, so she headed home and went to bed for some sleep. Under her pillow, she'd stashed a loaded handgun.

Allen crashed into the room about 3 a.m., waking Frankie with the sudden noise. He grabbed a lamp and threw it at her. "I asked him, 'Say, are you trying to hurt me?'" she told the jury. "'I don't want to hurt you and I don't want you to hurt me. Best place for you to go is to your mother.' He stood there and cursed me and said he wasn't going anyplace. I said, 'I'm the boss here, I pay the rent and I have to protect myself'. [2]

"He ran his hand in his side pocket, opened his knife and started round this side [of the bed] to cut me. I was standing there: pillow lays this way. Just run my hand under the pillow and shot him. Didn't shoot but once, standing by the bed." Recalling the event years later for a 1935 interview in *Daring Detective Tabloid*, Frankie added that Allen had beaten her badly a few nights before the killing. The judge had noticed her black eye in court, she said, and may have taken pity on her as a result. [3]

If we assume that both Frankie and Allen were trying to salvage what pride they could when relating the incident, there's no real contradiction in their two accounts. Allen – via Clay – tells us what happened up to the point when Frankie went home and Frankie takes up the story from there.

Allen staggered from the room when Frankie shot him and made it as far as the steps of his mother's house at 32 Targee Street before collapsing. He told her what had happened and – according to Clay – she began to scream "Frankie's shot Allen! Frankie's shot Allen!" By the time he was taken to City Hospital everyone in the neighbourhood knew that Frankie had got her man.

Police took Frankie to the hospital too, where Allen confirmed she was the one who'd shot him. Doctors found a bullet in his liver and he died there in the early hours of 19 October. Frankie was arrested and jailed, getting her hearing on 13 November 1899, where the verdict was justifiable homicide in self-defence. "I ain't superstitious no more," she later said. "I went to trial on Friday 13 and the bad luck omens didn't go against me. Why, the judge even gave me back my gun." [4]

The first ballad we know of telling this tale is Bill Dooley's "Frankie Killed Allen", which he's said to have written on the night after the shooting itself. Dooley, a black St Louis pianist and songwriter, had a knack for verses setting the city's juiciest news stories to a catchy tune and by all accounts this was one of his best efforts yet. He printed up copies of the finished song as crude single-sheet publications and set about hawking them at 10c a time as he performed the ballad for passing pedestrians all over St Louis's Chestnut Valley vice district.

It wasn't long before the surrounding bars and whorehouses all had a copy and were ordering their own pianists to play it too. Frankie soon came to hate the song. By Christmas 1899, she couldn't go anywhere in St Louis without hearing the damned thing played by a nearby street musician or blaring from the doorway of a crowded bar. She would never escape it again.

The ragtime musician Hughie Cannon, who'd had a big sheet music hit with his 1902 song "Won't You Come Home Bill Bailey", gave "Frankie & Johnny" its next big boost. In 1904, he published sheet music for a song he called "He Done Me Wrong", adding the subtitle "Death Of Bill Bailey" to try and capitalise on his earlier success. The tune's very similar to the "Frankie & Johnny" melody we know today and retains Dooley's "He Done Me Wrong" refrain. Cannon discarded the rest of the existing lyrics, however, substituting Mrs Bailey's tale of her husband's death from cholera.

By 1909, when the song collector John Lomax found a Texas version returning us to Frankie's own tale, her victim's name was no longer Allen, but Albert. Some sources insist this had been Britt's baptismal name all along – "Allen" being simply what he preferred to go by on the street – though I wonder if it's the song's own contraction of "Al Britt". In any case, he was rechristened again in Frank & Bert Leighton's 1912 sheet music for their vaudeville song "Frankie & Johnny" and that's the name which has stuck ever since.

These extracts are taken from The Leighton Brothers' version:

Frankie and Johnny were sweethearts,
They had a quarrel one day,
Johnny he vowed he would leave her,
Said he was going away,

Frankie she begged and pleaded,
Cried "Oh Johnny, please stay",

She says "My honey, I've done you wrong,
But please don't go away",

Johnny says "Listen now, Frankie,
Don't want to tell you no lie,
I've lost my heart to another queen,
Her name is Nellie Bly",

Frankie then said to her Johnny,
"Say man, your hour has come",
From under her silk kimono,
She drew a forty-four gun,

Johnny he dashed down the stairway,
Crying "Oh Frankie, don't shoot",
Frankie took aim with the forty-four,
Five times with a rooty-toot-toot,

"Send for your rubber-tired hearses,
Go get your rubber-tired hacks,
Take lovin' Johnny to the graveyard,
I shot him in the back". [5]

It's odd to hear Frankie telling Johnny that it's she who's done him wrong there, rather than the other way round. As we can see, Alice Pryar has already been rechristened Nellie Bly. Listeners would have known that name both from the title of Stephen Foster's 1850 minstrel song and from the by-line adopted by Elizabeth Cochrane, a famously enterprising reporter of Frankie's day. Singers tackling "Frankie & Johnny" may have simply found the substituted name easier to remember and pronounce. Frankie's generous wardrobe allowance for Johnny doesn't appear anywhere in the Leighton Brothers' version, but we know that was safely in place by 1916. A version the English song collector Cecil Sharp transcribed on a visit to North Carolina that year puts it like this:

Franky was a good girl since everybody knows,
She paid one hundred dollar bill,
For a suit of little Albert's clothes. [6]

The first audio recording of "Frankie & Johnny" seems to be the Paul Biese Trio's jaunty 1921 reading. By the time their vocalist, Frank Crumit, cut the song again as a solo disc six years later, all the remaining elements we're now used to were there. Crumit's version gives Frankie a much more robust view of where the real blame lies in this situation ("He was my man and he done me wrong"), cuts the Leightons' five shots down to the now-standard three and adds a couple of coda verses about Frankie's arrest. These briefly raise the spectre of the electric chair, but then explain that the law declined to punish her at all.

A few last refinements would follow in the next couple of years, but essentially Crumit's version is the same "Frankie & Johnny" we know today. He'd enjoyed a big hit with "Abdul Abulbul Amir" just a few months earlier, so the fact that he'd chosen "Frankie & Johnny" as its follow-up raised the song's profile to a whole new level.

Meanwhile, amateur musicians all over America were continuing to produce their own folk variants, each with its own unique twist on Frankie's tale. When Huston published his play's text in 1930 he added a dozen of these variants to boost the book's page count, no two of which tell the story in quite the same way. The most mutable detail of all is the name of Frankie's rival, who Huston's dozen ballads variously call Alice Blye, Alice Fry, Alkali, Alco Lize, Nelsie Fly, Katy Fly and Sara Slies. Frankie's own name is not sacred either, appearing as Amy in two of the ballads and Lilly in a third. The man she shoots is called Albert in nine cases – suggesting they date from quite early in the song's career – Johnny in two and Pauly in the last.

Whatever they decide to call him, Huston's ballads want us to know that Albert/Johnny/Pauly had some nasty habits. These verses were found in West Virginia:

Albert was a bad man,
He always liked to sin,
The only fault that Albert had,
Was drinking too much gin,

Albert was a bad boy,
He never did do right,
The only thing that Albert did,
Was gamble, drink and fight. [7]

These verses, collected in 1925, have Frankie finding Albert was partial to a spot of opium too:

Oh, I went down to the hop-joint,
An' I rung the hop-joint bell,
And there sat Albert a-hittin' the pipe,
A-hittin' the pipe to beat hell. [7]

After Frankie's shot her man, this Appalachian version summons her family to offer some comfort:

In came Frankie's father,
And says "What makes you sigh?
For every nickel and dime he gets,
He spends on Nelsie Fly,
He done you wrong,
He done you wrong",

In came Frankie's sister,
And says "What makes you weep?
If Johnny Gray had been a man of mine,
I'd a-killed him away last week!
He's done you wrong,
He's done you wrong". [7]

These verses are great fun, but Crumit's 1927 recording only underlined the fact that an agreed-upon version of the song's lyrics was now in place. Huston ensured his own play stuck closely to the same plot, carefully including the $100 suit of clothes, the couple's vow to remain as faithful as the stars and Johnny's dalliance with Nellie Bly. Frankie kills Johnny with the preferred three shots, giving him time to quote a verse from the ballad verbatim before he dies, and then goes uncomplaining to the gallows. Huston leaves the audience to decide exactly how Frankie's earned the money Johnny steals from her, but does nothing to deny that she's a prostitute.

He gives all his characters a phonetic Yosemite Sam accent throughout ("I was a-goin' to turn it over to ye in one lump sum a cash like ye allus wanted") and canters through the whole tale in a brisk 60 pages of double-spaced dialogue. He saves his most macabre touch for the end, when Frankie addresses the crowd gathered round her scaffold and offers to lead them all in one final dance. "I'll be showin' ye new steps in a minute," she promises as the hangman places the noose round her neck. "Steps ye've never seen before."

Huston took to staging his play as a puppet show, which became a big hit at New York's society parties of the Prohibition era. Writing in March 1930, the gossip columnist Deming Seymour revealed George Gershwin had paid Huston and his assistant $200 for a recent performance at the composer's home. Cartier's Jules Glaenzer and the philanthropist Paul Felix Warburg also hired him to stage the show for their own guests. I'm sure all three hosts had plenty of illicit hooch on hand, which may explain later rumours maintaining one of Huston's *Frankie & Johnny* stagings was interrupted by a police raid.

Just as with "Stagger Lee", Frankie's tale also produced an underground "toast" version of the song, far too filthy to be published in any respectable journal or recorded commercially. Fortunately, the anonymous compiler of an underground 1927 anthology called *Immortalia* liked "Frankie & Johnnie" enough to include it in his daringly raunchy book. The 18 verses there tell the same core story, but offer a far less squeamish account of what its two protagonists' lives must really have been like.

Frankie, we're told, is a "fucky hussy", whose johns keep her so busy that she "never had time to get out of bed". She gives all her money to Johnnie, "who spent it on parlour house whores", but still can't stop him "finger-frigging Alice Bly". The toast's Frankie shoots Johnnie five times – just as she'd done in The Leighton Brothers' 1912 lyrics – which suggests it was already in circulation long before the official song ever appeared on disc. "I didn't shoot him in the third degree," Frankie boasts to the judge in court. "I shot him in his big fat ass."

As far as I know, there's never been a recorded version of the toast's lyrics, but here's a couple of sample verses to give you the flavour. The first comes as Frankie takes a break from servicing her clients to hand over the cash she's earned:

> *Frankie hung a sign on her door,*
> *"No more fish for sale",*
> *Then she went looking for Johnnie,*
> *To give him all her kale,*
> *He was a-doin' her wrong,*
> *God-damn his soul!*

And here's what happens when she discovers the awful truth:

> *Frankie ran back to the crib-joint,*
> *Took the oilcloth off the bed,*
> *Took out a bindle of coke,*
> *And snuffed it right up in her head,*
> *God-damn his soul,*
> *He was a-doin' her wrong!* [8]

There are several variations on these lyrics, which add additional refinements such as Frankie shooting Johnnie in the balls or firing a bullet directly up his hole. In one version, she brings his penis back from the graveyard as a souvenir, explaining that it's "the best part of the man who done her wrong". In 1990, the writer and artist Daniel Clowes adapted these toast lyrics into a three-page comic strip picturing all their key scenes.

Brutal as the *Immortalia* version is, it's probably a lot closer to the truth. We know from contemporary press reports that cocaine was a popular drug in 1890s brothels, so it makes sense to imagine Frankie using the stuff. Street-level prostitution in any age is likely to be a fairly squalid and violent affair, so it's hard to accuse the toast of being unduly lurid on those grounds. It certainly isn't pretty, but then Frankie's real life must often have lacked decorum too.

Hoping to escape her new notoriety, the real Frankie fled St Louis in late 1900. She moved first to Nebraska and then to Oregon, but found the song followed her everywhere she went. "Everybody along Targee Street was singing that song," she later recalled. "I'd come out of my house and they'd follow me down the street, a-singing and a-singing. It followed me to Omaha and then to Portland. I couldn't get away from it." [9]

Frankie eventually settled down in Portland, running a tiny shoe-shine parlour there, where she'd sit in the window playing solitaire all day when business was slow. The ballad never went away – Mississippi John Hurt, Riley Puckett and Jimmie Rodgers all recorded it in 1928 or 1929 and the first film adaptation came out in 1930 – but for a while at least she was left in peace.

In 1933, all that changed. Paramount's *She Done Him Wrong* was Mae West's first starring vehicle and also the film which kick-started Cary Grant's career. Based on West's play *Diamond Lil*, it contains many of her best lines, as well as her own rendition of "Frankie & Johnny". Ads for the film make its debt to Frankie's ballad very clear. "Frankie and Johnny were sweethearts," their headlines blare. "He was her man, but ... She Done Him Wrong". West's character in the movie, a sexbomb singer called Lady Lou, underlines the connection again in her own dialogue. "Some guy done her wrong," she says of another woman at the saloon where she works. "The story's so old it should have been set to music long ago."

Prompted by the film's release, a *Salt Lake Tribune* reporter tracked Frankie down in Portland, where he found a "gray-haired, big-muscled woman" of quiet disposition who wanted only to be left alone. "She refused to discuss her past," he wrote. "The shining of shoes and the dealing of solitaire keeps her busy." [10]

When West's film reached Portland, Frankie found strangers gathering outside her home to point at her and stare. "I'm so tired of it all, I don't even answer any more," she told a reporter. "What I want is peace – an opportunity to live like a normal human being. I know that I'm black but, even so, I have my rights. If people had left me alone, I'd have forgotten this thing a long time ago."

Added to this irritation was Frankie's growing resentment that everyone seemed to be profiting from the story but her. She'd already persuaded herself that authors like Huston must be making a fortune from their books about her, and now here was Paramount capitalising on the case as well. "All these writing fellows and such have been writing about me for years," she complained. "One man made $25,000 on a book about 'Frankie & Johnny', and I never got a quarter from him writing me up that way. Not five cents! Here I am sick and almost broke and they're making money writing my life! I'm sore. They've got to pay me from now on." [11]

She sued both Paramount Productions and Mae West herself, asking for $100,000 in damages. "Mae West chuckled when informed in Hollywood of the suit," the *Harrisburg Telegraph* reported. "'What's she going to do?' asked Miss West. 'Sue everybody in the country who sings the song 'Frankie & Johnny'?'" Louis Phillips, the studio's trial counsel, added that the whole suit was "ridiculous".

For Frankie, though, her lawsuit was no laughing matter. She argued the song's account of her life – and therefore the movie too – was defamatory and full of factual errors. The shooting had happened at home, she said, not in a saloon as the song often claimed. Allen was a "conceited piano player" not a gambler, her gun had been a smaller calibre than the one described and she'd fired it only once, rather than the three times stated in the song. Most important of all, she had killed Allen not in the fit of sexual jealousy the song depicts, but because he was attacking her with a knife. She reminded everyone once again that the real verdict in the real case had been justifiable homicide in self-defence.

Taken as a whole, Frankie's counsel said, West's movie portrayed his client as "a woman of easy virtue, as the consort of gamblers and notorious criminals and as a murderess". It had brought her into "public scandal, infamy, shame and disgrace", he added, making Frankie an object of "hatred, ridicule, shame and contempt". Despite all these charges, the court was not convinced she deserved any compensation and Frankie lost her case. [12]

She sued a second time over Republic's 1936 film *Frankie & Johnny*, which starred Helen Morgan in another loose adaptation of the song's tale. Just like the Mae West release before it, Frankie argued, the new film presented a false and humiliating account of her life. This time, she sued the studio, Morgan, two of the film's other actors, its director, its screenwriter and two of Republic's distribution companies. She also upped the ante by asking for $200,000 rather than the $100,000 she'd demanded from Paramount.

In 1938, $200,000 had about the same spending power $3.4m would have today. But Frankie had no illusions about receiving the full sum. "My attorney's suing for $200,000, but you know how those costs are," she told the *Oregon Statesman*. "You've got to sue for a figure and then take a dime on the dollar. Those picture people made a lot of money out of that picture, and I think old Frankie Baker should get some of it." [13]

Frankie's lawyers, the black firm of McLemore & Witherspoon, filed papers to begin the action in April 1938. The studio stalled proceedings for as long as it could but finally, in August 1941, Judge Robert Aaronson sent Frankie's case for a jury trial at St Louis's Circuit Court. This gave both Richard Clay and Frankie herself a chance to once again give their first-hand accounts of what happened on the night of the shooting.

Clay's testimony confirmed that the ballad's sketch of Al Britt's character gets him just about right. "We was good friends," he said. "He was a great man with the girls and I told him once he'd better quit speaking to so many of them. He was a fancy dresser all right. Frankie was Al's main girl, older than he was and never had any trouble with nobody that I know of on the street. Yeah, I knew Alice Pryar. Al used to take her out too. She and Frankie had a little mix-up over Al. People said Frankie and Al used to fuss about her. I don't know. Frankie was a nice girl and behaved herself like a lady." [14]

When her turn in the witness box came, Frankie gave her own description of the man she'd killed. "He was a dark fella," she said. "Extremely dark and good-looking. He was a spare-built fella and a very good dancer. Although I knew he stepped out once in a while, I didn't shoot him because he was running round with any other woman." [15]

"I remember the night he was shot," Clay added. "I was in bed at the time, but got up and went down to Al's house. He was laying on the steps of his mother's house and people said he had run home from Frankie's. I was at the inquest too, but I didn't see much of Frankie after that. People said she left St Louis because the songs folks was singing all over town annoyed her." [16]

Republic fought its own side of the case by hiring a string of academics to testify that the ballad "Frankie & Johnny" pre-dated 1899, and therefore couldn't have been based on Al Britt's killing. Their evidence for this was flimsy at best, relying largely on a notion of precisely when the phrase "crib-man" became an archaic term. One of Republic's hired guns was the musicologist Sigmund Spaeth, whose testimony sat oddly with his contribution to a 1927 book called *American Mountain Songs*. In that book, which Spaeth edited, the ballad is actually titled "Frankie Baker" and described as "the St Louis classic". Despite this, Spaeth backed the studio's argument in court, and once again Frankie lost her case.

The verdict came on 24 February 1942, the jury taking just over an hour to reach its decision. "A unanimous verdict was reached on the third ballot," the *Ottawa Journal* reported. "The defence was based chiefly on testimony of research experts that the song originated many years before the St Louis episode." [17]

Frankie's chances of victory had always been pretty slim. Watching the two movies now, it's hard to see how she ever hoped to build a case. Frankie – or in Mae West's case, her stand-in Lady Lou – is presented as a sympathetic character in both films, who never actually kills anyone herself. The worst you can say of Lou is that she knowingly sends a man off to his death, but he's such a revolting character that we're encouraged to think it served him right. The Helen Morgan vehicle sticks closer to the real story, but makes Frankie a saintly figure who's saved from pulling the trigger by another character stepping in first.

The truth of the matter is that the damage Frankie suffered from these two films lay less in the plots they used than in the fact that they pulled the song back to the front of everybody's mind and made it even more famous than it had been before. *She Done Him Wrong* was a huge hit, pulling in $2.2 million on Paramount's investment of just $200,000, and that sort of box-office take in 1933 translated to a vast audience. That's what generated the sudden surge in curiosity about her which Frankie found so distressing, but it wasn't a close enough connection to win her any cash. [18]

Frankie lost her shoe-shine parlour in the 1940s, when Portland's city authorities demolished the condemned building where it was housed. By 1950 she was on relief and, aged 74, she moved into Oregon's Multnomah County Home. She was still perfectly lucid about killing Allen, but seemed confused about every other aspect of her life.

Officials at the home complained that she frightened and attacked other residents. In a May 1950 hearing in Portland, Judge Ashby Dickson ruled Frankie was a danger to herself and others, declared her insane and sent her to the state mental hospital at Pendleton, where she died 18 months later. Even in death, she couldn't escape the ballad: "Frankie of song fame dies at Pendleton," one headline announced. [19]

The real Frankie may be gone, but her fictional alter-ego seems as immortal as ever. A 1962 thesis by Bruce Redfern Buckley found no fewer than 291 versions of the ballad to study. Since then, we've had two more *Frankie & Johnny* movies, one starring Elvis Presley in 1966 and one starring Al Pacino and Michelle Pfeiffer in 1991. Though both were happy to exploit the song's title, neither bothered much with its underlying facts. Presley's offering puts Frankie, Johnny and Nellie on a Mississippi riverboat and lets them all live happily ever after when the credits roll, while Pacino's gives us a couple of knowing asides about the song ("Didn't they kill each other?") but crafts its own plot from scratch. One day, we may get a *Frankie & Johnny* movie casting black actors in its two title roles, but that hasn't happened yet.

Songwriters have not been shy to exercise artistic licence either. Sam Cooke's 1963 version – a top 30 hit on both sides of the Atlantic – had Frankie giving her beau a sports car and some "Ivy League clothes". Jimmy Anderson's 1969 blues take for Excello ends with her getting drunk in the bar where she'd found Johnny and then merely dumping him instead of killing him. Bob Dylan included the song on his 1992 album *Good As I Been To You*, but could not resist adding details of Frankie's execution on the gallows.

It's far from the only measure of a song's success, of course, but if it's accuracy you're after, then Mississippi John Hurt's 1928 "Frankie" is hard to beat. Recorded relatively close to the event, this version gets just about everything right. All the characters are given their real names, the row in the street which Clay describes is sketched out and Frankie leaves the court a free woman. True, Hurt has Frankie shoot Albert three or four times and sends her along to a funeral she never attended, but compared to the liberties taken elsewhere, these are very small offences.

By far the best "Frankie & Johnny" of recent years is the one Snakefarm recorded for their 1999 album *Songs From My Funeral*. Finding herself trapped in a bad publishing deal, the band's Anna Domino had decided to forego her own songwriting to work with her husband Michel Delory on giving some traditional American ballads a radical new treatment instead. She knew the strength of these songs well, and that the folk process often produced a result which no individual songwriter could hope to match.

"It takes a long time to produce a ballad that will stick," she told me. "It has to go through generations and genres, shed its copyright, be half-forgotten and then rediscovered." It's this process of constant tempering that gives such songs their extraordinary power and the reinterpretations they get from each new generation that keeps them alive. [20]

"One day, while waiting to cross Canal Street in New York, I announced to Michel that I would try recording some of the old songs, but with modern rhythm sections," Domino said. "By next morning, I had sketches of three songs with rhythm, bass, vocals, basic arrangements. Those three songs were 'St James Infirmary', 'Streets Of Laredo' and – I think – 'Stagger Lee'. 'St James Infirmary' came first and arranged itself, which is how you know when things are working.

"It truly surprised me that these verbose songs could put up with strong rhythms. I'd always understood that the stronger the rhythms, the simpler the vocals had to be. Of course, I'd taken great liberties with the songs, but that's what public domain is for. These songs are deathless. They're endlessly mutable. Uncountable numbers have been lost and forgotten, of course, but the themes never die."

Domino's first exposure to these songs came when spending time with her Ozarks grandparents as a child. "My grandfather sang after dinner sometimes," she said. "Songs that went on for 30 verses or so. One that stuck with me had the refrain 'And they laid her down in a lov-el-ly grave'. The songs Snakefarm covers are the ones I've been playing since I got my first guitar in my early teens."

Hearing as they prepared the album that Nick Cave was already working on his own version of "Stagger Lee", Snakefarm shelved that track for the time being. Even so, *Songs From My Funeral* has plenty of murder ballads, including not only "Frankie & Johnny" itself but also "Tom Dooley" and "Banks Of The Ohio" among its ten tracks. Throughout, the band's approach is to give these songs a dark, trancey setting, full of atmospheric soundscapes and bluesy guitar. The effect is to sweep away a century of over-familiar traditional interpretations to render the songs once again as mysterious and disturbing as they were always meant to be.

"American traditional ballads are particularly morbid, cruel and heartbreaking because America was a very scary place," Domino said. "All those immigrants with their own customs, traditions and religions poured in to face an unassailably strange, wild and unknowable land that was almost lawless. They'd left their families and homes forever and entered a place of great hardship and mystery. I never singled out songs of murder particularly – there are just a lot of them."

For "Frankie & Johnny" itself Snakefarm sticks close to the lyrics' established tale, which Domino sings in a sweet, breathy voice. The mournful backing traces the border between jazz and blues, easing itself slowly along with bongo drums and a prominent bass. There's a touch of twang in the guitar, a wisp of ghostly flute here and there to underscore the song's essential sorrow and a quietly reflective instrumental passage as Frankie drinks in the enormity of what she's done.

"We got some friends in from New York to help fill out my initial arrangement," Domino recalled. "It changed a lot in the process, going from a more aggressive electronic beat to something softer. As dreamy as an opium high, or – as I thought of it while doing the vocals – what was going through Johnny's mind as he lay wounded and dying on that hardwood floor. I got Michel to sing very quietly behind me in the refrain to try and bring Johnny in.

"Stephen Ulrich added his distinctive, unexpected guitar accents, Paul Dugan brought his upright bass in to ground and smooth out the rhythmic feel, and Paul Shapiro's flute is a lovely whisper here and there. The only thing left of the original electronic beat is the bongos."

It's no coincidence that the track's prevailing mood recalls the jazz soundtracks used in the great crime movies of Hollywood's noir era. "It grew out of the instrumental part with the finger snaps," Domino said. "That set a rhythm and a feel that infected the rest of the song. And it doesn't hurt that the lyrics tell a damned good suspense story."

Here's how Snakefarm handles the moment of Frankie's terrible discovery:

Frankie went down to the corner,
Just for a bucket of beer,
She said to the fat bartender,
"Has my lovin'est man been here?"
He was her man, but he done her wrong,

"I don't want to cause you no trouble,
 And I don't want to tell you no lies,
But I saw your man here an hour ago,
With a gal named Alice Blye,
If he's your man, he's doin' you wrong",

Frankie looked over the transom,
And found to her great surprise,
That there on the bed sat Johnny,
And he was lovin' up Alice Blye,
He was her man, but he done her wrong. [21]

We all know what happens next – and anyone who's had their own partner cheat on them may recognise the anger which drives Frankie's hand towards her gun. For most of us, that moment of blind rage passes with no fatal results, but Frankie was not so fortunate. "The song describes a very human experience," Domino said. 'But she actually goes through with it and loses everything but her liberty. It's desperation that drives her to kill. Everyone suffers tragedies of necessity in these songs. Frankie loses the love of her life twice over. Poor Johnny dies in agony. We are fascinated by our own suffering and that's what these songs represent."

Doing her right: 10 great versions of Frankie's story

"Leaving Home", by Charlie Poole & The North Carolina Ramblers (1926). Poole's retitled version of "Frankie & Johnny" gives the song a jolly hillbilly treatment, courtesy of Ramblers' fiddler Posey Rorer. Poole makes Frankie the villain of the piece, having her shoot Johnny in the back for threatening to leave her and then begging to be jailed afterwards.

"Frankie", by Mississippi John Hurt (1928). As with his reading of "Stagger Lee" – based on another St Louis murder of the 1890s – Hurt gives his subject all due gravitas. The gentle beauty of his guitar picking is never allowed to disguise what a sad and wasteful episode he is describing. Far from glorifying the sensational aspects of murder, Hurt's version is full of human sympathy.

"Frankie & Albert", by Leadbelly (1933). Recorded at Angola prison by John and Alan Lomax, Leadbelly gives us a half-sung, half-spoken version set to the steady strum of his own guitar. Frankie's a cook in the white folks' kitchen here and Alice Pryar is given her real name. Albert's mother gets a walk-on part too, as Frankie apologises for killing the woman's only son.

"Frankie & Johnny", by Sammy Davis Jr (1956). Notable not only for its determined use of jazz lingo ("He was her mate / But he wouldn't fly straight"), but also for Cyd Charisse's stunningly sultry dancing. The 1956 MGM musical *Meet Me In Las Vegas* has Sammy singing the story while Cyd slinks through Frankie's role in a big production number which is sexy, witty and inventive. She's never been more of a "queen sport" than this.

"Frankie's Man Johnny", by Johnny Cash (1958). Cash casts Johnny as a touring guitarist who leaves his faithful woman at home to have some fun on the road – just as Cash himself was doing at the time. Powered along by the Tennessee Two's trademark chug, Johnny tries to seduce a redhead at one of his gigs only to discover it's his sweetheart's sister checking up on him. It's a near-miss, but he's Frankie's man and "he still ain't done her wrong".

"Frankie & Johnny", by Sam Cooke (1963). Blasting horns and a smouldering bassline help Cooke nudge the song towards the era's popular teen death anthems. Johnny's updated sports car and Ivy League clothes can't save him from Frankie's assumptions of infidelity, but he dies protesting his love for her anyway.

"Frankie & Johnny", by Elvis Presley (1966). Presley sings the ballad from Johnny's point of view, confessing to his dalliance with Nellie Bly, getting shot by Frankie and telling us all about it – quite possibly from beyond the grave. This version outdid Sam Cooke's chart success with the song, reaching number 21 in the UK against Cooke's number 30.

"The New Frankie & Johnny", by The Innsiders (1983). Not a great version, perhaps, but worth hearing all the same. This finger-clicking barbershop quartet transplants the story to New York and replaces Nellie Bly with Sinatra's Miss Annabelle Lee. Imagine Homer Simpson's Be Sharps covering the song and you won't be far out.

"Frankie & Johnny", by Snakefarm (1999). Singer Anna Domino takes it slow for this brooding, bluesy version. Frankie's love and pride in Johnny is evident in Domino's delivery, as is her crushing disappointment when he proves so faithless. The trancey, late-night feel of the accompanying music reminds us that this tale's a tragedy for killer and victim alike.

"Frankie", by Beth Orton (1999). Recorded live at Nick Cave's *Meltdown* festival in London, Orton accompanies herself on acoustic guitar in a fragile, keening rendition that's clearly determined to do Frankie justice. Quieting her guitar to near-silence as she switches to first-person narration in the song's final few lines, she lets her voice alone send Frankie's pain and regret reverberating through the hall.

3 - Knoxville Girl

"Thus I deluded her again,
Into a private place,
Then took a stick out of the hedge,
And struck her in the face,

But she fell on her bended knee,
And did for mercy cry,
'For heaven's sake, don't murder me,
I am not fit to die.'"
"The Berkshire Tragedy" – (1744).

It's the fragility of Charlie Louvin's voice that does it. He was 79 years old when he entered a Nashville studio to re-record "Knoxville Girl" for his self-titled 2007 album and he sounds like a breath of Tennessee wind could blow him away. There's a palpable sadness in his voice as Louvin's character confesses his old crime, but absolutely no attempt to excuse what he's done. The result is one of the most exquisite readings the song's received in its 90-year history on disc.

Like almost every other version, Louvin's sticks closely to the template set by Arthur Tanner on the song's first commercial release in 1927. "Knoxville Girl" was already well-known in the South by the time Tanner's record came out, but it was his Columbia Records 78 which froze it in its enduring form. The version of events Tanner gave us has been adhered to by almost every singer who followed him and it goes like this:

The narrator meets a girl in Knoxville and spends every Sunday evening at her home. One evening, they go for walk and he begins beating her with a sturdy stick. She begs for her life, but he ignores her pleas, continues the beating even more viciously and doesn't stop till the ground is awash with her blood. He dumps her dead body in the river, then returns home, fending off his mother's queries about his stained clothes by insisting he's had a nosebleed. After a tortured night, he's thrown in jail for life. His last words before the music fades out are to assure us that he really did love her.

Louvin first tackled this grim little tale with his brother Ira in 1956, when they worked as a bluegrass duo called The Louvin Brothers. Ira was long dead by the time Charlie revisited the song, and the partner he chose for 2007's session was Will Oldham, better known as Bonny "Prince" Billy. Oldham, who wasn't even born when the Louvins first cut "Knoxville Girl", wisely avoids trying to mimic the brothers' blood-born harmonies, contenting himself instead with some restrained background singing and few lines of the lead vocal when Charlie takes a breather.

Despite the 43-year difference in their ages, the two men clearly see the song through very similar eyes, and that's one clue to why it's survived so long. Like a shark, "Knoxville Girl" seems to have reached a peak of evolution many generations ago, finding an unchanging form which suits each new decade as well as the last. Young singers find the song just as irresistible as their grandfathers did, and show just as little inclination to meddle with its established form. You have only to check iTunes to see that new recordings of "Knoxville Girl" appear there almost daily, as do freshly-packaged compilations exploiting the song's long back catalogue.

Fifteen years into the 21st century, it's clear that everyone still wants a piece of this unfortunate lass. Even now, though, when you play the song to someone who hasn't heard it before, they all ask the same question: why did he kill her?

The song certainly doesn't spell out any motive, moving from an innocent country walk to the start of the beating in two consecutive lines. The Louvin Brothers' 1956 lyric – which I'm going to use as my model throughout this chapter – puts it like this:

> We went to take an evening walk,
> About a mile from town,
> I picked a stick up off the ground,
> And knocked that fair girl down. [1]

It's as simple and as brutal as that: one minute they're walking quietly along, the next he's bludgeoning her with a makeshift club. To see why he's doing this, we have to consider some clues from the rest of the song. Take this couplet from the opening verse:

> *And every Sunday evening,*
> *Out in her home I'd dwell.*

Then there's the victim's words as she begs for mercy:

> *Oh Willard dear, don't kill me here,*
> *I'm unprepared to die.* [2]

And finally, this verse:

> *Go down, go down, you Knoxville Girl,*
> *With the dark and roving eye,*
> *Go down, go down, you Knoxville Girl,*
> *You can never be my bride.*

Put these three fragments together and things begin to get a little clearer. The killer didn't just visit this girl's home on Sunday evenings, he dwelt there, which carries a definite suggestion that he stayed the night. Faced with imminent death, the girl says she's "unprepared to die", which tells us she's not yet had a chance to make her peace with God about some recent sin that's troubling her mind. Her "dark and roving eye" hints that – in the killer's mind at least – she's a bit of a temptress. Although she can now never be his bride, that possibility's evidently been raised, or why else would he mention it?

So, we've got a young man who's slept with his girlfriend, come under some pressure to marry her and then kills her instead. To understand why, we need to rewind the clock to 17th century Shropshire and two of that century's English diarists.

Philip Henry was a non-conformist clergyman living about 25 miles from the Shropshire town of Shrewsbury. The town was also known as Salop in those days and, on 20 February 1683, Henry wrote this in his diary:

> I heard of a murther in Salop on Sabb. Day ye 10. instant, a woman fathering a conception on a Milner was Kild by him in a feild, her Body laye there many dayes by reason of ye Coroner's absence. [3]

Henry, like everyone else in England, then used the Julian calendar, which ran ten days "behind" the modern Gregorian calendar adopted in 1752. Making this adjustment confirms that his 10 February 1683 really was a Sunday. He's a contemporary witness describing a recent event, so there's good reason to take his account seriously.

The next piece of the puzzle comes from the third volume of Samuel Pepys' collected ballads. Pepys was a keen collector of the printed ballad sheets which were then sold on every London street corner and amassed over 1,800 examples in his personal archive. At some point between 1666 and 1688, he added one called "The Bloody Miller", which came complete with this introduction:

> A true and just Account of one Francis Cooper of Hocstow near Shrewsbury, who was a Miller's Servant and kept company with one Anne Nichols for the space of two years, who then proved to be with Child by him and being urged by her Father to marry her he most wickedly and barbarously murdered her. [4]

Sounds familiar, doesn't it? Hocstow, is a 17th century spelling of Hogstow, a village about 12 miles south-west of Shrewsbury, so the place, the killer's profession, the date and the deed itself all match Henry's account. It's fair to conclude that both documents are describing the same crime, and now we can put a name to each of the main players. The murderer was called Francis Cooper, his victim was Anne Nichols and he killed her because he'd knocked her up and didn't want to marry her.

Checking the Shropshire burial records, I discovered a good deal of evidence to support this account. With the help of county archivist Jean Evans, I found a woman called Anne Nicholas who had been buried in

Westbury on 1 March 1683. Given the vagaries of 17th century spelling, "Nichols" and "Nicholas" are a good match, and Westbury lies just five miles from Hogstow itself.

Not only that, but the parish register shows a note of "*truculenter occisa*" against Anne's burial, indicating that she met a violent death. The handwritten register's official print transcript renders this simply as "murdered". Three weeks after her burial, on 24 March, a boy named Ichabod was baptised in the parish, his parents being listed as "Francis Cooper, homicide, and Anne". I was delighted at these details – particularly as I seemed to be the first person who'd dug them out of the archives.

There could hardly be a more appropriate name than Ichabod for Francis and Anne's son. It means "no glory" and comes from the *First Book Of Samuel*, where the wife of Phinehas delivers a son just after hearing its father has been killed in battle and her people defeated. She calls the child Ichabod to reflect the grim circumstances of its birth and then promptly dies herself.

Our records of UK executions don't go back far enough to confirm the ballad's claim that Francis was hanged, but that seems his most likely fate. It would certainly explain why I was unable to find any burial record for him. Like all executed murderers, he'd have been refused burial on sacred ground and hence never entered in the register. I've since visited the Westbury parish church of St Mary's where Anne was probably buried, but its earliest surviving gravestones date back only to about 1800, so there's nothing further to be learned there.

One thing I can't explain is how young Ichabod managed to survive long enough to be baptised. Did Francis wait till just after his son's birth to kill Anne, then abandon the baby to die of starvation or exposure in that Shropshire field? Was the pregnancy so far advanced that someone managed to cut a living child from the dead mother's womb? Whatever the truth of the matter, I suspect he ended up in the care of the church, and that's how he came to be given such a Biblically-appropriate name.

The match of names, places, crimes and dates given in our three documents is too close to dismiss as mere coincidence. The details in Westbury's parish register provide documentary proof there really was a Shropshire murderer called Francis Cooper in 1683, that the ballad sheet identifies his victim correctly, and that Francis really did impregnate her. The delay between Anne's 10 February murder and her burial on 1 March can be explained by the "many dayes" she was left waiting for the coroner and then the inquest conducted when he finally arrived.

Neither Francis nor Anne are given names in "The Bloody Miller"'s verses, which call them simply "I" and "she" throughout. The young miller who narrates the tale spots an attractive girl in his home village and, despite her virtuous nature, persuades her to sleep with him. She discovers she's pregnant and her father sends her round to the miller's cottage to demand he marries her. The miller suggests they find a quiet country spot where they can discuss the matter in private. He then murders her horribly and is eventually hanged for the crime.

The similarities with "Knoxville Girl"'s plot are striking enough, but it's the wording and scansion of the two songs that really establishes "The Bloody Miller" as "Knoxville Girl"'s earliest ancestor. Before we come on to that aspect, though, we need to look at another old English ballad too.

Gallows ballads like "The Bloody Miller" were a popular form in Pepys' day, and often claimed to be an authentic record of the killer's last confession or his dying words on the scaffold. These were composed by workers in every large town's print shops, run off the presses the night before the execution and sold at the base of the gallows itself while the hanged man's body was still swinging. The goriest ballads, which tended to sell particularly well, would be endlessly rewritten and adapted to extend their shelf life, often incorporating local details or adapting themselves to new atrocities as time passed and the sellers travelled from town to town.

"The Bloody Miller" spawned other ballads very quickly and the most significant of these is "The Berkshire Tragedy". The National Library of Australia has an Edinburgh copy printed in 1744, but it's probably a good deal older than that. The ballad tells the same basic story as "The Bloody Miller", but sets its tale in Wytham, just across the border from Berkshire in the next-door county of Oxfordshire. Although the 1744 sheet sticks closely to "The Bloody Miller"'s template, it claims to be the last confession of a Wytham man called John Mauge, who'd just killed his sweetheart Anne Knite and was about to hang for it. If so, then even this very early version of the printed ballad is an amalgam of two quite separate crimes.

"The Berkshire Tragedy" adds several new elements to the tale which are not present in "The Bloody Miller", but which crop up again a century later in the first versions of "Knoxville Girl". Most significantly of all, its narrator describes his victim as "an Oxford lass" – Oxford's about four miles from Wytham – and that's a development which would steer much of the song's later history. It's not clear why it's called "The Berkshire Tragedy" when neither of the main characters lived there, but perhaps "The Oxfordshire Tragedy" was simply thought too unwieldy a title.

Let's recap for a moment. We've got "The Bloody Miller", collected by Pepys in around 1685, complete with an introduction identifying both killer and his victim, plus an independent contemporary account of the crime itself and documents confirming Francis and Anne's names. By 1744, this ballad had produced an alternative version called "The Berkshire Tragedy", which adds many of the details we're familiar with in "Knoxville Girl" today, but which may also draw on a second crime quite separate from the one Pepys' sheet describes.

The ballad scholar George Laws draws precisely this family tree for "Knoxville Girl" in his 1957 book *American Balladry From British Broadsides*, linking the song directly back to 17th century England. "The ballad in all its forms preserves the same stanzic pattern, the same basic sequence of events, many of the same descriptive and narrative details and even the same phrases and rhyming words," he points out. [5]

The clearest way to illustrate this point is to assemble a composite version of "The Bloody Miller" and "The Berkshire Tragedy", using the two English ballads' original wording, but setting each verse against its equivalent in the American song. You can see the result and just how closely it fits "Knoxville Girl", on the page opposite.

The English ballads are a lot more long-winded than their American cousins and tend to go in for a lot more moralising. But cutting all this out, as I've done in my composite version, still leaves all the key elements of "Knoxville Girl" in place. The private walk's there and so's the stick, the plea for mercy and the fact that she's not yet made her peace with God. The sadism of the killing itself is present too, as are the hair, the river, the forestalled wedding, the return home, the nosebleed, the candle, the restless night, the trip to jail and the bad end.

One element which was lost when the English ballads started to be shortened was an unambiguous statement of what caused all the trouble. "The Bloody Miller" has:

KNOXVILLE GIRL

"The Bloody Miller" (c, 1685) /
"The Berkshire Tragedy" (1744)

By chance upon an Oxford lass,
I cast a wanton eye,
And promis'd I would marry her,
If she would with me would lie,

This I deluded her again,
Into a private place,
Then took a stick out of the hedge,
And struck her in the face,

But she fell on her bended knee,
And did for mercy cry,
"For heaven's sake, don't murder me,
I am not fit to die",

From ear to ear I slit her mouth,
And stabbed her in the head,
Till she poor soule did breathless lie,
Before her Butcher bled,

And then I took her by the hair,
To cover this foul sin,
And dragg'd her to the river side,
Then threw her body in,

Thus in the blood of innocence,
My hands were deeply dy'd,
And shined in her purple gore,
That should have been my bride,

Then home unto my mill I ran,
But sorely was amaz'd,
My man thought I had mischief done,
And strangely on me gaz'd,

"How come you by that blood upon,
Your trembling hands and clothes?"
I presently to him reply'd,
"By bleeding at the nose",

I wishfully upon him look'd,
But little to him said,
But snatch'd the candle from his hand,
And went unto my bed,

Where I lay trembling all the night,
For I could take no rest,
And perfect flames of Hell did flash,
Like lightning in my face,

The justice too perceiv'd the guilt,
Nor longer would take bail,
But the next morning I was sent,
Away to Reading gaol,

So like a wretch my dayes I end,
Upon the Gallows Tree,
And I do hope my punishment,
Will such a warning be,
That none may ever after this,
Commit such villany.

"Knoxville Girl", The Louvin Brothers (1956).
Lyrics: Trad / Public Domain.

I met a little girl in Knoxville,
A town we all know well,
And every Sunday evening,
Out in her home I'd dwell,

We went to take an evening walk,
About a mile from town,
I picked a stick up off the ground,
And knocked that fair girl down,

She fell down on her bended knees,
For mercy she did cry,
"Oh, Willard dear, don't kill me here,
I'm unprepared to die",

She never spoke another word,
I only beat her more,
Until the ground around me,
Within her blood did flow,

I took her by her golden curls,
And I drug her round and round,
Throwing her into the river,
That flows through Knoxville town,

Go down, go down, you Knoxville girl,
With the dark and roving eyes,
Go down, go down, you Knoxville girl,
You can never be my bride,

I started back to Knoxville,
Got there about midnight,
My mother she was worried,
And woke up in a fright,

Saying, "Dear son, what have you done,
To bloody your clothes so?"
I told my anxious mother,
I was bleeding at my nose,

I called for me a candle,
To light myself to bed,
I called for me a handkerchief,
To bind my aching head,

Rolled and tumbled the whole night through,
As troubles was for me,
Like flames of hell around my bed,
And in my eyes could see,

They carried me down to Knoxville,
And put me in a cell,
My friends all tried to get me out,
But none could go my bail,

I'm here to waste my life away,
Down in this dirty old jail,
Because I murdered that Knoxville girl,
The girl I loved so well.

She did believe my flattering tongue,
Till I got her with Child. [6]

And "The Berkshire Tragedy" has:

For the damsel came to me and said,
"By you I am with child,
I hope, dear John, you'll marry me,
For you have me defil'd." [7]

Whoever put the earliest versions of "Knoxville Girl" together retained the source ballads' scansion and that means my composite version can be sung to "Knoxville Girl"'s modern tune. In this form, "The Berkshire Tragedy" looks much more significant than "The Bloody Miller", accounting for 40 of the composite's 44 lines. But remember that, without "The Bloody Miller", we'd never have had "The Berkshire Tragedy" in the first place. It's also "The Bloody Miller" which is most directly connected to the real Anne Nichols' death and which first coined this whole family of songs' most distinctive and enduring image:

But when I saw this for my fact,
Just judgement on me passed,
The blood in Court ran from my nose,
Yea, ran exceeding fast.

Every later version, starting with "The Berkshire Tragedy", shifts this scene to the killer's return home, where he uses the nosebleed excuse to fob off questions about his bloodstained clothes. "The Berkshire Tragedy" has him holding this conversation with a servant, but that would hardly have been a credible circumstance for the early Scottish and Irish settlers who first brought this song across the Atlantic. "Knoxville Girl" sets the conversation in simple family surroundings instead, having the killer confronted by his worried mother:

Saying "Dear son, what have you done,
To bloody your clothes so?",
I told my anxious mother,
I was bleeding at my nose.

This nosebleed recurs in almost every version of "Knoxville Girl" and it's the single most reliable DNA "signature" establishing that all the branches of this song's family tree lead back to "The Bloody Miller"'s trunk. In its first usage, it may have been intended as an omen of the killer's ill fortune – in this case, his imminent execution.

This is a belief from English folklore which goes back at least as far as 1180, when Nigel de Longchamps' *Mirror For Fools* has a character interpreting his nosebleed as a sign of bad luck to come. The same idea appears again in John Webster's *Duchess Of Malfi* from 1614 and in Samuel Pepys' 1667 diary. On 6 July that year, Pepys writes: "It was an ominous thing, methought, just as he was bidding me his last Adieu, his nose fell a-bleeding, which run in my mind a pretty while after." [8, 9, 10]

We know this notion was still current when "The Bloody Miller" was written, because 1684 produced *The Island Queens*, a play by the restoration dramatist John Banks, with this exchange:

> **DOWGLAS:** "No sooner was I laid to rest, but just three drops of blood fell from my nose and stain'd my pillow."
> **QUEEN MARY:** "That rather does betoken some mischief to thyself."
> **DOWGLAS:** "Perhaps to cowards, who prize their own base lives. But to the brave, 'tis always fatal to the friend they love." [11]

Anyone who beats a woman to death while she's carrying his child would certainly count as a coward rather than a brave man, so perhaps that's the idea "The Bloody Miller"'s original composer was trying to convey. Equally, it could be simple foreshadowing, creating tension in the audience's mind just as the ominous chords of a horror movie's soundtrack do for us. Either way, the nosebleed is now cemented deep into "Knoxville Girl"'s foundations and it's still the surest sign of every variation's parentage.

Once "The Berkshire Tragedy" had got the process underway, "The Bloody Miller" quickly spawned a dozen competing versions of its basic story. These had titles like "The Cruel Miller", "Hanged I Shall Be", "The Wittham Miller" or "Ekefield Town", and all reported the killer's nosebleed when he returned home. The strength of the core story ensured these songs remained in the ballad sellers' stock for many years and continued to sell well. "The Berkshire Tragedy" itself was still being hawked around London as late as 1825, when a print copy was cheekily retitled to claim the crime had happened just a few months before.

Recycling like this was part and parcel of the ballad seller's trade. "The ballad printers of America and Britain apparently ransacked the old ballad sheets for anything that was usable," Laws says. "Frequently, an archaic ballad could be given local application, or could be redesigned to fit a predetermined amount of space."

It's not clear which version of the song reached America first, but the strand I'm going to follow is the one which starts with "The Berkshire Tragedy"'s description of its victim as "an Oxford lass". We don't know exactly when a version called "The Oxford Tragedy" first appeared. But, given "The Berkshire Tragedy"'s unambiguous setting in Oxfordshire and the fact that the two counties are right next door to each other, the transposition must have suggested itself almost immediately.

Laws suggests that "The Oxford Girl" appeared full-blown in the US, perhaps as a variation of Ireland's similarly-named "Wexford Girl", which again derives from "The Bloody Miller". To me, it makes much more sense to imagine an English version of the song called "The Oxford Tragedy" morphing into "The Wexford Murder" for Irish consumption and then both songs crossing the Atlantic to establish a foothold there. Singers in the New World would presumably have been imagining Oxford, Mississippi, rather than Inspector Morse's dreaming spires, but the song was none the worse for that.

The first proven American original we have is "The Lexington Miller", printed as an early 19th century broadsheet in Boston and currently held by the Harvard College Library. This describes a miller in Lexington, Kentucky, who promises to marry a local girl if she'll sleep with him. We all know what happens next and events here unfold just as they did in "The Berkshire Tragedy" a century before.

Unlike later American versions, "The Lexington Miller" retains many of "The Berkshire Tragedy"'s less important details, such as the Devil tempting our narrator to commit murder, the victim's sister accusing him and the killer's final execution. Once again, though, it's got exactly the same metre we know today from "Knoxville Girl", as a couple of sample verses will demonstrate:

Now she upon her knees did fall,
And most heartily did cry,
Saying "Kind Sir, don't murder me,
I am not fit to die",

I would not harken unto her cries,
But laid it on the more,
Till I had taken her life away,
Which I could not restore. [12]

"Berkshire" is pronounced "Barxshire" in Britain, and my own theory is that the various places where the song touches down – Oxford, Wexford, Lexington, Knoxville – are determined more by that "X" sound in their names than by any more subtle consideration. Once "The BarXshire Tragedy"'s OXford lass found her way into the title and lyrics, any place name lacking that distinctive consonant simply sounded wrong, and that's a tradition the song's offspring have obeyed ever since.

Whatever the reason for its precise setting, by 1831 America's singers had a bloody miller of their own. All they needed now was a home-grown murder they could tie into the song and, by the end of the century, they'd found one.

Mary Lula Noel lived with her parents in Pineville, Missouri, about eight miles from the town which bore her family's name. On Wednesday, 7 December 1892, she was staying with her sister, Mrs Sydney Holly, at the Holly family's nearby home, when a Joplin man named William Simmons arrived to visit her. Simmons was still there on Saturday, 10 December, when Mr and Mrs Holly left to collect Mary's parents for a trip to the town of Noel itself. That meant spending the night away, and the Hollys suggested that Simmons might like to accompany them part of the way and then return to Joplin alone. Perhaps they feared what the two young people would get up to if left alone in the house overnight.

Simmons said he'd rather walk as far as Lanagan and then take a train home from there. Mary said she'd stay with him at the Hollys' Mann Farm home until he left and then follow the Hollys on to her father's house if the Elk River was not running too high. If the crossing was impossible, she'd stay on that side of the river with one of the many relatives the Noels had scattered about there.

Judge J. A. Sturges, who relates this story in his 1897 *History of McDonald County*, tells us the river's ford was then too flooded for vehicles, but could be negotiated on horseback. "About 8 o'clock in the morning Holly and his wife started away, leaving Simmons and Miss Noel together at their house," he adds. "This was the last ever seen of her alive." [13]

Instead of returning home on the Sunday, as they'd originally planned, Mr and Mrs Holly stayed with Mary's parents for the next few days. There was no sign of Mary, but everyone assumed she was safe with one of the family's relatives across the river. On the Monday, they began asking around, but could find no trace of her. They sent a letter to one of Mary's uncles in Webb City, about 40 miles away, because they knew she sometimes stayed with him. When he replied that he hadn't seen her, the horrible truth began to dawn. "Their beautiful daughter and sister was gone, lost," Sturges says. "No-one knew where and only those who have experienced the feeling can realise the agony which clung to them day and night."

Mary's father and Mr Holly went to Joplin on the Friday of that week to make enquiries. Holly later testified that he'd seen Simmons there and confronted him with the words: "Will, your girl's gone".

"Simmons trembled violently a few seconds and replied, 'Is that so?'" Sturges reports. "He asked no questions concerning her and appeared to be desirous of avoiding the conversation. When asked if she came away with him he replied that she did not. They stood in silence for a few moments when Simmons remarked: 'You don't suppose the fool girl jumped in the river and drowned herself, do you?'"

Noel and Holly returned to Pineville and, on the morning of Saturday 17 December, began a systematic search. The Noels were a prominent family in McDonald County and hundreds of volunteers joined the effort, most now assuming that Mary had been deliberately killed. Soon, the search gravitated towards the river, where the deepest stretches were dragged and every spot searched. Here's Sturges again:

The deep holes were dragged, giant powder exploded and every spot examined for some distance up and down the stream. Finally, about 2 o'clock in the afternoon, in a narrow, swift place in the river at the lower end of a large, deep hole of water, the body was found where some of the clothing had caught in a willow that projected into the water. It was but little more than quarter of a mile below her father's house and within a few feet of the road along which her parents had passed that fateful Saturday afternoon, unconscious of the great tragedy that had been enacted.

On examination afterwards conclusive evidence of a violent death were found. A bruise on one temple, one spot on one cheek and three or four on the other, as though a hand had been placed over her mouth to stifle her screams, finger prints on the throat, were all plainly visible. Besides a bruise the size of the palm of one's hand on the back of her head and her neck broken. The lungs were perfectly dry and all evidences of drowning were absent.

The searchers also found recent tracks made by a man and a woman between the Hollys' house, where Simmons and Mary had last been seen together, to the river's edge, near the deep area where the body was found. Their conclusion was that the couple must have walked down there together to see if the nearby ford was usable.

Simmons was arrested in Joplin, just as he was getting ready to leave town, but it was feared he'd be lynched if sent back to Pineville, so he went to the jail in Neosho instead. He was tried for first-degree murder in May 1893, but the hotly contested case produced a split jury and a re-trial had to be arranged. That came in November, when the prosecutor indicated that he'd accept second-degree murder, on the grounds that the killing could have been done without the deliberate forethought and intent needed for a first-degree charge. The new jury accepted this, returned a guilty verdict and Simmons was sentenced to ten years.

In 1927, the folklorist Vance Randolph collected a "Knoxville Girl" variant from a Mrs Lee Stevens in Missouri. She called this song "The Noel Girl", and it begins:

'Twas in the city of Pineville,
I owned a floury mill,
'Twas in the city of Pineville,
I used to live and dwell. [14]

The rest of the song canters through the familiar tale, mentioning every important milestone along the way. There's the false promise of marriage, the private walk, the sudden attack, the plea for mercy, the river, the candle, the nosebleed – everything. The Pineville reference and the song's title aside, it's a straightforward reading of "Knoxville Girl" as everyone came to know it from Arthur Tanner's 1927 recording, with exactly the same details of "The Bloody Miller" and "The Berkshire Tragedy" left intact.

It's obviously nonsense to suggest, as some people do, that Mary Noel's death is the prime source for "Knoxville Girl". Even so, you can see why her case got drawn into the song's mythology. The real facts of this killing form an almost uncanny echo of the one described half a world away and 200 years earlier.

Just as in "The Berkshire Tragedy", Simmons really did take his unsuspecting victim "from her sister's door", beat her viciously round the head "and dragged her to the river side then threw her body in". Holly, encountering the killer in Joplin, may well have asked himself "what makes you shake and tremble so," just as "The Berkshire Tragedy"'s servant asked of his master. And Mary's body really was found "floating before her father's door". Sturges tells us Mary was "young (and) extremely handsome", with "lady like manners", while "The Bloody Miller" calls its own victim "a fair and comely maid, thought modest, grave and wise".

It's almost as though William Simmons arrived at Mann Farm with a copy of "The Berkshire Tragedy" stuffed into his pocket and set out to re-enact it as closely as he could. There's no suggestion in the 1897 account that he killed Mary because he'd made her pregnant, but it's possible that Judge Sturges avoided this issue for the sake of delicacy. He was writing at a time when Mary's father was still alive, and may have wished to avoid embarrassing one of the county's leading families. He offers no alternative motive for Simmons' deed, however, so we certainly can't rule out an unwanted pregnancy as the cause of it all.

In 1917, the English song collector Cecil Sharp visited another Pineville, this one in Kentucky, where he persuaded two women named Wilson and Townsley to sing a song they called "Flora Dean".

What emerged was a missing link between the British and American versions of the song, retaining the servant/master relationship of the English original, but setting its tale firmly in America. The miller becomes a miller's apprentice here, and is confronted about the blood by his boss rather than by his mother. There's no doubt where it's all taking place, though, as these lines show:

> I fell in love with a Knoxville Girl,
> Her name was Flora Dean. [15]

The rest of the story plays out in its familiar way, with the sudden unprovoked attack, Flora begging for her life, the disposal of her body in the river and the killer's nosebleed. When Flora's body is eventually found, it's:

> A-floating down by her father's house,
> Who lived in Knoxville town.

Ten years later, with Tanner's record, Knoxville became the accepted setting for this tale and all the other locations sank to footnote status. Once a song's been committed to disc and widely heard on the radio, that rapidly becomes the official version and any deviations from its line are seen not merely as variations, but mistakes.

Tanner's record might never have reached the market at all if it hadn't been for an earlier 1925 hit by Vernon Dalhart called "The Death Of Floyd Collins". This told the tale of a young man who got himself trapped in Kentucky's Sand Cave in February 1925 and whose plight was avidly followed by newspaper readers and radio listeners throughout America. Collins died of exposure before he could be rescued and Columbia scored a big hit with the Dalhart record that followed in May. [16]

Henry Sapoznik, writing in the sleeve notes for Tompkins Square's *People Take Warning* compilation, says Dalhart's record "set in motion a rage for country-tinged exploitation event songs which made 78s and sheet music the broadside ballads of the post-Industrial Age". Looking for more of the same, Columbia had Tanner re-record the same version of "Knoxville Girl" they'd scrapped from his session three weeks earlier, and that's when the song took off. Sixteen years later, when The Louvin Brothers started their radio career, "Knoxville Girl" quickly became the most requested song in their set. Two decades after that, it proved just as popular for Ralph and Carter Stanley, who included it on their classic 1969 live album *The Legendary Stanley Brothers*.

Even in old age, Charlie Louvin was keen to see audiences take the song in the sombre mood he intended, and to give full attention to the story it told. The country singer Ruth Gerson – who included "Knoxville Girl" on her 2011 album *Deceived* — has seen him perform it twice at New York gigs, and never forgotten the experience.

"I saw Charlie Louvin play it at the Rodeo Bar," she told me. "He was upset at a group of young men at a table laughing, and he shook his finger at them. I saw him again in New York at his 80th birthday album release party, where he took time to explain why the woman in the song dies. It was serious to him. He instructed the audience to listen carefully to the words – she dies because she had dark and *roving* eyes." [17]

Ralph Stanley, who first heard "Knoxville Girl" as a small boy in the early 1930s, was just two days short of his 88th birthday when I spoke to him about the song on the phone from his home in Virginia. Like Louvin, he believes it's the girl's "dark and roving eye" which reveals her killer's motive: "He probably got jealous of her, I guess," Stanley told me. "It could have happened that way and they just wrote about it. A lot of [murder ballads] are true songs. Back then, if something happened, they wrote songs about it." [18]

Did the song get a good reaction when he and Carter played it live? "Oh, yeah," he replied. "It's been a good seller all down through the line for years. It's a good song, it's about a good subject. I don't know if it was the words or the melody or what: it was just a good song and a good seller."

Stanley's son, Ralph II, is now a songwriter and a recording artist in his own right, stepping into his late Uncle Carter's shoes to sing alongside his father in The Clinch Mountain Boys on their late 90s tours. "Knoxville Girl" wasn't a regular part of the set in those years, but every now and again someone in the audience would request it and Ralph II stepped up to oblige. "I just tried to put it across," he told me. "I tried to do it in the same manner my Uncle Carter did when I was singing it with Dad there, trying to fill the void. I always loved that song."

His own first taste of "Knoxville Girl" had come just as early as his father's, in this case from listening to that Stanley Brothers live album as his mother played it in the family car. "I was probably four or five years old," Ralph II said. "I thought it was kind of spooky when I was a kid, but I enjoyed it. Later on, I heard The Louvin Brothers do it, but I was really fond of Dad and Carter's version. It's an eerie song, you know? Gives you a cold chill when it's sung right like they sung it."

The Stanley Brothers were great champions of murder ballads throughout their career, recording not only "Knoxville Girl" but also "Pretty Polly", "Poor Ellen Smith", "Death Of The Lawson Family" and "Banks Of The Ohio". Ralph II was hearing those songs as a toddler too and he's continued their tradition by covering Stonewall Jackson's "Bluefield" on his 2012 album *Born To Be A Drifter*. This tells the story of a real incident in West Virginia, when a deputy sheriff who also happened to be the area's biggest moonshiner took a shot at one of the lawmen raiding his still. The man he killed turned out to be his best friend, the sheriff himself.

Ralph II believes it's this grounding in real events and everyday tragedy which makes country and bluegrass such a natural home for murder ballads. "Bluegrass is real, it speaks of real life and it tells the story of life," he said. "The story of the Lawson family was a big to-do that happened in North Carolina that Dad and Carter had heard about. I don't know who wrote the song, but they had heard about it and they sung it. It's a true story. 'Knoxville Girl'? They're great, great lyrics and the bands that sung it put a real good melody to it. It's just dead-on, keeps you into the song all the way through."

Those strengths make it all the more surprising that – unlike many of the other songs in this book – "Knoxville Girl" has never managed to conquer the pop charts. The closest it's come is with Olivia Newton-John's "Banks Of The Ohio", which reached number 6 in the British charts in October 1971 and remained in the Top 50 for 17 weeks. The link with "Knoxville Girl" lies in "Banks Of The Ohio"'s almost identical plot.

A couple go for a private walk by the river, one of them produces a knife and ignores the other's protest about being unprepared for eternity. After the stabbing, the victim's body is dragged into the river and the killer returns home protesting true love. But there are differences too. This time, it's the murderer who wants to get married and the victim who refuses. When the knife appears, the victim seems almost eager to die, pushing on to the blade as it pierces flesh.

The fact that "Banks Of The Ohio" is so often sung by a woman produces some twists too. Newton-John casts herself as the murderer ("I killed the only man I love / He would not take me for his bride"), but Kristin Hersh plays the victim ("He drew his knife across my breast / And in his arms I gently pressed"). Snakefarm's Anna Domino seems to be singing as a male killer ("I asked your mother for you dear / And she said you were too young"), but the more I listen to her carefully ambiguous lyrics, the less certain I am. Couldn't that "lily hand" she mentions equally belong to a young man killed by a besotted older woman?

Song scholars trace "Banks Of The Ohio" back to an older song with an identical plot called "The Banks Of The Old Pee Dee", first collected in 1915. The best-known river of that name originates in the Appalachian Mountains of North Carolina, a region where we know "Knoxville Girl"'s source songs had been adapted for American use since the early 1800s. Somewhere along the way, "Banks Of The Ohio" discarded its tell-tale nosebleed, but the family resemblance remains unmistakable.

For all its debt to the old English ballads, there's no doubt that "Knoxville Girl" is a much better song than any of its predecessors. It's much sharper and more concise than the English originals, and gains all the more punch from that. The 12 verses of "Knoxville Girl" in its classic form are far easier for a singer to memorise than the 44 verses he'd have to contend with in "The Berkshire Tragedy"'s original text and present far less of a challenge to the modern audience's patience.

Where the flavour of the English songs is one of cheerful tabloid vulgarity, "Knoxville Girl" replaces this with a stoic fatalism that quietly acknowledges the Devil lurks inside us all. The line describing Knoxville as "a town we all know well", suggests the song is an intimate confession to the singer's close neighbours, and that's a feeling missing from the earlier versions too. If he prefers not to spell out his tale's sexual content in graphic detail, then that just hints at a thwarted small-town decency which makes it all the more heartbreaking.

Death was an everyday reality for the subsistence farmers who first brought "Knoxville Girl" to America's southern states, and their harsh Calvinist religion offered no illusions about the rewards sin would bring. The few pleasures they could hope for – sex, moonshine and fiddle tunes – seemed only to promise eternal damnation. The folk tradition has written these qualities into every note of "Knoxville Girl" and it's that which accounts for its extraordinary power.

If you doubt me on this point, just ask Gerson. "*Deceived* is a collection of songs about the bad things that happen to 'bad girls'," she told me. "'Knoxville Girl' was one of the first songs that inspired the album. The first time I heard it was a Nick Cave version, then I listened to The Louvin Brothers – and threw up from being so disturbed. We think the murder of those weaker and unable to defend themselves is wrong, but we accept it. We do not scream out against it. We sing and dance to it. 'Knoxville Girl' is an incredible song, but it shakes me down everytime I sing it."

Loved so well: 10 Knoxville knockouts

"Knoxville Girl", by Arthur Tanner & His Corn Shuckers (1927).
The first commercial recording and the one which set the lyrics in stone
for everyone that's followed. Tanner's vocals are surprisingly clear for
such an old record and the fiddle and guitar accompaniment keeps
everything moving along nicely.

"Knoxville Girl", by The Louvin Brothers (1956). Bearing a clear
influence from The Blue Sky Boys' 1937 version, the Louvins add a
shuffling beat and produce the song's single most essential version. The
Everly Brothers idolised Charlie and Ira Louvin and this record tells you
why.

"Knoxville Girl", by Charlie Feathers (1973). The former Sun
Studios session musician and self-styled "King of Rockabilly" brings
a touch of Elvis to this hillbilly rap version. There's a stop/start beat,
a knowing melodrama to his spoken-word vocals and some enjoyably
twangy guitar. It should be a mess, but actually it works rather well.

"Knoxville Girl", by Kevin Williams & Friends (1997). Each
musician takes the lead for a verse or two in this rather lovely instrumental
version. Williams' mandolin and Craig Duncan's hammered dulcimer
describe the slaughter, while Glen Duncan's fiddle is left to mourn the
results.

"Knoxville Girl", by Mark Jungers (2003). A busy acoustic guitar
lurches us into this flat-out rockabilly treatment. Jungers and his band
take the course at 90 MPH, conjuring up a picture of sweaty quiffs,
heavily-tattooed arms and a drummer who stands up to play. Splendid
stuff.

"The Oxford Girl", by Waterson:Carthy (2004). That's Norma
Waterson and Martin Carthy, of course, who give us this rare recording
of "Knoxville Girl"'s ancestor. Tim van Eyken's melodeon sets an
appropriately mournful tone as Norma sings her way to the gallows.

"Knoxville Girl (Parting Gift)", by Jennie Stearns (2005). Not a version of the original song, but Stearns' meditation on the "Knoxville Girl"'s fate and the baffling cruelty of men. The gift, it turns out, is Stearns' song itself, placed like a gentle flower on the victim's grave. It's every bit as sweet as it sounds.

"Knoxville Girl", by Sheila Kay Adams (2005). Sheila learned this song as a child in the evocatively-named town of Sodom, North Carolina and her a cappella version is one of the loveliest I've heard. Clear, steady and tuneful, it's a little gem.

"Knoxville Girl", by Charlie Louvin & Will Oldham (2007). Young bands often revel in the brutality of "Knoxville Girl", but Louvin's sombre solo reading is a chastening reminder of what violence really means. Make way for a grown-up, children.

"Knoxville Girl", by Rachel Brooke (2009). Brooke coats this recording with surface noise to mimic the 78s she so obviously loves, which creates a pleasing old-time feel. She gives a clever twist to the lyrics too, turning the story into one about a girl murdering the woman her true love prefers. "Tom Dooley"'s Ann Melton would have sympathised.

4 - The Lonesome Death Of Hattie Carroll

"This is a true story. This is taken out of the newspaper."
Bob Dylan, introducing "Hattie Carroll"
at Manchester Free Trade Hall in May 1965.

"The song was a lie. Just a damned lie."
William Zantzinger, quoted in
The New Yorker, 26 January, 2009.

On 28 August 1963, Dr Martin Luther King led 250,000 civil rights marchers to Washington in what *The New York Times* called "the greatest assembly for the redress of grievances that this capital has ever seen". King delivered his historic "I have a dream" speech at the foot of the Lincoln Memorial, President Kennedy praised the marchers' dignity, and a young folk singer called Bob Dylan sang two of his own songs for the crowd.

Like every newspaper in America, Baltimore's *Afro-American* led on the march. Building the front page round a close-up of a young black marcher with the US flag artfully reflected in his sunglasses, it chose the banner headline "Cry for Freedom". Beneath this were other headlines spotlighting various aspects of the event: "241,000 join in fervent appeal to the Congress"; "March praised by press"; "JFK vows push for more jobs". Only one unconnected story made it above the fold that day, and its headline read: "Cane-killer gets off with six months".

The killer in question was William Zantzinger, a prosperous Baltimore tobacco farmer, who had got very drunk at a society dance there six months earlier. He'd called one of the barmaids a "black bitch" and then hit her with his cane when she asked him to wait for a moment while she finished serving another customer. The barmaid, Hattie Carroll, had died a few hours later from a brain haemorrhage brought on by Zantzinger's assault, he'd been convicted of manslaughter, and his sentence happened to be announced on the day of the march.

Many thought Zantzinger's thuggish behaviour at the dance should have brought a murder conviction, and believed it was only his position in Baltimore's rich, white elite which got him off so lightly. Right from the start, Carroll's death had been seen to symbolise every injustice the Washington marchers wanted to overturn. "The case was drawn in shades of black and white," the *Afro-American* remarked. "Not only because of the racial identification of the victim and her accused slayer, but because it seemed to place the rich against the poor, the haves against the have-nots." [1]

Dylan had already penned two songs about racist white-on-black murders in the past 18 months – "The Death Of Emmett Till" and "Only A Pawn In Their Game" – and included one of these in his short Washington set. "Pawn" was about the murder of black civil rights activist Medgar Evers, who'd been gunned down in Jackson, Mississippi, in June 1963. Dylan portrayed the killer as poor white trash, sucked into committing a racist murder by the paranoia cynical white politicians had fed him. He was less to be hated than pitied, Dylan suggested, and that made the song a gutsy choice for the Washington rally.

Evers' death was still a raw memory when Dylan stepped up to the Lincoln Memorial's forest of podium mikes to sing, and his widow was there as one of the rally's key speakers. And yet here was a white singer, telling an 80% black audience that they should look on her husband's killer with a degree of understanding. Even with this challenging message, though, the song went down well, winning Dylan applause and cheers as he slipped back into the crowd.

As with many of his early songs, "Pawn"'s words and music were first published in *Broadside*, a tiny Greenwich Village magazine whose mimeographed pages were filled with radical songs. *Broadside* wanted songs which "mirrored an America becoming ever more deeply involved with the great national struggles of war or peace, civil rights and [...] the plight of the unemployed and poor". Songs like these, the editors added, should "reflect an America of still increasing violence and death, inflicted especially on the Negro people and their white allies". [2]

In February 1962, when *Broadside* made its debut, that meant contemporary American folk music and, for a while, Dylan was very happy to follow the magazine's agenda. In its first 18 months alone, he gave them 16 new songs, including "Masters Of War", "Talking John Birch Society Blues" and "Blowing In The Wind".

The fanzine writer Paul Nelson, who tended to be sceptical about glib protest songs, heard Dylan play "Pawn" at a small gathering in the summer of 1963 and took this opportunity to challenge the singer about it. "These songs were like fish in the barrel stuff," Nelson later wrote. "It's like patting yourself on the back music. [...] Dylan was arguing 'No, no, this is really where it's at'. But he also made the point that the easiest way to get published if you wrote your own songs was to write topical songs, 'cause *Broadside* wouldn't publish [you] if you didn't." [3]

It's worth remembering that the Bob Dylan of August 1963 was not the global superstar we know today. He was then just 22 years old, only two albums into his career, and would have to wait another 20 months for his first chart hit. The debut album had sold poorly enough for Columbia to discuss dropping him, and the second – already on the shelves for three months – was only now beginning to shift.

Dylan's career could have gone either way at that point, and *Broadside* gave him a useful platform to show off his skills, establish his ownership of each new song and polish up his radical credentials. I don't doubt his civil rights songs were driven by genuine outrage – no intelligent young artist could fail to be moved by such turbulent times – but there were also sound career reasons to keep those songs coming. In October 1963, he decided Hattie Carroll would be his next subject.

On Friday, 8 February 1963, the night she met her death, Carroll was working as a barmaid at Baltimore's Emerson Hotel. The 51-year-old grandmother had done occasional work at the hotel for the past six years, stepping in whenever they needed extra staff for a big function like that evening's Spinsters' Ball. It promised to be quite a night: a white tie charity affair, with 200 guests from Maryland's most prominent families invited and the prestigious Howard Lanin Orchestra providing the music.

Two of the guests, William Zantzinger and his wife Jane, started their evening with a pre-dinner drink at the city's Eager House restaurant. Zantzinger, 24 years old and over six feet tall, was the son of a rich tobacco farming family in Southern Maryland. His parents could trace their ancestors back both to Maryland's earliest white settlers and to a former governor of the state. His sister had been given not one, but two coming-out balls, both of which were covered in *The Washington Post*. Jane came from similarly up-market stock.

Eyewitness accounts from other diners at Eager House that night describe the couple guzzling whiskey at the bar before they sat down and continuing to do so throughout their meal. Soon, they were so unruly that the restaurant's barman simply refused to serve them anymore. With this source of booze cut off, Jane invaded a group of strangers' table and began slurping from their drinks instead. Meanwhile, Zantzinger took to lunging unsteadily at any member of the restaurant staff who happened to be carrying a tray of drinks, deliberately striking several of them with his wooden cane. This cane – the same one he'd later hit Carroll with – was a cheap carnival souvenir rather than a walking stick, but still heavy enough to inflict pain. [4]

Their meal complete, they moved on to the Spinsters' Ball. Walking in, Zantzinger announced himself with a roar of: "I just flew in from Texas. Gimme a drink!" He was still fooling around with the cane, knocking it on the table's silver punchbowl whenever he wanted more booze, swiping it across the black bellhop's rear end and running its tip over any pretty woman who happened to walk by. Meanwhile, he continued working his way through a steady stream of bourbon and ginger ales from the open bar.

When they tried to dance, the couple collapsed in a tangled heap, and Zantzinger started hitting his wife on the head with a shoe. Some of the other guests intervened, one of whom later testified he "knocked Zantzinger cold" when the oaf took a swing at him. Dusting herself off, Jane allowed the hotel staff to lead her away to an empty bedroom upstairs where she could recover herself. Her husband returned to their table, where he resumed drinking, and swiped George Gessell, the hotel's black bellhop, across the behind with his cane.

By now, it was about 1:30 on Saturday morning and Zantzinger's mood was turning darker. He approached Ethel Hill, a black waitress clearing one of the tables near his, and asked her something about a fireman's fund. She said she didn't know what he meant, and Zantzinger snarled: "Don't say 'No' to me, you nigger, say 'No, sir'". He flailed at her with his cane, chasing her as she fled back towards the kitchen and hitting her on the arm, thighs and buttocks.

Working alongside Carroll that night were three other Emerson barmaids: Marina Patterson, Grace Shelton and Shirley Burrell. All three women witnessed Zantzinger's behaviour, and later testified in court about what they'd seen. "I heard Mrs Hill say 'What is wrong with you? Leave me alone'," Patterson recalled. "Then I heard him say 'Nigger, what's wrong with you?' Then I saw him whack her across the buttocks with the cane. She ran out of the room crying 'Somebody help me. This man is killing me!'" [5]

Ten minutes after this incident, Zantzinger shoved his way through to the bar again and began calling for more bourbon. Carroll, who was busy serving another customer, asked him to wait for a moment. "Mrs Carroll was fixing another drink," Patterson testified. "So she didn't serve him immediately. He said 'Nigger, did you hear me ask for a drink?' He said 'I don't have to take that kind of shit off a nigger'. He took the cane and struck her on the right shoulder. She leaned against the bar. Mr Zantzinger stood at the bar for a while, then he picked up his drink and left. She seemed to have been in shock. She said 'That man has upset me so, I feel deathly ill'."

"He hit her. He struck right down and hit her," Burrell confirmed. "It was a hard blow. So hard that I couldn't understand how she could stand up. [...] She handed him the drink, and then she stood there for a minute, and then she fell on me. I was so shocked I couldn't say anything to her."

"Zantzinger yelled 'Why are you so slow, you black bitch?' then hit Mrs Carroll with the cane," Shelton added. "We were petrified. We were dumbfounded."

Shelton and Burrell helped Carroll back into the privacy of the kitchen. "She said her arm was hurting and 'I'm losing my grip'," Shelton remembered. "I asked her to hold on to my arm, but I could feel her hand slipping off. Her speech became thick and garbled, and her words were running together." Carroll complained her right arm felt numb, so the two women tried to massage it back to life.

Meanwhile, someone else was calling both an ambulance and the police. One of the other guests, Hal Whittaker, forced Zantzinger's cane away from him and snapped it into pieces. "I saw that lady being taken out on a stretcher and I became upset," he later told the court. "I didn't want him to use it again." Years afterwards, Whittaker told his son this story, saying Zantzinger had struck the boy's pregnant mother earlier in the evening. [6, 7]

The unconscious Carroll was taken to Baltimore's Mercy Hospital. Two cops arrived at the Emerson Hotel to arrest Zantzinger, who loudly protested his innocence, and were leading him out through the hotel lobby when Jane reappeared. Still very drunk, she tumbled down a flight of five stairs, knocking both her husband and Officer Warren Todd to the ground. Crawling across the floor to grab Zantzinger's legs, she cried "You can't take my Billy Boy away! He beats me, but I still love him!" The police responded by arresting her too and bundling the couple off to Baltimore's Pine Street Police Station. [8]

There, Jane was charged with disorderly conduct, and allowed to go home after providing a $28 collateral. Zantzinger, charged with disorderly conduct, plus two charges of assault against Ethel Hill and Hattie Carroll by striking them with a wooden cane, was left to cool off in the cells for what remained of the night.

A few hours later, now sporting a black eye and still wearing the remains of his bedraggled white tie outfit, Zantzinger appeared before Judge Albert Blum at the city's Municipal Criminal Court. As the hearing began, Carroll was still unconscious at Mercy Hospital, and Blum left instructions that he was to be told of any change in her condition immediately. Zantzinger pleaded not guilty to all the charges against him, and was released on $3,600 bail.

As Zantzinger walked out of the courtroom that Saturday morning, Carroll was already dead, but news of this fact did not reach Blum until it was too late to stop the accused man leaving. The judge later said he would never have allowed such low bail if he'd known this was now a potential murder case, and police blamed hospital staff for being too slow in passing on the information.

One of the last people – perhaps the very last person – to speak to Carroll, was Yvonne Ross, another Emerson Hotel worker, who'd ridden with her friend in the ambulance to Mercy. "I stayed with her at the hospital for a while," she recalled in court. "She was unconscious. Then she woke up. The last thing I heard her say was 'Help me please'." [9]

Carroll died at 9.15 on the Saturday morning, less than eight hours after Zantzinger had attacked her. "It all happened so fast," one eyewitness said of the assault. "He was like a wild animal. After he had knocked her unconscious, he became even more belligerent. Now she is dead. And all because she didn't serve him fast enough." The hospital confirmed that Carroll had suffered a brain haemorrhage, but said her official cause of death would have to wait for the autopsy. Matters were complicated by the fact that she'd long suffered from an enlarged heart, hardened arteries and high blood pressure.

The police issued a warrant for Zantzinger as soon as they realised Carroll was dead, adding another warrant for Jane, who'd failed to turn up for her own disorderly conduct hearing. Next morning's *Baltimore Sun* splashed this news with the headline: "Caning Suspect, Wife Sought State-Wide In Death Of Barmaid: Charles County Man Is Charged With Homicide". The story beneath added that police had failed to find Zantzinger at his Mount Victoria farm, about 70 miles south of Baltimore, and now "had no idea of his whereabouts". [10]

Reading between the lines of that report, it's pretty clear the paper was hoping the Zantzingers had gone on the run, creating a police chase which would yield much juicy copy in the weeks to come. In fact, Zantzinger gave himself up the very next day, walking into Baltimore's Central District police HQ with his lawyer Claude Hanley just after noon on Sunday. He was arrested, handcuffed and returned to lock-up to wait for another hearing next day.

At that hearing, Judge Robert Hammerman ordered that Zantzinger should be held without bail until a trial could be scheduled. But Zantzinger's lawyers persuaded the superior City Court to overturn this ruling. That court's Judge, Dulany Foster, set Zantzinger's bail at $25,000 (worth close to $200,000 today), and allowed him to go free till the trial date. William O'Donnell, Maryland's state prosecutor, did not oppose bail. By now, George Gessell, the Emerson's bellhop, had added his own assault complaint against Zantzinger, bringing his full sheet to one charge of homicide, two of assault (the other victim being Ethel Hill) and one of disorderly conduct. Hammerman insisted Zantzinger pay an additional $500 bail for the Gessell assault, but was then forced to release him.

As the *Afro-American* reminded its readers, the homicide charge at this point was a general one, which could eventually lead to a conviction for first-degree murder, second-degree murder or merely manslaughter. Which of those three categories Zantzinger's case belonged to – and hence the punishment he received – would be decided by the court only after it had heard all the facts at his trial.

Jane Zantzinger had to forfeit her earlier $28 but she, too, was granted bail again – this time of $603 – as she awaited her own trial for disorderly conduct. Maryland's most charming couple was back on the street.

Carroll's funeral was held on an overcast February afternoon at West Baltimore's Gillis Memorial Church, where she'd been a deacon and sung in the choir. Reporters put the crowd there at 1,600 mourners, only about half of whom were able to fit in the church for the service itself. White police, there to control the crowd, looked on as organisers grimly distributed flyers for a rally to protest Carroll's death. "Who will be next?" the flyers asked.

Although there were no white faces in the crowd, the National Council of Christians and Jews did send representatives to the funeral, and so did the Emerson Hotel. Messages of sympathy came in from as far away as Alabama, confirming that Carroll's case was now getting national attention. Inside the church, Reverend Theodore Jackson preached that her death would mean more to the city of Baltimore than any other it had seen. "The ministers of this city, the doctors, lawyers, all people should come together as never before and let people know that coloured citizens are not going to stand for certain things," he thundered from the pulpit. "We are in the hands of a just God, but not in the hands of a just people." [11]

The emotional peak of the service came when the Gillis Young Adult Choir sang "He Leadeth Me", Carroll's favourite hymn. Tearful relatives were then helped to the 34 cars in her waiting funeral procession, which took the body to Baltimore's National Cemetery, where her husband James' military service had earned Carroll a place. Crowds lingered outside the church long after the cars had disappeared, reluctant to break this last connection with a woman many of them had never known. [12, 13]

Photographs from that day show a smartly-dressed black crowd, standing 10 deep on the sidewalk opposite the church for what looks like a full city block. In the foreground are a small group of Muslim women, with long scarves covering their hair and draping down their backs. The men wear hats and long overcoats and everyone is sombre-faced. A second photo shows weeping mourners exiting down the steps from what had evidently been a packed service.

Perhaps the most telling photograph from that day's paper, though, is the *Afro-American's* full-length shot of Hattie Carroll herself. Often reduced to a head-and-shoulders, the full frame shows a middle-aged woman in an elegantly simple black dress and heels. She's wearing a lace-trimmed hat with a necklace and a brooch, and clutching a shiny evening bag. She looks like exactly what she was: somebody's Mum, dressed up in her Sunday best and posing for her proud husband or daughter to take a quick snap before they leave the house. It's a tiny ceremony that's been duplicated in a million homes all over the world, but never to quite such touching effect as this.

Zantzinger's next court appearance came at Baltimore's Central Homicide Court, where Judge Basil Thomas took only 85 minutes to decide the charges against him were serious enough to refer the case to a Grand Jury. Speaking to a tense and packed courtroom, Baltimore assistant medical examiner Dr Charles Petty testified that Carroll's fatal brain haemorrhage had been induced by the fright, fear or anger caused by Zantzinger's blow. "Emotional reaction to the blow caused her death," he said. [14]

Shelton and Burrell, Carroll's two colleagues at the Emerson Hotel's bar, gave their accounts of Zantzinger's behaviour that night, describing all the details we've already seen. Burrell broke down and wept as she told the court about Zantzinger's attack. He had been loud, abusive and belligerent all evening, she said.

Deputy state attorney Charles Moylan – perhaps stung by rumours that his office had already decided to settle for a manslaughter conviction – insisted that his witnesses' detailed testimony was essential because it established malice on Zantzinger's part. "Malice is the essential element which distinguishes murder from manslaughter," he reminded the court.

The Grand Jury hearing a few days later formally indicted Zantzinger on a homicide charge. A tentative date of 28 March was set for his criminal trial, but no-one seemed to think anything would really happen that soon. As the *Afro-American* pointed out, anyone facing a potential death penalty charge in Maryland was entitled to request a change of venue if they thought bad publicity or ill-feeling would make it impossible for them to get a fair trial in their home jurisdiction. Baltimore's newspapers had been making hay with the Zantzinger story for over a month by that time, so he was thought almost certain to invoke this right.

In the middle of April, state prosecutor William O'Donnell confirmed that Zantzinger had succeeded in moving his trial out of Baltimore, and said Hagerstown in Western Maryland would be the replacement venue. His office had chosen Hagerstown, O'Donnell explained, because it had court time open and local accommodation available. It remained to be seen whether the defence would ask for a jury trial or a court trial, where the verdict would be left to a panel of judges alone.

At this point, the charge sheet against Zantzinger comprised one charge of homicide, three of assault (one each against Carroll, Hill and Gessell) and one of disorderly conduct. Jane faced one charge of assaulting Officer Warren Todd and one of disorderly conduct, but her trial would remain in Baltimore

A s the legal process ground on, Dylan was singing his latest songs on various New York radio stations and giving their lyrics to *Broadside*.

The magazine's 20th issue, dated February 1963, gave its front page over to his "Masters Of War", illustrating the song with a couple of his girlfriend Suze Rotolo's scrawled drawings. Late February's *Broadside* 21 ran Dylan's "The Rise & Fall Of Hollis Brown", and the magazine's two March editions had "John Brown" and "Train A-Travellin'" respectively. That last issue though – *Broadside* 23 – is less notable for the Dylan song on its front page than the Don West composition nestling within. [15]

West, a socialist campaigner and poet, had composed nine verses of polemic which he called "The Ballad Of Hattie Carroll", suggesting it be sung to the tune of "Wayfaring Stranger". Compared to the song Dylan would write six months later, West's effort is a plodding, awkward thing, more concerned with parading its writer's conscience than adding any poetic resonance to the event. It bluntly describes its story as one of "brutal murder", describing a powerful rich man who "flailed away" with his cane and "beat to death" Hattie Carroll.

Zantzinger's criminal trial hadn't even been scheduled, let alone resolved, when this issue of *Broadside* was published – so no-one yet knew whether the law would ultimately view him as a murderer or not. Although West doesn't name Zantzinger anywhere in the song, he does give Hattie Carroll's name in full, leaving no-one who'd read the papers in any doubt about who his song's killer must be. Just to ram that point home, *Broadside* stuck a photocopied press clipping under West's lyric. This story, headlined "Rich Brute Slays Negro Mother of 10", is by-lined Roy H Wood.

Wood was a former secretary of Washington DC's Communist Party, who had been campaigning for local black families as long ago as 1949 and was forced to testify before Joe McCarthy's Committee on Un-American Activities in the following year. "His personal first commandment was that all people were created equal," Wood's daughter Calla told me in 2011. "The thing that distressed him most about his beloved Baltimore was the deep-rooted racism among its white population." [16]

Wood's story begins like this:

BALTIMORE – Mrs Hattie Carroll, 51, Negro waitress at the Emerson Hotel, died last week as the result of a brutal beating by a wealthy socialite during the exclusive Spinsters' Ball at that hotel. Mrs Carroll, mother of 10 children [...] died in the hospital where she had been taken after being felled from blows inflicted by William Devereux Zantzinger, 24, owner of a 600-acre tobacco farm near Marlsboro, Md.

Mrs Carroll was one of two waitresses whom Zantzinger struck with a wooden cane at the society affair. [...] He strode to the bar and rained blows on the head and back of Mrs Carroll who was working there. The cane was broken in three places. [17]

Other employees called the police, Wood reports, then adds: "Zantzinger's father is a member of the state planning commission in Maryland. Others of his relatives in the Devereux family are prominent in politics here. The judge who released Zantzinger on bond has already permitted his attorney to claim that Mrs Carroll died indirectly as a result of the attack rather than directly. There is speculation here that attempts will be made to get Zantzinger off with a slap on the wrist."

Wood is clearly angry about the way Carroll was treated, and wants to make sure his readers get angry too. He takes every chance to paint Zantzinger that night as a rich, spoilt thug – which he was – but goes a little too far in how he describes the attack itself. All the court evidence describes a single blow to Carroll's right shoulder rather than the many blows on her head and back which Wood reports. Is he indulging in a bit of clever juxtaposition when he implies Zantzinger actually broke his cane on Carroll's back, or simply unaware of Hal Whittaker's intervention? He clearly wants us to think the judge was corrupt in "permitting" Zantzinger's attorney to argue Carroll's death had not been caused directly by the blow, but given the woman's known medical history, what other ruling was possible?

Dylan could hardly have been more involved with *Broadside* at this point. He was spending all his time in New York and contributing new songs to every issue of the magazine. The March 1963 issue which contained West's "Ballad Of Hattie Carroll" had Dylan's own "Train A-Travellin'" on its front page, a song he'd put on tape for the magazine's Sis Cunningham just a few months earlier. It's fair to assume he would have been seeing every issue of the magazine at this point, if only to check out his own work there and keep a wary eye on the competition.

As we'll see in a moment, *Broadside's* Wood clipping became one of Dylan's prime sources in writing "The Lonesome Death Of Hattie

Carroll". Many of its details – the two main characters' ages, the size of Zantzinger's family farm, how many children Carroll had – would appear almost verbatim in the song six months later. Whether you view the more colourful aspects in Wood's account as deliberate distortions or justifiable hyperbole, they played a key role in shaping Dylan's lyric and, through that, Wood continues to influence the way we all think of the case to this day. The host of tiny decisions he made sitting at his typewriter in February 1963 cast a longer shadow than he could ever have imagined.

Zantzinger opted for a court trial rather than a jury one and proceedings began in Hagerstown's 19th century courthouse on 19 June 1963. The three-man panel of judges who'd decide his fate was headed by Judge David McLaughlin, who shared the bench with Judges Irvine Rutledge and Stuart Hamill. The *Afro-American* sent reporter James Williams along to set the scene for its readers.

Maryland's white aristocracy was well-represented in the crowded courtroom, many guests at the Spinsters' Ball having been summoned to give testimony. Most of them looked thoroughly uncomfortable at being dragged into court, but Zantzinger and his wife seemed almost uncannily calm. Williams noted that Zantzinger was in a dark lightweight suit, while Jane wore stripy blue linen with a white blouse and shoes.

"The state has obviously gone all out to make the case stick against Zantzinger by bringing to this Western Maryland town some 30 witnesses and using its top legal talent in Baltimore city to prosecute the case," Williams wrote approvingly. He also praises McLaughlin, reminding readers the judge was chief justice of Washington County, saying he was held in great respect there and acknowledging the calm, impartial way he handled Zantzinger's trial.

State prosecutor William O'Donnell and deputy state's attorney Charles Moylan certainly don't seem to have pulled their punches. O'Donnell called Zantzinger "the lord of the manor, lord of the plantation" and Moylan claimed he had never been able to accept the South's Civil War defeat and the end to slavery which that brought.

The two prosecutors questioned Marina Patterson, Grace Shelton and Shirley Burrell as they built their case, hearing more of the testimony I've quoted above. They saved Charles Petty, the doctor who'd carried out Carroll's autopsy, for their final witness, questioning him on the Thursday as they prepared to close the prosecution's case. Moylan asked him whether he believed Zantzinger's blow with the cane had caused Carroll's fatal stroke. "Yes," Petty replied. "My opinion is there was a definite relationship. The assault occurred some minutes before the onslaught of the symptoms. I feel there is a definite cause and effect between the two."

The defence team produced two doctors of its own, who both testified that Carroll's stroke could have been caused by something other than Zantzinger's behaviour, and a series of character witnesses to speak on his behalf. They did all they could to draw attention to Carroll's history of health problems and painted their client as an honest, hard-working man.

The defendant himself gave evidence on Friday, with Zantzinger keen to portray himself as a simple country farmer who'd gone to Baltimore for a rare chance to let his hair down and ended up drinking so much that he had no recollection of striking Carroll at all. It was this claim which gave the *Afro-American* its next banner headline. "Cane-Killer Forgets," its front page screamed incredulously. "He can't remember fatal blow."

The defence closed its case on Friday and then broke for the weekend, leaving only Monday morning's final arguments before the three judges could begin considering their verdict. That came on Thursday 27 June, when McLaughlin walked back into the courthouse to announce Zantzinger's fate. "We find that Hattie Carroll's death was not due solely to disease, but that it was caused or hastened by the defendant's verbal insults, coupled with an actual assault," he said. "And that he is guilty of manslaughter."

McLaughlin also announced that Zantzinger had been found guilty of the three assault charges, but all anyone was interested in was the manslaughter ruling. What did it all mean? "The court accepted medical testimony that the caning itself was not enough to cause death," next day's *New York Times* explained. "But the combination of shock, produced by Zantzinger's abusive language and the blow with the cane were sufficient to cause a sudden blood pressure increase and fatal brain hemorrhage. [...] The verdict involves a possible maximum sentence of ten years in prison and a $500 fine." [18]

In fact, sentencing was going to have to wait. Zantzinger's lawyers quickly lodged an application for a new trial, claiming that the medical evidence left room for reasonable doubt on the cause of Hattie Carroll's death. Sentence could not be pronounced until this application had been considered and the probation office completed its report. In the meantime, Zantzinger was left to go free on his existing $25,000 bail because, as McLaughlin noted in his judgement, this was a busy time of year on the family's farm.

The same three judges who'd presided at Zantzinger's trial dismissed his defence team's application to re-try the case and, by the end of August, they were ready to announce a sentence. "A review of this case discloses this was involuntary manslaughter, similar to manslaughter by automobile," McLaughlin announced. "We don't feel that Mr Zantzinger is an animal type. Our problem is to view this case from the type of punishment Mr Zantzinger should have." [19]

Finally, the sentence was announced: six months in jail and a fine of $500 in the Carroll case, plus additional fines totaling $125 for assaulting George Gessell and Ethel Hill. The jail time, McLaughlin added, would not start until 15 September, a dispensation again designed to let Zantzinger finish gathering in his farm's crops. Zantzinger took the news stoically, though Jane fell into silent tears and his mother looked stunned.

The *Afro-American* was fairly stunned itself, headlining the resulting story "Cane-killer gets off with six months" and giving it all the prominence left available by the same day's Washington freedom march. "Some observers expressed the opinion afterwards that it was an unexpectedly light penalty," the story's second paragraph dryly remarked.

A few weeks later *The New York Herald Tribune* speculated that Zantzinger's sentence had deliberately been kept under a year to ensure that he went to county rather than state prison. The majority black population in Maryland's state jail, the paper guessed, would have ensured Zantzinger didn't survive long there. Whatever the reason, it was decided that he should serve his time at Washington County Jail, about 70 miles from Baltimore. A particularly diligent *Afro-American* reporter later discovered he'd been given work in the kitchens there. [20, 21]

The same *Herald Tribune* piece interviewed Zantzinger and Jane as he prepared to leave home to start his sentence. The paper found Zantzinger in arrogant mood, declaring that all he was going to miss out on during his winter incarceration was "a lot of snow". He also told the reporter that he had much more respect for some black people than for the "white niggers" he knew, and added: "Hell, you wouldn't want to go to school with Negroes any more than you would with French people". Stepping in to defend her husband's generosity, Jane said: "Nobody treats his niggers as well as Billy does around here." For some reason, she seemed to think that would be helpful.

Dylan returned to New York after the Washington rally, where he may well have seen *The New York Times'* 29 August report of Zantzinger's six-month sentence. By then, he was going out with folk singer Joan Baez, and at the end of September 1963 he flew out to California to stay with her there. She maintains he wrote "Hattie Carroll" while living at her California home during that visit, though Dylan himself says he wrote the song at an all-night restaurant in New York. [22]

Either way, there's nothing in the lyrics that he couldn't have gleaned from a combination of Wood's account (which either he or Baez had presumably saved from *Broadside*) and *The New York Times* story. Wood's account of both the killer and his victim's ages, the size of Carroll's family, the high-society nature of this hotel dance, Zantzinger's wealth, the precise acreage filled by his family's tobacco farm, the Zantzingers' political connections in Maryland and the suggestion that this trial had been fixed, all find their way directly into Dylan's lyrics. The fact that he follows Wood in claiming Carroll had birthed 10 children (when other sources give nine, 11 or even 13 as the true total) is one more bit of evidence how much trust he placed in *Broadside's* clipping.

Unfortunately, Wood's story was a little too politically-committed to be an entirely reliable source of the facts and all Dylan added from *The New York Times* was the length of Zantzinger's sentence. What little caution Wood does display in his own story – by avoiding the word "murder" for example – tends to get swept away in Dylan's version of events.

No wonder Clinton Heylin – a leading analyst of Dylan's work – calls the song "a million dollar libel case waiting to happen". He argues that, because it wasn't literally Zantzinger's blow with the cane that directly caused Carroll's death, he can't fairly be described as the killer. I wouldn't go quite that far, but there's no denying Dylan took a risk linking Zantzinger with first-degree murder when he'd been convicted only of manslaughter – a far less serious crime. [23]

Heylin is sceptical about the excuses sometimes made for Dylan here, pointing out that any initial anger he might have felt at reading of Carroll's death must long since have faded by the time he wrote the song nearly eight months later. Even if we assume *Broadside's* reproduction of the clipping was the first time Dylan ever heard of Carroll's case, then six months would have passed.

I put some of these points to the British songwriter Billy Bragg, who repurposed Dylan's song for his own "The Lonesome Death Of Rachel Corrie" in 2006. Bragg's song tells the story of a young American activist killed by an Israeli bulldozer while protesting the destruction of Palestinian homes on the Gaza Strip. What responsibility does he feel Dylan – or any other songwriter – bears to get their facts right when tackling a topical song about real people?

"This is folk music we're talking about here," Bragg told me. "It's more about the storytelling. It's a folk song: you're trying to make a moral point. You've got to smooth some of the lines out a little bit to make it cohesive – and you're allowed to do that. I'm sure I didn't get all the facts exactly right in 'The Lonesome Death Of Rachel Corrie'. The Israeli Defence Forces would certainly question the way I put the story together. But I think people generally realise that a song is trying to tell a story, rather than report a story directly.

"Dylan's song displays what went down – a very privileged man killed a black woman and got off lightly. That's the story. And if William Zantzinger is stupid enough to give Bob Dylan all the publicity he needs for his song by suing him, then more fool him." [24]

Biographer Howard Sounes credits Dylan with "the economy of a news reporter" in writing "Hattie Carroll", and that's true as far as it goes. But any reporter taking Dylan's story to his editor would have got a severe bollocking for being so careless. If the story had been allowed into print without his errors being corrected, the paper employing him would have been forced into either printing a very embarrassing correction or coughing up a big out-of-court settlement to make the case go away. The last words ringing in the reporter's ears as he cleared his desk would have been the editor's forceful reminder that he'd even spelt the killer's name wrong!

It's this last discrepancy which is most puzzling of all. What possible purpose could be served by mis-spelling his name? All we know for sure is that the Wood story and *The New York Times* report Dylan was working from both spell Zantzinger's name correctly, with the "t" in place, as does every other newspaper story I've seen from that time. The first official version we have of Dylan's lyrics, which appear in typewritten form on the front page of *Broadside's* April 1964 edition, spells it correctly too. And yet, in every version I've ever heard, from its first studio recording in 1963, through the *Rolling Thunder Review's* 1975 performance to a 2006 Arizona bootleg, Dylan sings "Zanzinger". That's also the way it's written on the lyrics page of his own official website.

Did Dylan always have the name spelt this way, only to find a helpful *Broadside* staffer "correcting" it for him before publication? Was it a simple typing error on his part which no-one noticed until the record was already out? Did he imagine that mis-spelling Zantzinger's name would confer some magical defence against any legal action the song might prompt? Was "Zanzinger" simply easier to pronounce when singing?

Whatever the answer, Dylan has now performed "Hattie Carroll" so often that I doubt he could sing "Zantzinger" even if he wanted to. Ever since writing the song, he's seldom let a year's touring slip by without including it in at least a handful of his set-lists. He's put it on at least two official live albums too. And in every one of those renditions, the name he sings is "Zanzinger".

However you spell his name, Zantzinger's very seldom spoken in public about Dylan. Sounes got one of his very few comments on the subject for his 2001 Dylan biography. "He's just like a scum of a bag of the earth," Sounes quotes a spluttering Zantzinger as saying. "I should have sued him and put him in jail".

Though he never did sue over the song, evidence emerged in 2009 suggesting Zantzinger's lawyers threatened action against both Dylan and his record label when "Hattie Carroll" was first released. Pleasingly enough, this evidence comes from David Simon, the writer and producer behind HBO's *The Wire*, a series which has made him the poet laureate of Baltimore crime.

Simon, then a crime reporter with *The Baltimore Sun*, spent 1988 shadowing the city's murder police for a book about their work which later inspired the TV show *Homicide: Life On The Street*. The relationship he built up with Baltimore's cops during this time let him examine Carroll's old case file, where he found a surprising note. Intrigued, he made an appointment with Zantzinger and raised the issue face-to-face.

Writing about this encounter for a 2009 *New Yorker* article, Simon recalls his opening gambit of disparaging Dylan. "That son of a bitch libelled you," he told Zantzinger. "You could've sued his ass for what he did." Zantzinger responded by saying he had planned a major libel action, firing off steely letters to the singer and his label alike. Dylan, Zantzinger claimed, had been running scared when he decided he couldn't face any more courtrooms in his immediate future and let the matter drop.

That's when Simon showed Zantzinger the note he'd found in Carroll's old case file: a cover sheet, dated just a few months after "Hattie Carroll"'s release, explaining that the attached letter was from a New York folk singer anxious for more information about the case. But the attachment itself was missing. Had this been a letter from Dylan himself, perhaps later stolen from the files by a souvenir-hunting fan? It seems very likely and, if so, he clearly had the issue of his song's accuracy in mind. "His letter was the re-action of a worried young man," Simon concludes. "Zantzinger enjoyed that immensely." [25]

Dylan first recorded "Hattie Carroll" on 23 October 1963, as part of the New York sessions for his third album *The Times They Are A-Changin'*, giving it a live debut at Carnegie Hall just three days later. The album was released in January 1964, complete with a take of "Hattie Carroll" which Dylanologist Christopher Ricks calls "a perfect song, perfectly rendered, once and for all". Other songwriters seemed to agree, with Judy Collins rapidly nabbing the song for her own 1964 Town Hall concert, and Phil Ochs using a *Broadside* essay to praise Dylan's skill. [26]

Billy Bragg was just six years old when *The Times They Are A-Changin'* came out, and so would have to wait another decade before discovering it for himself. "That album was a very big album for me," he said. "The whole idea of what Dylan was doing with that album entered deeply into my consciousness: that idea of telling a story, making a point, offering a different perspective. It was probably one of the seminal records in the making of Billy Bragg, and 'Hattie Carroll' was one of the stand-out tracks in that because it made a moral point.

"Although the Dylan album was nearly a decade old by the time I heard it, it still had its contemporary power because it spoke about the Civil Rights movement. 'Hattie Carroll' had a resonance because it spoke of the inequalities in the American system, particularly with regard to race."

We've already seen that the song may not have stood up to the cold scrutiny of the libel courts – which make no distinction between a tale set to music and one set in type – but it remains an absolute triumph when judged simply as art. It's the work of a superb craftsman who's already starting to leave his contemporary rivals far behind.

Dylan himself has cited "Hattie Carroll" as one of the new breed of more ambitious songs he was inspired to write by Brecht and Weill's *The Threepenny Opera*. In his book *Chronicles*, he recalls watching a New York staging of this show around 1961, and being particularly struck by "Pirate Jenny". In the opera, this song's sung by a downtrodden skivvy who fantasises that a pirate ship will one day come to slaughter all the men and women who treat her like dirt. When all her tormentors are dead, Jenny decides, she'll sail off on the pirates' black freighter as its beautiful new captain.

Impressed by what he calls the "big medicine" of Brecht's lyrics, Dylan set about dissecting "Pirate Jenny" to try and understand how it worked its magic. One of the things he noticed was the structure provided by its recurring chorus, sung with a slight variation each time to mark the black freighter's unstoppable approach. Without what he'd learned from "Pirate Jenny", he says, many of the songs he'd write over the next couple of years simply wouldn't have been possible – and "Hattie Carroll" is one of the six specific examples he gives. [27]

One clear sign of this influence is the three-line section Dylan adds to the end of each verse denying listeners permission to weep at Carroll's fate. It's not Carroll's death that's the greatest outrage here – so don't cry yet. It's not Zantzinger's casual attitude to the crime either – not yet, not yet – and nor is it Carroll's lowly duties. For Dylan, the greatest outrage is the fact that Zantzinger was allowed to get away with it and it's only when we've drunk in that final abomination that he's prepared to allow us any release. Few other songwriters would have had the wit to even attempt that, let alone the restraint to pull it off so effectively.

"It's 'Hold back – there's something worse coming'," Bragg said. "Something even worse than what happened to this poor person. There's something worse, and you should hold back. He tells the story, gets you to sympathise with Hattie and then nails the establishment for not doing her justice. That's what's clever about it – he doesn't just want you to be angry about what happened to Hattie Carroll. He wants you to be angry about the state's inability to come up with a fair sentence for William Zantzinger."

Another big strand feeding into "Hattie Carroll" is Dylan's long grounding in British and American folk music. That's a tradition Bragg's been educating himself about ever since his mid-teens, when he discovered a stack of Topic Records samplers at his local library. "Listening to the Topic samplers was a bit like going to a museum," he said. "One of them specialised in murder ballads, so I was hearing things like 'Knoxville Girl' and those kind of tracks too. That's something I connected with very early on – that murder ballads were part of the folk tradition.

"Dylan makes 'Hattie Carroll' sound like an old song by using that repetitive chorus, that storytelling chorus. He clearly understands the tradition and how to write a song that fits neatly into that. I think he does a really good job of recreating that in a new setting. 'Hattie Carroll' is in that tradition of songs that tell a story, like 'The Ballad Of Maria Marten' and I suppose I connected with that. But the thing about Dylan was that it wasn't like going to a museum."

Another striking aspect of the song, as Sounes points out, is that Dylan never feels it necessary to spell out that Zantzinger was white and Carroll was black. In the troubled racial atmosphere of 1963 America, he knew he could rely on listeners to automatically fill in that information for themselves. In that year alone, Alabama police had fire-hosed peaceful black demonstrators, Medgar Evers had been killed by a white sniper and a Klan bomb had slaughtered four black children in a Birmingham church. Of *course* an arrogant rich man would be white. Of *course* the servant who emptied the ashtrays his tobacco farm filled would be black. What need was there to say so?

"The song is really about privilege rather than about murder," Bragg said. "It's a privilege ballad disguised as a murder ballad. It's not just that a poor person was murdered – that's nothing to do with you – it's suddenly become about all of us, because of the way the system is gamed by the rich and the powerful. The courts are there to fix what happened to Hattie Carroll, but this is bigger than that and we should all be concerned about it. I think that's why it's a song that still resonates with people."

Dylan himself evidently realised he had something a bit special in "Hattie Carroll", because that's the song he chose to sing when *The Steve Allen Show* gave him his first national television appearance in February 1964. Perched on a stool next to Allen for a brief interview, Dylan looks nervous and fidgety. He regains his composure only when he's allowed to sing "Hattie Carroll" instead of talking about it.

Zantzinger completed his six month sentence, and was released from jail about a month after Dylan appeared on *Steve Allen*, but his notoriety showed no sign of going away. In January 1964, the Carroll family filed a civil suit against him demanding $1m in damages, and the *Afro-American* continued to carry letters drawing attention to the light sentence he'd received. A *Broadside* editorial in July 1964 surveyed all the violence America had suffered in the past two years, saying its victims had ranged "from a humble hotel maid to the President of the United States".

In October that year, the *Afro-American* led an inside page with news that Jane Zantzinger was planning a fund-raiser for 1964's Republican Presidential candidate Barry Goldwater, who'd opposed Kennedy's civil rights legislation. Despite Jane's protests that her husband had nothing to do with the event, this story was headlined: "Killer of Hotel Barmaid Raising Funds for Goldwater". Every time Zantzinger's name appeared in the papers from that day onward, this was how he'd be described.

After a spell running the family farm, Zantzinger switched into real estate, moving first to Waldorf and then to Port Tobacco, but never leaving Charles County. He had three children, then divorced Jane and married again. By 1991, he owned a nightclub in La Plata, an antiques shop and a White Plains auctioneer's business called W&Z Realty. He drove a Mercedes with the vanity plate "SOLD2U" and cultivated his reputation as a fun-loving good ol' boy with an annual pig and oyster roast. In October 1983, the Internal Revenue Service took the income stream he was receiving from his mother's trust to clear a little over $78,000 in unpaid federal taxes.

Every now and again, one reporter or another would notice the anniversary of Hattie Carroll's death had come around again and approach Zantzinger for an interview, but he always refused. It's a tribute to Simon's skills as a journalist that he persuaded Zantzinger to see him at all in 1988, but his first impression was less dramatic than the reporter might have hoped. Zantzinger had acquired a generous pot belly since his 1963 prime and his hair was thinning.

Zantzinger ran Simon through the details of Dylan's song, listing its equivocations as he went, and confirmed that he'd paid the Carroll family an out-of-court settlement many years ago. Heylin puts the size of that settlement at $25,000, but it's not clear how – if at all – that relates to the $1m civil suit I mentioned earlier or to the family's silence ever since. The only clue we have to their attitude today is a 2009 message board post from Talya Carroll, Hattie's great grand-daughter. "I would like for you all to know that the Carroll family did not get the justice we deserved in that trial," she wrote. "I witness fallout between members of our family, and also her children are dying by the years. Many of her 13 children moved out of the Baltimore area and have not been in contact with the others, leaving our family broken." [28, 29]

Zantzinger returned to the headlines in April 1991, when the *Maryland Independent* carried a front-page story saying he'd been collecting rents of $200 a month on some beat-up old wooden shacks in Patuxent Woods which he hadn't actually owned since 1986. Charles County had confiscated the shacks that year because Zantzinger owed it over $18,000 in unpaid property taxes. The six shacks, which Maryland's Real Estate Commission described as "reminiscent of slave quarters", had no running water, no sewers, no outhouses and no heating. They were occupied by poor black families, who had to empty their chamber pots in the woods near the shallow wells they relied on for drinking water. [30]

The Washington Post calculated that Zantzinger had illegally collected from $600 to $10,364 per household on these shacks after they were confiscated by the county, the sums reaching over $64,000 in total. He'd even succeeded in suing John Savoy, a 61-year-old black tenant living on welfare, for unpaid rent of $240 on a shanty which he –

Zantzinger – no longer owned. "He carried me to court, and he didn't even own the place," a bemused Savoy told reporters. [31]

Zantzinger was served a summons charging him with deceptive trade practice, including one count of making a false and misleading oral statement. The maximum sentence was one year in jail, plus a $1,000 fine. Soon after this, he was indicted for rent theft on a charge sheet that now comprised two counts of felony theft and 50 of unfair and deceptive trade practices. A second development at Indian Head was cited alongside the Patuxent Woods properties, adding an extra $4,750 to the rent Zantzinger had wrongly collected. He was arrested and released on personal bond. "Each felony count carries a maximum penalty of 15 years in prison and a $1,000 fine," *The Washington Post* noted.

The case reached court in November 1991, with Zantzinger pleading guilty to the misdemeanours and prosecutors dropping his two felony charges in return. Evidence presented in court revealed he had concealed the Patuxent Woods income stream in his 1988 divorce, explaining that he no longer held title to the properties. This scuppered any possible argument that he had continued collecting rents there in good faith. The court also heard about Zantzinger's manslaughter conviction in the Hattie Carroll case, as well as his three more recent court appearances for drunk driving.

Judge Steven Platt sentenced him to 18 months on work-release in the county jail, plus 2,400 hours of community service with local housing charities and penalties or fines totalling $62,000. This time, the judge denied his request for time to set his affairs in order and Zantzinger was led away in handcuffs to begin his sentence immediately. A few months later, the Maryland Real Estate Commission declined to renew Zantzinger's licence and levied a $2,000 fine of its own against him. [32]

When Bragg was preparing to write his own Rachel Corrie tribute in 2006, "Hattie Carroll" immediately came to mind as the template he should use – and that's the sign of a song that's still very much alive and still earning its keep in the world.

"'Hattie Carroll' pointed a way towards using songs to explain things to people," Bragg told me. "Dylan realised that folk music could have that role. You've got to remember that in the 20th century, for young people, music was how we communicated with one another, it was how we gathered our thoughts together. Music was our social medium, so Dylan was doing a really amazing job with that reportage.

"The thing that interested me most about 'Hattie Carroll' was that it has this second focus of the anger which is not on what happened to Hattie Carroll, but on the sentence that was passed on William Zantzinger. I thought it was very interesting the way he'd done that, and that's what I tried to do when I wrote the Rachel Corrie song."

The key to understanding Bragg's approach here is that it was not Corrie's death in 2003 which prompted his song, but rather the news three years later that a New York theatre had abruptly cancelled plans to stage a play based on her letters and journals. "That's the thing that really outraged me – quite apart from what happened to her," Bragg said. "People who were trying to bring her story to a wider audience were being censored and in some sense the people in New York were doing to her what the Israeli government had done to the Palestinians – make her into a non-person.

"It seemed to me that it would fit 'Hattie Carroll''s shape: 'Wait, wait, there's something worse coming.' Not every murder or case of injustice will fit that kind of treatment, but what happened to Rachel Corrie and the cancelling of the play in New York did fit it. So, when I was looking for a way to put that across, Dylan's format seemed to be a pretty handy way to get into it. I think I was on an aeroplane at the time. I didn't have a guitar, so already having a format made it a lot easier to fit the story to what I was trying to do."

The resulting song borrows both "Hattie Carroll"'s tune and its chorus, which Bragg uses to split his tale into three sections. The first tells us how Corrie died – but don't cry yet. The second gives a brief sketch of her life and her idealism – not yet, not yet. It's only after this final section that Bragg lets us release the tension Dylan's structure has helped him build:

The artistic director of a New York theatre,
Cancelled a play based on Rachel's writings,
But she wasn't a bomber or a killer or fighter,

But one who acted in the spirit of the Freedom Riders,
Is there no place for a voice in America,
That doesn't conform to the Fox News agenda?
Who believes in non-violence instead of brute force,
Who is willing to confront the might of an army,
Whose passionate beliefs were matched by her bravery,
The question she asked rings out round the world,
If America is truly the beacon of freedom,
Then how can it stand by while they bring down the curtain,
And turn Rachel Corrie into a non-person? [33]

Bragg was touring in the US when he wrote "Rachel Corrie". He began trying out the song at shows on that tour, recorded it fast and released it immediately as a free download which *The Guardian* stepped in to distribute. "In the old days, if I wrote a topical song, I might have to wait six months till I made an album for it to come out. Now it's all very different. We had a day off in Detroit on that tour, so we booked a studio and I went in and recorded it – got it out there. That's a real boon to a topical songwriter.

"Every now and again, something about Rachel Corrie comes up, and people use the song to draw attention to that. They tag it on to a tweet or something like that. You can use a song to gather people together to express their solidarity by coming together for an issue and feeling they're not alone. Good music can do that, as well as entertain and make people dance and laugh and cry and all those other things. It also has a role that sometimes you can make an interesting moral point – or make a point that isn't necessarily in the papers. And Dylan does that with 'Hattie Carroll'."

Carroll herself has been gone for over 50 years now, Zantzinger died in 2009, Dylan's over 70 and pretty soon all three will have moved beyond living memory. "Stagger Lee" and the other old murder ballads in this book must have gone through a similar process, as anyone with direct knowledge of the crime or its participants died out and the legend that song preserved took over from cold, hard fact.

There's no doubt that "Hattie Carroll" is a good enough song to survive into the next century, and by then few people will have any interest in digging back through the history screens to check the niggling details I've discussed here. The danger is not that people will muck about with "Hattie Carroll" – that approach just breathes new life into the song – but that too many interpreters will stifle it with reverential solemnity. Even the "rag" chorus which Bragg found so crucial to his own adaptation turns out to be expendable – as Angela Correa proved with her 2010 Les Shelleys recording. She and Tom Brosseau, her partner in the duo, drop Dylan's chorus altogether, yet the song emerges unscathed.

"Our version is really spare and quiet, almost a whisper of a song," Correa told me. "Once you hit that chorus chord it changes the feeling from a hypnotic, trance-like tale into something quite different, quite bold. It's a shift from telling a story to pointing a finger, and we thought it was more interesting without the chorus, both melodically and story-wise. It leaves the listener to make their own opinion of what's just been shared." [34]

Even listening to Dylan himself, you can hear the song tearing itself free of its roots. The performances recorded at his 2005 and 2006 gigs show him delivering "Hattie Carroll"'s lyrics in a rather mannered, distancing way. It's as though he's already begun letting go of the song's history, handing its more earnest aspects over to the younger singers who've adopted it for themselves.

Whenever he's taken to task for distorting the truth in one of his songs about real people, Dylan counters that he's merely working in the tradition of romanticised old outlaw ballads like Billy Gashade's "Jesse James". Perhaps he's just got his eyes fixed further into the future than the rest of us, looking to how a song like "Hattie Carroll" will fare not in a few weeks' time, but in a few decades' time, when it can function as legend alone. The small lies which "Hattie Carroll" tells in service of a much greater truth will then be forgotten, and in the end this magnificent song's own verdict is the only one that's going to matter.

A whole other level: 10 great versions of Hattie's story

"The Lonesome Death Of Hattie Carroll", by Bob Dylan (1963).
The song's masterful original recording appears on Dylan's *The Times They Are A-Changin'* LP, and this remains its definitive version. "It would have to be in the top 20 songs of his pre-electric period," Billy Bragg told me. "He was still in connection there with what Woody Guthrie was doing. He was doing Woody's work."

"The Lonesome Death Of Hattie Carroll", by Judy Collins (1964). Collins was quick to realise just what a remarkable song this is, adding it to her March 1964 New York Town Hall concert which was being recorded for a live album. She performs it solo, her bell-clear voice resonating through the hall. The audience listens in such rapt silence that it seems almost to be holding its breath.

"The Lonesome Death Of Hattie Carroll", by Bob Dylan (1975). Another live recording, this one from a Boston show on the 1975 Rolling Thunder Revue tour. It's a pacey, muscular version, with Rob Stoner's bass driving the song along and Dylan himself in fine, attacking voice. A perfect example of the added power his early songs gained when "Judas" went electric.

"The Lonesome Death Of Hattie Carroll", by Martin Carthy (1998). Carthy's calm vocals and careful diction put clarity at the heart of this rendition. He wants to be sure you understand exactly what happened here, knowing that once that's been achieved the anger will take care of itself. His sparse but inventive guitar playing underlines key words, but it's always Dylan's lyrics he puts to the fore.

"The Lonesome Death Of Hattie Carroll", by Michael Rose (2004). Black Uhuru's former frontman does his bit to chant down Babylon with this pretty reggae version. His sweet voice joins with a propulsive bass line, background stabs of piano and a gentle sax solo to integrate the song into reggae's own long tradition of protest music. It's a good fit.

"The Lonesome Death Of Rachel Corrie", by Billy Bragg (2006).
Bragg rewrites Dylan's lyrics – but keeps his chorus – to protest the censorship of a New York play about a young American activist killed on the Gaza Strip. Written fast, recorded fast and first released as a free download via *The Guardian's* website, it still helps draw attention to her case today. "The format of 'Hattie Carroll' was ideal", Bragg told me.

"The Lonesome Death Of Hattie Carroll", by Mike Leslie (2008).
Listening to this recording, I imagine Leslie sitting next to me in a grotty bar, toying with a shot glass, as he growls out a half-drunk story I never asked to hear. There's someone strumming an acoustic guitar in the background, true, but that seems a world away from his unhurried spoken-word vocals.

"The Lonesome Death Of Hattie Carroll", by Michel Reis (2009).
Of all the approaches that might suit "Hattie Carroll", instrumental jazz is not the first you'd think of. Reis makes it work, though, producing a lovely piano ballad that reminds you how strong Dylan's tune is even without the words.

"The Lonesome Death Of Hattie Carroll", by Les Shelleys (2010).
LA duo Les Shelleys – better known as Tom Brosseau and Angela Correa – offer a beautifully-harmonised, almost a capella, version of the song. The pair omit Dylan's chorus to merge all his remaining lines into a single long verse, accompanied only by the most minimal acoustic guitar. The result is haunting, and quite gorgeous.

"The Lonesome Death Of Hattie Carroll", by Cage The Elephant (2012). Singer Matt Shultz delivers the song in an eerie, high-pitched whisper, punctuated at the start only by handclaps and a tumble of echoey drums. Slow and stately throughout, the music behind him builds in both intensity and volume, culminating in a storm of discordant guitars as the six-month sentence is announced. The weather's broken at last, and here comes the rain of those falling tears.

5 – Tom Dooley

The New York Herald, 2 May 1868,
on Wilkes County, North Carolina.

Sometimes, it's not the information a song contains which gives it its power, but precisely what it chooses to leave out.

The Kingston Trio's 1958 recording of "Tom Dooley" scored a top five hit on both sides of the Atlantic and dragged the burgeoning folk revival from a few Greenwich Village cafes to the global stage. Shorn of repetitions, the song is a sparse 16 lines long – just 78 words in all – and the sheer economy this forces on its bare-bones tale guarantees that the record will raise many more questions than it answers.

We're introduced to a man called Tom Dooley and told he's due to hang tomorrow morning for stabbing an unnamed beauty to death. If it hadn't been for this Grayson fellow, he'd have been safe in Tennessee instead. Listen again, and you may pick up from the spoken word introduction that some sort of romantic triangle was involved.

It's not much, is it? And yet this rudimentary tale was enough to ensure the record sold six million copies round the world, topping the charts not only in America, but in Australia, Canada and Norway too.

Only Lonnie Donegan's canny decision to quickly cut his own competing version – itself a sizable UK hit – kept the Trio's original from scoring the top spot in Britain too. Dooley's ballad and the killing that inspired it have been firmly cemented in the public imagination ever since, spilling over into movies, comedy, theatre and every other medium. In his 1997 book *Invisible Republic*, Greil Marcus calls the Trio's record "insistently mysterious" and suggests it's the very paucity of information it offers which makes the song so fascinating. [1]

The singer clearly sympathises with Dooley – "Poor boy, you're bound to die" – and invites us to do likewise. But how can we oblige when he refuses to tell us who it was that Dooley killed, why he did so or what the extenuating circumstances might be? Where did all this happen? And when? Who was Grayson, how did he thwart Dooley's planned escape and what's so special about Tennessee? And why have these innocent-looking preppy boys, with their short hair, slacks and crisp stripy shirts, chosen such a violent song?

A quick glance at the discs surrounding "Tom Dooley" in the US chart that autumn confirms how awkwardly it sat with the era's sugary norm. Dooley's tale of slaughter and despair made a strange bedfellow for "Rockin' Robin", "Queen Of The Hop" and "The Chipmunk Song". Conway Twitty's cornball country reading of "It's Only Make Believe" was the single that preceded "Tom Dooley" at number one and it was The Teddy Bears' winsome "To Know Him Is To Love Him" that dislodged it. Small wonder, as Marcus says, that Dooley's disc prompted such a nagging question in listeners' minds whenever it was played: "What *is* this?" [2]

That question was only heightened by the many bizarre spin-offs which Dooleymania produced. The first to show through were a batch of late fifties answer songs, such as Merle Kilgore's "Tom Dooley Jr", Russ Hamilton's "The Reprieve Of Tom Dooley" and The Balladeers' "Tom Dooley Gets The Last Laugh". These were typically facetious attempts to cash in on the original hit's popularity. On The Balladeers' disc, for example, Tom's hanging rope turns out to be so long that he's left balancing tip-toe on the ground beneath. [3]

Columbia Pictures was keen to exploit the original song's success too, and released a 1959 movie adaption called *The Legend Of Tom Dooley*.

This cast Michael Landon – best-known as *Bonanza's* Little Joe – in the title role, but cheerfully made up its own story from scratch. In this telling, Dooley and his Confederate army friends are framed for murder after what they take to be an honourable wartime shooting and Tom kills his unfortunate girlfriend in a tragic accident.

Ella Fitzgerald got in on the act too, slipping an unexpected snatch of "Tom Dooley" into her 1960 recording of "Rudolph The Red Nosed Reindeer". Listeners to that year's *A Swinging Christmas* album were startled to hear Ella replying to the track's short piano break by singing the improvised lines: "Hang your nose down, Rudy / Hang your nose and cry". If nothing else, this shows how firmly Dooley's ballad had already lodged itself in America's collective mind, and suggests that even the finest jazz singer of her generation had found its chorus ringing through her head.

Still we were no closer to discovering what the true story was. The folk music covers which started to appear in the next couple of years took a more serious approach, but many were content to simply copy The Kingston Trio's template. Where these did manage to slip in an extra bit of information – Lonnie Donegan's reference to "Sheriff Grayson" for example – it often turned out to be untrue.

Mike Seeger's New Lost City Ramblers went back to an earlier folk version of the song for their 1960 recording, adding the news that Tom had been a fiddle player, naming his victim as Laura Foster, and giving us the rough dimensions of her shallow grave. The blind country singer Doc Watson contributed a third version in 1964 – perhaps an even older one – which claimed Tom was innocent of any crime and condemned to hang only because someone was determined to persecute him. Just who that someone was, Watson declined to say.

Really determined listeners could consult the few printed sources then available with Tom's story, but these proved just as impossible to reconcile as the songs. John and Alan Lomax had included "Tom Dooley" in their 1946 collection *Folk Song USA*, printing the same words The Kingston Trio would use 12 years later, but their account of the case behind the song relied more on folklore than fact. Rufus Gardner's 1960 book *Tom Dooley: The Eternal Triangle* located the tale firmly in North Carolina, but was determined to whitewash the reputation of everyone involved. When the newspapers deigned to print a background article about Dooley's song, they simply reproduced the same mistakes and tall tales these two books contained. [4, 5]

In 1957, no-one outside North Carolina had even heard of Tom Dooley. Five years later, his name was known around the world, and many millions of people were at least dimly aware that he'd been accused of killing his girlfriend and later hanged for it. Hardcore folk fans may also have grasped that the killing happened in North Carolina's Wilkes County in 1866. For every "fact" that emerged, though, there was another one alongside to contradict it, and that meant Dooley's identity in the mass media became more confused every day.

Here was a folk song – a folk song, for God's sake – that had somehow managed to top the charts and sell six million copies. Here was a tale of murder and judicial execution sung by three clean-cut young boys any mother could admire. Here were novelty records, movies, books and a story which contradicted itself with every new telling and yet never seemed to change. With every drop of a needle on to vinyl, every flickering image of Landon's face on a cinema or TV screen, Marcus's question resounded anew: "What *is* this?"

I'm glad you asked...

Tom Dula was born in 1844 among the "ignorant, poor and depraved" hill folk *The New York Herald* would later condemn. His home was near the mouth of Elk Creek in North Carolina's Wilkes County, a community we now call Elkville. Like any family thereabouts whose surname ended in "a", Tom's was pronounced in the local dialect with a long "ee" at the end: "Dooley".

Lotty Foster and her brood of five illegitimate children lived about half a mile from the Dulas' cabin. As John Foster West explains in his 1993 book *Lift Up Your Head Tom Dooley*, Lotty's whole family was illiterate and she herself was known to be both an easy lay and a drunk. Her daughter Ann was married by the age of 15, choosing a local farmer called James Melton as her husband. [6]

Not long after the wedding, Lotty caught Tom and Ann in bed together, at a time when Tom would have been about 15 and Ann perhaps a year older. "He jumped out and got under the bed," she recalled seven years later. "I ordered him out. He had his clothes off". [7]

Ann's adultery with Tom didn't stop there. James kept three beds in his single-room cabin and he often slept alone in one while Tom and Ann shared another. The third bed was occupied by Ann's cousin Pauline Foster, who later testified she'd seen Tom slipping into Ann's bed many times and spending the night with her there. James didn't seem to object – perhaps because he was scared of his wife's ferocious temper.

"Ann Melton was a unique character, possessing almost all the faults one woman could have," West writes. "In addition to her promiscuity, [she] was temperamental, demanding and aggressive." She was also the area's reigning beauty, and the fact that Tom was handsome enough to bed her let him cut a swathe through Elkville's other young women too. He was a talented fiddle player, which may also have helped with his seduction technique.

The 1860 census shows Tom's mother Mary as head of their household, suggesting his father was already dead. Tom showed little interest in cultivating the family's patch of rocky ground, opting instead to follow his two older brothers into the Civil War. In March 1862, he enlisted with the Confederate cause, joining Company K of the North Carolina Infantry's 42nd regiment. His companions there found him a gallant fighter, but also someone with a rather dark and desperate side to his character. "Among them, it was generally believed he murdered the husband of a woman at Wilmington [...] during the war, with whom he then had criminal intercourse," *The New York Herald* reported. [8]

By February 1864, Tom had been promoted from private soldier to musician, indicating he was responsible for drumming out the charge or retreat in battle. He saw a lot of action in the year that followed, fighting at Cold Harbor, Petersburg and Kinston. In March 1865, he was captured by Unionist troops and sent to a Yankee POW camp.

The Civil War ended a month or so later, but Tom was not released until 11 June. Already, his own regional pronunciation of the family name was causing confusion and he found the oath of allegiance he was required to sign to the newly-restored USA listed him as "Dooley". He put his mark to that spelling rather than risk his release, but could not resist scrawling "Dula" above it as well. It's also this document which gives us our most reliable description of Tom's appearance: 5ft 9½ ins tall, with dark brown curly hair and brown eyes.

Returning home to Elkville after his imprisonment, Tom found times there were harder than ever, with old Civil War resentments playing themselves out in the surrounding hills and starvation a very real prospect for the poor. Many Elkville folk had no choice but to replace former slaves at the big plantations lining the Yadkin river, becoming sharecroppers or tenant farmers there.

One man who did this was Wilson Foster, who shared a cabin with his daughter Laura. Folklore describes Laura as a beautiful girl with chestnut hair and blue – or green or brown – eyes and a noticeable gap between her two front teeth. By the ripe old age of 20, she'd secured a reputation for "round heels" – a mountain term denoting the ease with which she could be toppled on to her back.

Wilson first found his daughter in bed with Tom in March 1866, and later testified the young man would come calling on Laura about once a week. Often, he'd spend the night with her, alternating these visits with his customary trips to Ann's bed. It was also in March 1866 that Ann's cousin Pauline arrived from next-door Watauga County to work as a live-in housekeeper at the Meltons' place. Pauline's heels were even rounder than Ann or Laura's, which meant it wasn't long before Tom was screwing her too.

So, let's review for a moment. In the spring of 1866, Tom was sleeping with Ann, Laura and Pauline. Ann was also sleeping with her husband James and – if the Elkville gossip's to be believed – a couple of other men as well. Pauline, we know, also slept with Ann's brother Thomas and was said to have bedded her own brother Sam. Tom's the only bedmate of Laura's we can put a name to, but her reputation suggests there were others.

None of this merry bed-hopping would have mattered in the least if it hadn't been for one awkward fact: Pauline had syphilis.

Pauline had contracted the disease before leaving Watauga County and come over the border to Elkville to seek medical help. George

Carter, the only doctor for miles around, lived nearby and she'd taken the Meltons' housekeeping job to pay for the blue stone, blue mass and caustic he prescribed. No-one but Carter seems to have known Pauline had "the pock".

It takes about three weeks from catching syphilis to the first appearance of its tell-tale chancre on the penis and that's precisely the symptom Tom presented at his own visit to the doctor around 31 March. "He had the syphilis," Carter later testified. "He told me he caught it from Laura Foster."

No doubt that's what Tom believed, but he would have known nothing about Pauline's disease. She'd arrived in Elkville on 1 March and, assuming a week or so passed before she and Tom first slept together, the timing would be about right for the infection to have come from her. Soon, Ann and Laura were both showing symptoms of syphilis too and Ann claimed she'd also passed it on to James. "We all have it," Pauline would later declare.

Tom told a neighbour in the middle of May that he intended to kill the woman who'd given him this horrible disease. Ann made a similar threat, telling Pauline that she planned to kill Laura in revenge for her own infection via Tom. Throughout that month, Tom and Laura were locked in a series of private and intense-sounding conversations, culminating in Laura announcing to a neighbour that Tom had promised to marry her. Some take this proposal as evidence that Laura was carrying Tom's baby, others that he was simply looking for an excuse to get her alone in the woods so he could kill her in private.

On Thursday 24 May, Pauline was alone at the Melton house when Tom turned up to get some alum for the sores on his mouth and borrow a canteen. She handed the two items over and Tom passed the empty canteen to man named Carson McGuire, telling him to fill it with moonshine liquor.

His next stop was Lotty's place, where he borrowed a heavy digging tool called a mattock. He told Lotty he wanted to "work some devilment out" of himself. Soon after this, a local woman called Martha Gilbert saw Tom swinging the mattock on a path about 100 yards from the Dula cabin. He told her he was working to widen the path there.

McGuire delivered the full canteen to Ann at the Melton house at about 10 a. m. After the family's noon meal, she took a swig from it, announced she was going to take the canteen to Tom, and then left for her mother's cabin. Tom arrived at Lotty's – without the mattock – soon after Ann and they left together about 3 p.m. Neither was seen again till dawn the next day.

Ann arrived home about 5.30 on the Friday morning and went straight to bed. Meanwhile, Tom was waiting to speak to Laura outside her father's cabin. She sneaked out to talk to him, then returned to her bedside where she quickly got dressed and bundled a few spare clothes together. She threw a cape over her shoulders to hide the syphilis welts already showing there and slipped out the door.

Laura loosed the rope tethering her father's mare outside and rode down the track towards the meeting place Tom had chosen. She was just a mile into her six-mile journey when she met Betsy Scott, the same neighbour she'd confided in a few days before, and told her she and Tom had agreed to meet at "Bates's Place" – a spot in the woods where an old blacksmith's shop had once stood. Betsy, perhaps thinking how short-lived a promise of marriage from Tom might prove, urged her to get there fast. Meanwhile, Tom was walking along a short-cut towards Bates's Place, which cut the distance to about five miles. As always, he carried a six-inch Bowie knife in his coat pocket.

He stopped briefly to chat with neighbours three times along the way, including Hezekiah Kendall who asked if he was still pursuing his plans for revenge against Laura. "No, I have quit that," Tom replied. He was next seen at the Meltons' cabin, when Pauline stepped inside from her field work to fetch a milk pail and found Tom standing over Ann's bed, talking to her in low, urgent tones. He left soon after Pauline saw him, taking a route which could lead either to his own cabin or to Bates's Place once again.

Wilson was up and about by then too, and angry to find both his daughter and his horse had gone missing. He followed the mare's tracks for a while, but then lost the trail and went off to cadge some breakfast at a friend's house instead. After his meal, he walked on to the Meltons', where he found Ann still in bed. Tom had just left. All these encounters, from Tom's conversation with Kendall on the road to Wilson's arrival at the Meltons' cabin, came between about 7.30 and 8.30 a.m.

Tom wasn't seen again till noon, when Mary Dula returned to the cabin they shared to find her son lying in bed. They ate lunch together and Tom remained in Mary's company till about 3 p.m., when she went out to deal with the cows. Ann's mother Lotty and her brother Thomas both testified later that they'd seen Tom heading up towards Bates's Place while Mary was preparing supper that evening. Tom returned home in time to eat supper with Mary, but then left again just after dark, staying out for what she said was about an hour. The distance between the Dulas' cabin and Bates's Place was less than a mile, so he'd have had enough time to get there and back on either occasion.

We know Ann was still in bed alone at home around 8 on Friday morning, but we have no other account of her movements until nightfall, when Wilson returned to the Meltons' cabin for a party with her, James, Pauline, Thomas and three other men. He stayed at the party for two or three hours, then spent what was left of the night at his friend Francis Melton's place. When he returned to his own cabin on Saturday morning, he found his mare already waiting there. It had chewed through its halter rope, about three feet of which was still hanging from its headcollar. No-one ever saw Laura alive again.

Tom returned to the Meltons' cabin on Saturday morning, where he spent half an hour talking quietly with Ann. Laura's disappearance had set Elkville gossiping that she and Tom must have run off together, but when Pauline mentioned this he just laughed and said, "I have no use for Laura Foster". Later that morning, Ann told Pauline she'd slipped out of the cabin overnight without anyone noticing. "She'd done what she said," Pauline concluded. "She'd killed Laura Foster."

As soon as people realised Tom was still in Elkville, the gossip switched to claims Laura had been murdered. By 22 June, a local family called Hendricks was openly saying that Tom had killed her. "They would have to prove it," he laughed in response. "And perhaps take a beating besides."

Calls for his arrest started circulating a few days later, and a search party was organised to look for what everyone now assumed would be Laura's remains. At Bates's Place, they found a piece of rope tied to a dogwood tree, chewed through at its dangling end and matching the rope Wilson's mare had trailed home. Nearby, there were a couple of piles of horse dung – suggesting the mare had stood there for some time – and a small patch of discoloured ground which the searchers believed was stained by Laura's blood.

Next day, Tom called at the Meltons' place around nightfall. He spoke privately to Ann outside, then came back in to retrieve a knife she'd hidden for him under one of the beds' headboards. When Pauline asked what was wrong, Tom said the Hendricks clan was falsely claiming he'd killed Laura and that meant he was going to have to get out of Wilkes County. After a final tearful embrace between himself and Ann, Tom left. He stopped in Watauga County for a few days and then walked on towards Tennessee.

By the time Tom left Watauga, Elkville's Justice of the Peace – a man called Pickens Carter – had issued a warrant for his arrest on suspicion of murder. Sheriff William Hix dispatched two deputies, Jack Adkins and Ben Ferguson, to track the fugitive down and bring him home. He also arrested Ann and two of Tom's cousins on the same charge, but all three were found not guilty at Carter's 29 June hearing and allowed to go free.

Tom arrived in Tennessee on 2 July after a week of hard walking. He pitched up at a farm owned by Colonel James Grayson, a former soldier who sat in the state's legislature. Tom, now claiming his surname was Hall, took a job as a field hand there. A week later, he'd earned enough to replace his ruined boots so he moved on again, this time heading west towards Johnson City.

Adkins and Ferguson arrived at Grayson's farm a few days after Tom had left and Grayson realised the man they were describing was his old field hand. Grayson rode off with the two deputies to find Johnson County's sheriff, knowing they'd need his authority to arrest Tom outside their own North Carolina jurisdiction. Discovering the sheriff was away on official business, the three men rode on after Tom anyway.

They found him camped by a creek at Pandora, about nine miles west of Mountain City and told him he was under arrest. Tom, seeing that Grayson carried a gun, thought it best to surrender. One recent *Appalachian Heritage* article claims Adkins and Ferguson were both keen to hang him on the spot, but that Grayson insisted on taking him back for trial. Grayson mounted Tom on his horse behind him, tying his feet beneath its belly to keep him there, and the whole party headed back east. Next day, Adkins and Ferguson locked Tom in the Wilkesboro jail cell which tourists still visit today. [9]

Hearing of Tom's capture around 14 July, Pauline fled from Elkville back into Watauga County. Ann dragged her home a few days later, explaining forcefully that panic like this would just make them all look guilty. Back in Elkville, she urged Pauline to help her ensure no further evidence against Tom came to light. "I want to show you Laura's grave," she said. "I want to see whether it looks suspicious."

Ann insisted that Pauline went with her, saying she would dig up Laura's body and rebury it in her cabbage patch if necessary. Pausing at a pine log part way up what it is now Laura Foster Ridge, Ann announced the grave was just a little further on. Pauline, now more scared than ever, refused to take another step.

Ann marched on alone. She returned a few minutes later, apparently having satisfied herself the grave would draw no attention and cursed her cousin for cowardice all the way back home. Pauline was falling apart fast now, tormented by the knowledge that she may have given Tom the infection that cost Laura her life, and often drunk enough to make her more unpredictable than ever.

About a week later, Ann and Pauline were together at the Meltons' cabin when Adkins and Ferguson turned up to question them. Ferguson told Pauline he believed she'd helped Tom kill Laura and that was why she'd fled across the county line. "Yes, I and Dula killed her and I ran away," Pauline drunkenly replied. "Come out, Tom Dula and let us kill some more! Let us kill Ben Ferguson!" Seeing the state she was in, the two deputies ignored her outburst and Pauline later insisted it had all been meant as a joke.

The authorities decided a few nights in jail might be just the push Pauline needed to make her talk. Locked in a cell and told she'd be prosecuted for murder, she cracked, describing her trip up the ridge with Ann and agreeing to help the next search party find Laura's grave. A few days later, a party of over 70 men followed Pauline to the pine log where she and Ann had parted company. She pointed up the hill in the direction Ann had gone and the men split into pairs for the search that followed.

One of these pairs was Colonel James Isbell and his elderly father-in-law David Horton. They searched their section of the ridge meticulously for an hour and then, about 75 yards on from the log where they'd started, Horton's horse began to snort and rear up.

"My father James Isbell noticed the horse back and shy away," Robert Isbell later wrote in *The Lenoir News-Topic*. "He called to Major Horton to rein the horse back from the spot it had shied from and when he did the horse refused to go. My father [...] went forward and stamped the spot with his boot heel, turned up a side of turf and found Laura about two feet under the ground, cramped in a short grave." [10]

This spot was only about 250 yards from the path Tom had been seen working with Lotty's mattock back in May. "After taking out the earth I saw the prints of what appeared to have been a mattock in the hard side of the grave," James Isbell said at Tom's trial. "The flesh was off the face. Her body had on a checked cotton dress and a dark-coloured cloak or cape. There was a bundle of clothes laid on the head."

The two men called Dr Carter over and he examined the body where it lay, finding the slit of a knife in the fabric over Laura's left breast and a corresponding stab wound between her third and fourth ribs. "The body was lying on its right side, face up," Carter later testified. "The hole in which it lay was two-and-a-half feet deep, very narrow and not long enough for the body. The legs were drawn up."

After three months in the ground, Laura was too decomposed to tell for sure whether the knife had penetrated her heart or not, but Carter confirmed it certainly could have done so and that such a wound would have killed her outright. If he saw any sign that she was pregnant when she died, then he seems to have kept it to himself.

The body was taken to Elkville's general store where it was formally identified by both Pauline and Wilson, who recognised Laura by the gap in her teeth and what was left of her clothes. Ann was arrested and given the same Wilkesboro cell next to Tom's which Pauline had just vacated.

The discovery of Laura's body gave her story a convenient punctuation point and that's when the case's first ballad emerged. This was written by Happy Valley's Captain Thomas Land, who Gardner calls "a local poetical celebrity". Land doesn't mention Tom or Ann by name in the 84

Stagger Lee's tale became a graphic
novel in 2006. Art for both images
by Shepherd Hendrix. (© *Derek
McCulloch & Shepherd Hendrix, used
with their permission*)

Left: Furry Lewis brought Stack and Billy's gambling to the fore. (*Advert from* The Chicago Defender, *21 April 1928*)

Below: Mississippi John Hurt's 1928 recording of "Stack O'Lee" is full of rueful wisdom. (*Everett Collection Historial/Alamy Stock Photo*)

Bottom: Mick Harvey with Nick Cave in 1998. "'Stagger Lee' is such a *separate* kind of song," Harvey says. (*Ebet Roberts/Getty Images*)

Hollywood has always found "Frankie & Johnny"'s story irresistible.
(*GAB Archive/Redferns*)

Top left: Cary Grant and Mae West in 1933's *She Done Him Wrong*. Frankie sued Paramount Studios over the film's inaccuracies. (*AF Archive/Alamy Stock Photo*)

Top right: The real Frankie Baker was a St Louis prostitute. "She was a queen sport," one former neighbour told the judge. (St Louis Post-Dispatch, *14 February 1942*)

Above: Snakefarm's 1999 recording of "Frankie & Johnny" gives the song a noirish setting. "The lyrics tell a damn good suspense story," says the band's Anna Domino. (*Judith Burrows/Getty Images*)

Above: "The Bloody Miller", shown here in its illustration from a 17th Century ballad sheet, is the song which ultimately became "Knoxville Girl". (*17th century woodcut*)

Left: Judge J. A. Sturges gave Americans a "Knoxville Girl" murder of their own to hang the song on. (Source: *Illustrated History Of McDonald County*, 1897)

Below: England's 17th century parish records confirm that the real killer behind "Knoxville Girl" was Francis Cooper, and that his victim was Anne Nichols. (*Parish Register Extracts*)

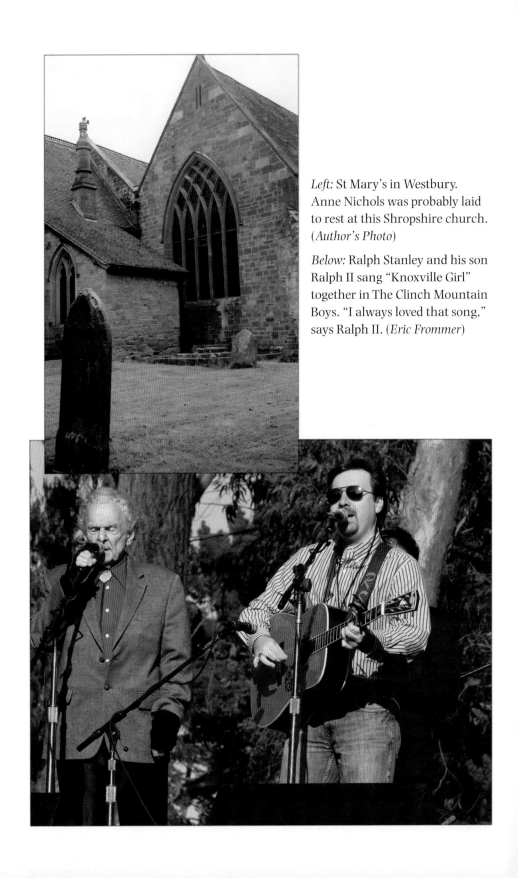

Left: St Mary's in Westbury. Anne Nichols was probably laid to rest at this Shropshire church. (*Author's Photo*)

Below: Ralph Stanley and his son Ralph II sang "Knoxville Girl" together in The Clinch Mountain Boys. "I always loved that song," says Ralph II. (*Eric Frommer*)

Above left: Billy Bragg with Martin Carthy. Bragg repurposed "The Lonesome Death Of Hattie Carroll" for his own Rachel Corrie song in 2006. (*Bryan Ledgard*)

Above right: The Wire's David Simon questioned William Zantzinger about Dylan's song in 1988. "We were going to sue him big time," Zantzinger claimed. (*Michael Ventura/ Alamy Stock Photo*)

Left: William Zantzinger was sentenced again in 1992, this time to 18 months for collecting rent on properties he no longer owned. (*Larry Morris/ The Washington Post/Getty Images*)

Left: Judy Collins recognised what a great song "The Lonesome Death Of Hattie Carroll" was and quickly added it to her own live set. (*ABC TV* Hootenanny, *1963*)

Below: Bob Dylan with Joan Baez at the Civil Rights March on 28 August 1963, where Dylan sang two songs and Dr Martin Luther King gave his famous "I have a dream" speech. It's said Dylan wrote "The Lonesome Death Of Hattie Carroll" at Baez's home in California. (*Everett Collection Historial/Alamy Stock Photo*)

rather plodding lines he composed and his effort bears no resemblance to the Tom Dula song we know today. But he is clear that Laura was murdered by the lover she'd hoped to marry and that this man did not act alone:

> 'Ere sun declined toward the west,
> She met her groom and his vile guest,
> In forest wild, they three retreat,
> And look for parson there to meet. [11]

The local audience who first read Land's verses would have known full well that Tom was the groom he had in mind and been equally sure that his "vile guest" must be Ann. Throughout the poem, Land shows the pair acting together in Laura's murder and disposal, using plural phrases like "*those* who did poor Laura kill", "*they* her conceal" and "to dig the grave *they* now proceed". By doing this, he ensures that Ann is thoroughly implicated in the whole rotten business.

Laura herself is depicted as a sweet, innocent girl, too full of childlike love to imagine Tom could ever wish her harm:

> Her youthful heart no sorrow knew,
> She fancied all mankind were true,
> And thus she gaily passed along,
> Humming at times a favourite song.

Happy Valley's residents would have known that the real Laura was a good deal raunchier than that, but swallowed the lie for the extra narrative satisfaction it offered. The more of a saint Laura could appear, the more villainous Tom and Ann looked by comparison and that's what delivered the story's disreputable thrill.

Land takes us – somewhat laboriously – through the various stages of Laura's discovery, then closes with a bit of tidy alliteration and one last pious thought to ensure we don't have nightmares:

> The jury made the verdict plain,
> Which was, poor Laura had been slain,
> Some ruthless fiend had struck the blow,
> Which laid poor luckless Laura low,

Then in a church yard her they lay,
No more to rise till Judgement Day,
Then, robed in white, we trust she'll rise,
To meet her Saviour in the skies.

The poem, which he called *The Murder Of Laura Foster*, was written to be read rather than sung, but I have heard one musical setting of it. This appears on Sheila Clark's 1986 album *The Legend Of Tom Dula And Other Tragic Love Ballads*, where Clark gives us a lovely a capella rendition of Land's full 21 verses, with nothing but a short fiddle phrase to divide each of its three sections. She negotiates the more awkward lines with admirable style and it's a tribute to the sweetness of her voice that the track's nine minutes and fifteen seconds of rather trite versifying passes with so little pain.

Legal proceedings against Tom and Ann began on 1 October 1866, when North Carolina's Superior Court met at Wilkesboro under Judge Ralph Buxton. Tom was charged with murdering Laura, and Ann with both encouraging him to commit the crime and harbouring him afterwards. The prosecution quickly agreed to drop Ann's harbouring charges, leaving just the first accusation against her.

No-one knows how Tom managed to recruit Colonel Zebulon Vance to defend him, but it certainly represented a bit of a coup. A former Democratic Congressman, Vance had commanded the 26th Regiment of North Carolina's Infantry in battle for a while – not the 42nd where Tom served – and then spent the remainder of the war as state Governor. He'd spent two months in a Federalist jail after the war, returned to freedom an almost penniless man and set up his Charlotte law practice in March 1866.

In the six months since then, Vance had built a considerable reputation as a courtroom orator. No doubt he had a certain amount of sympathy for any Confederate soldier down on his luck. Perhaps, as West suggests, he simply relished the prospect of a fight with the Republican Unionists who led the prosecution's team. None of them had seen any military service at all, so if you want to imagine Vance sharing Jack Nicholson's attitude in *A Few Good Men*, I'm not going to argue with you.

Tom's Wilkesboro trial began on 4 October and Vance got the ball rolling by arguing that feelings against Tom and Ann were running so high in Wilkes County that a change of venue was required. The court agreed and arranged for the trial to be moved across the Iredell County line to Statesville, about 30 miles away. A week later, Sheriff Hix moved Tom and Ann to Statesville jail, an old building on Broad Street with a pillory, whipping post and stocks out front. Eight extra guards were hired to make sure Tom couldn't escape.

The Statesville proceedings began on 19 October 1866, again with Judge Buxton presiding. Twelve jurors were selected from a panel of 100 Iredell County freeholders – all men – and Vance stood up to speak once again. This time, his point was that Tom and Ann's cases should be heard as two completely separate trials. Ann had made several incriminating statements since Laura's death, he pointed out and often these statements had been made when Tom had no opportunity to challenge them immediately. Allowing those statements to be heard as part of the evidence in a joint trial would inevitably make Tom look guilty too, Vance said. The judge agreed and Tom was tried alone from that moment onwards. Ann's own trial would have to wait.

These preliminaries dealt with, District Attorney Walter Caldwell gave his opening statement. The state's case, he said would be that Tom had caught syphilis from Laura, that he'd communicated that disease to Ann and that his own infection had prompted Tom to take Laura's life as an act of revenge. "By these circumstances and others, I expect to prove Thomas Dula, the prisoner, committed the murder, instigated thereto by Ann Melton, who was prompted by revenge and jealousy," Caldwell told the jury.

The trial had lined up 83 witnesses in all, though it's not clear how many were actually called. Pauline Foster, Dr George Carter, James Melton, Wilson Foster, Lotty Foster, Jack Adkins, James Isbell and Betsy Scott were all heard, though, and gave their evidence just as I've quoted above. Despite her questionable character, the prosecution relied heavily on Pauline's testimony, which fills a third of the summary transcript Buxton later prepared. My guess is that the prosecution told Pauline that if she didn't co-operate to the fullest possible extent, she'd end up in the dock herself.

"The witnesses generally appeared impressed with the idea that Dula was guilty," *The New York Herald* reported. "Though some of them appeared anxious to affect his acquittal through fear of some of his reckless associates in the mountains."

Ann was allowed to attend the court throughout Tom's trial but not to testify. Even so, Buxton allowed statements she'd made to various witnesses to be admitted in evidence and over-ruled Vance's objections every time he challenged this. It's hard to reconcile this with Buxton's reputation for meticulous care and some take his rulings as evidence that the law was determined to railroad Tom for a crime he didn't commit.

Vance made the most of Tom's Civil War record throughout the trial, presenting his client as a brave ex-soldier and Laura as the crafty slut who'd seduced him. When the prosecution fought back by invoking Laura's "lonely grave on the hillside", Vance replied by asking the jury what they'd achieve by sending Tom to a grave there too. Right through the trial, Tom maintained he was innocent and refused to implicate anyone else in Laura's death either. [12]

Closing his case for the defence, Vance asked Buxton to instruct the jury that any circumstantial evidence they used to convict "must exclude every other hypothesis" and remind them they must be convinced of Tom's guilt beyond all reasonable doubt. Buxton agreed and told the jury exactly that. After hearing two days of evidence, they retired just after midnight on Saturday, 20 October and spent the rest of the night debating the case.

The jury returned at daybreak with a verdict of guilty. "Governor Vance and his assistant counsel for the defence made powerful forensic efforts which were considered models of ability," *The New York Herald* told its readers. "But such was the evidence that no other verdict than that of guilty could be rendered." *The Daily Dispatch* in Wilmington agreed, saying: "All the evidence that led to the conviction was entirely circumstantial, but so connected by a concatenation of circumstances as to leave no reasonable doubt on the minds of the jury". [8, 13]

Buxton set Tom's execution date for 9 November. That appointment looked unlikely to be met, though, because Vance had already appealed for a new trial on the grounds that Buxton had admitted a good deal of evidence he should not have allowed the court to hear. The judge agreed to refer this request to North Carolina's Supreme Court, but rejected the stay of judgement Vance had also requested. In the unlikely event that Tom's bid for a new trial could be definitively ruled out in just 19 days, his 9 November hanging would go ahead.

There were no court stenographers in North Carolina back in 1866, so Buxton worked with his clerk of the court to prepare a summary of the trial, quoting testimony from 18 of the witnesses called. It's this summary, now held in the state archives, which still provides our best record of Tom, Ann and Laura's movements on those crucial two days in May 1866. West was the first to transcribe the summary and publish it in full, which makes his book a key resource for anyone interested in the facts of the case rather than its mythology.

Now that Tom had been convicted of Laura's murder, Wilkes County's balladeers felt free to name him as her killer. Not only that, but Buxton's sentence meant they could stir the prospect of his execution into their lyrics too.

Frank Brown's collection of North Carolina Folklore, gathered between 1912 and 1943, includes three versions of "Tom Dula" contributed by a North Carolina woman called Maude Sutton. She begins with a mention of Land's verses, but it's her second entry – a banjo tune – which interests us here. "It was very popular in the hills of Wilkes, Alexander and Caldwell Counties in 1867," she says. "Many mountain ballad singers still sing it." She adds that the song was composed by an elderly black musician called Charlie Davenport, and sung to an existing tune from the state's slavery days. [14]

Sutton then quotes three verses from Davenport's song, which she simply calls "Tom Dula". You may recognise them:

Hang down your head Tom Dula,
Hang down your head and cry,
You killed poor Laura Foster,
And now you're bound to die,

You met her on the hill-top,
As God Almighty knows,
You met her on the hill-top,
And there you hid [her] clothes,

You met her on the hill-top,
You said she'd be your wife,
You met her on the hill-top,
And there you took her life.

A slip of the pen in Sutton's letter had Tom hiding his own clothes rather than Laura's, but I've corrected that above. She'd collected this version from a Lenoir man called Calvin Triplett, a surname which Ann's mother used on some early census forms. We don't know exactly what Calvin's relationship to the family was, but it's reasonable to assume he was kin of some sort. It's also unclear whether Sutton's three verses comprise the whole of the song as she found it, or just the first half. The 1867 verses she quotes, though, still survive almost untouched in many modern readings of the song.

Sutton seems to have seen this coming, telling Brown this is just the kind of story to be written in a ballad and sung for generations. "It has all the ballad essentials: a mystery death, an eternal triangle and a lover with courage enough to die for his lady," she adds.

The third ballad Sutton contributes – here called "Tom Dula's Lament" – is the one which folklore insists Dula composed himself and sang to the waiting crowds on his way to the gallows. It opens by giving Tom an instrument no one in the historical record ever mentions him playing:

I pick my banjo now,
I pick it on my knee,
This time tomorrow night,
It'll be no more use to me.

The remaining five verses, all narrated by Tom in the first person, tell us that the banjos helped him pass the time in jail, that Laura used to enjoy hearing him play it and that he was too much of a fool to realise how much she loved him. It's only the opening verse that still survives today though, sometimes with the instrument corrected to become a fiddle before it's allowed a place in the main ballad.

By 1867, then, we've already got much of the ballad we know today. The chorus The Kingston Trio made famous is already 90% complete and at least one of their three verses is substantially finished too. As Tom waited in Statesville jail for news of his appeal, the balladeers were still at work and it wouldn't be long before they had all the song's remaining elements in place.

North Carolina's Supreme Court ruled that Buxton had been wrong to admit some of the evidence he'd allowed his jury to hear and granted Tom a new trial as a result. The new trial date was set for 17 April 1867 and Tom had to wait in jail with Ann until that day arrived.

In fact, he had to wait a lot longer than that. When the court gathered on 17 April, three of the defendant's witnesses failed to turn up. Vance argued that these three individuals' testimony was crucial to his client's case and persuaded Judge Robert Gelliam to postpone the trial till 14 October as a result. The court then met only twice a year – Spring Term and Fall Term – so this was simply the next date available.

When 14 October came round, it was the prosecution's turn to object. This time, the missing witnesses included James Grayson, who Caldwell was not prepared to do without. He won his bid for another continuance, but this time the state governor decided on drastic action. He ordered a special court of *Oyer et Terminer* ("hear and determine") be set up to clear the Supreme Court's growing backlog and demanded that court must hear Tom's case on 20 January 1868. By that time, Laura would have been dead for 20 months.

The new court convened on time, with Judge William Shipp presiding. The evidence presented was much the same as that heard at Tom's first trial – presumably without the inadmissible stuff Buxton had allowed – and the new jury found Tom guilty all over again. Shipp set his execution date for 14 February, but granted Vance's request to appeal the verdict. On 13 April 1868, North Carolina's Supreme Court ruled there was no error in Shipp's proceedings and yet another execution date was chosen. This time the date – 1 May 1868 – would stand.

Eliza Dula, Tom's sister, arrived at Statesville jail with her husband on the night before the hanging. Ann was still in jail too, waiting for her own trial, but Tom refused to say anything that would either implicate her in Laura's murder or clear her from it. Eliza passed Tom a note via his jailers, which contained his mother's plea that he should at last tell the full story behind Laura's death. Only this, Mary Dula said, would give her the peace of knowing once and for all whether her son was a murderer. Tom asked the jailers if he could speak to Eliza in person, but when this was refused he opted to say nothing more.

The case was attracting international attention now, with even regional British newspapers like *The Hampshire Telegraph* and *The Sheffield Independent* finding room for it. It was already recognised as one of America's most famous crimes of passion and *The New York Herald* thought only Harvey Burdell's high society murder in 1857 could stand comparison. The paper was so confident of the Dula case's appeal that it dispatched a reporter to Statesville to give readers a first-hand description of Tom's final hours.

"He still remained defiant, nor showed any sign of repentance," the paper's man said of Tom on that final evening. "He partook of a hearty supper, laughed and spoke lightly. But, ere the jailer left him, it was discovered that his shackles were loose, a link in the chain being filed through with a piece of window glass, which was found concealed in his bed. While this was being adjusted, he glared savagely and, in a jocose manner, said it had been so for a month past."

With this last hope of escape gone, Tom seemed to change his mind about the confession everyone was nagging him to make. He called for Captain Richard Allison, one of Vance's assistants on the defence team, and handed him a short pencil-written note, its letters scratched together in Tom's own crude, unskilled hand. Tom made Allison swear not to let anyone see the note until after the execution. "Statement of Thomas C. Dula," it read. "I declare that I am the only person that had any hand in the murder of Laura Foster. April 30, 1868."

Left alone in his cell overnight and now with just hours to live, Tom lost the composure he'd maintained for so long. He spent the night pacing up and down as far as his leg chain would allow and managed to grab only the odd half hour of fitful sleep. He'd refused to see any clergymen throughout his time in jail, but all that changed as his hanging day dawned. "After breakfast, he sent for his spiritual advisers and seemed for the first time to make an attempt to pray," *The New York Herald* tells us. "But still, to them and to all others, denied his guilt or any knowledge of the murder. His theory seemed to be that he would show the people that he could die game."

Tom allowed the Methodist minister he'd been given to baptise him and then dropped to his knees in fervent prayer. "When left alone [he] was heard speaking incoherently, words occasionally dropping from his lips in relation to the murder, but nothing that was intelligible," *The New York Herald* wrote. "Thus wore away the last hours of the condemned."

Because Tom's trials had been dragging on so long and because people from at least three different counties had been involved, news of his hanging spread throughout the region, drawing a large crowd to Statesville as spectators. I can't improve on *The New York Herald's* vivid description of the day's events, so I'm simply going to reproduce some extracts from it here:

> By eleven o'clock, A. M., dense crowds of people thronged the streets, the great number of females being somewhat extraordinary. [...] A certain class, indicated by a bronzed complexion, rustic attire, a quid of tobacco in their mouths and a certain mountaineer look, were evidently attracted by that morbid curiosity to see an execution, so general among the ignorant classes of society.
>
> The preliminaries were all arranged by Sheriff Wasson. A gallows constructed of native pine, erected near the railway depot in an old field – as there is no public place of execution in Statesville – was the place selected for the final tragedy. A guard had been summoned to keep back the crowd and enforce the terrible death penalty and for the better preservation of order, the bar rooms were closed.

Rather than the "white oak tree" mentioned in Tom's ballad, Statesville had built him a simple gallows from two upright poles, set about ten feet apart, with a crossbar linking them at the top. The crossbar was placed high enough to let the cart they planned to use for Tom's transport draw up directly beneath it, leaving him to dangle there when the cart pulled away again.

The New York Herald's man must have been moving through the crowds at this point, stopping to quickly interview any spectators who looked promising and jotting down their replies as he went. He was obviously struck by the unusual number of women in the crowd – drawn, no doubt, by Tom's sexual charisma – and mentions this several times in his report. He puts the crowd overall at nearly 3,000 people of Tom's "own race and color", but makes no attempt to estimate the number of black people also attending.

We have other eyewitness accounts of Tom's hanging too, the best of which comes via a man called Hub Yount, whose father and aunt were both present. Yount, whose family then lived in nearby Catawba County, passed on his father's account to Gardner, who reproduces it in his book. "Thousands and thousands of people gathered to see the execution," Yount writes. "Statesville was a small town then and [there were] many fist and skull fights, old enemies meeting. There were several gun battles on the streets that day." [15]

It's while patrolling this lively crowd that *The New York Herald's* man met Tom's former army companions, noting their "anxious and singular curiosity" to see how their old comrade would meet his end. "Few were those who pitied him dying, as they believed him, guilty without a confession and none sympathised with him," he wrote.

Tom was led out of the jail just before quarter to one and once again, *The New York Herald's* man was there to watch:

> With a smile upon his features, [the condemned man] took his seat in the cart, in which was also his coffin, beside his sister and his brother in law. The procession moved slowly through the streets, accompanied by large crowds, male and female, whites and blacks, many being in carriages and many on horseback and on foot.
>
> While on his way to the gallows, he looked cheerful and spoke continually to his sister of the Scriptures, assuring her he had repented and that his peace was made with God. At the gallows, throngs of people were already assembled, the number of females being almost equal to that of the males. The few trees in the field were crowded with men and boys and under every shade that was present, were huddled together every imaginable specimen of humanity.

The folklore surrounding Tom's execution often claims he performed his own self-composed ballad for the crowd's amusement as his tumbrel crawled along. Most likely, this element of the tale arose from ballad sellers' long-standing habit of claiming that any song hawked at a public execution was written by the condemned man. It's inconceivable that *The New York Herald's* reporter could have watched Tom busking his way to the scaffold and yet never thought that fact worth mentioning in his long and detailed account. You've only got to read his copy to see the man was determined to report every bit of colour he could find on the day, so why would he miss out such a striking incident as that?

As the procession came within sight of the gallows, official horsemen rode fast into the field to disperse the crowds. This cleared the way for Tom's cart, which halted under the gallows' frame at eight minutes past one. Told by Sheriff Wasson he could address the crowd if he wished, Tom stood up in the cart, the noose already round his neck and spoke in what *The New York Herald* calls "a loud voice that rang back from the woods".

He spoke for nearly an hour, discussing his early childhood, his parents, his time in the army and the secessionist politics that still bedeviled his home state. He accused several witnesses at his trial of telling lies against him – reserving particular ire for James Isbell – and said it was only those lies which had put him on the scaffold today. His written confession, remember, was still a secret between himself and Allison, who'd sworn not to make it public till Tom was dead.

"The sheriff allowed Tom Dooley to make a long talk," Yount confirms. "At the conclusion, an old white-bearded man pointed his finger at Dooley and repeated his song that had been sung many times for the six months prior. I don't remember the words, except the old man pointed and sang: 'Oh Tom Dooley, hang down your head and cry. Because you killed poor Laura Foster and now you must die'." I doubt Yount's got those words exactly right, because they're impossible to scan to the tune we know was already used. They're certainly close enough to confirm Sutton's dating of something very like this chorus at 1867, though, and that's quite useful in itself.

Concluding his speech, Tom bade an affectionate farewell to Eliza, who was taken off the cart, and then watched as the rope dangling round his neck was thrown over the gallows' cross beam and fastened.

The cart pulled away, leaving Tom to hang. Here's *The New York Herald* again:

> The fall was about two feet and the neck was not broken. He breathed about five minutes and did not struggle, the pulse beating for ten minutes, and in thirteen minutes life was declared extinct by Dr Campbell, attending surgeon.
>
> After hanging for twenty minutes, the body was cut down and given to the afflicted relatives of this terrible criminal. Thus closed the career of a man who, though young in years, ignorant and depraved in character, was one of the most confirmed and hardened criminals of the age in which he lived.

Eliza and her husband placed Tom's body in the waiting coffin and arranged for it to be buried on a patch of land then owned by Bennett Dula III, Tom's cousin. The grave's in a meadow between Ferguson and Elkville, alongside what's now Tom Dula Road. Tom's confession was made public shortly after the hanging, although not in time to make *The New York Herald's* 2 May report.

Ann's trial finally came in the autumn of 1868, again with Vance defending, but Tom's confession meant the case against her was quickly dismissed. She'd already been in jail for two years by that time. "The gallows would have added little to her punishment," *The Statesville American* pronounced. [16]

The fact of Tom's confession is quite enough to explain Ann's acquittal on its own, but folklore likes to credit her extraordinary beauty too. In her letter to Brown, Sutton reports talking to an old man in Statesville who remembered the trial from his youth. Ann Melton, he said, was "the purtiest woman I'd ever looked in the face of. She'd a-been hung too, but her neck was just too purty to stretch hemp. [...] If there'd a-been any women on the jury, she'd a-got first degree. Men couldn't look at that woman and keep their heads."

That description's backed by *The New York Herald's* reporter, who calls Ann "a most beautiful woman". Despite her lack of education, he adds, she "has the manner and bearing of an accomplished lady and all the natural poise would grace a born beauty". As West points out, this description is all the more remarkable for the fact that *The New York*

Herald's man was meeting Ann after she'd been locked in a primitive jail cell for two years. What must she have been like in her full pomp?

Ann died in about 1875, after a long period of bedridden illness, and this episode has entered local folklore too. There are various accounts – some of which claim to stem from eye-witnesses at Ann's bedside – reporting she suffered the hallucinations, violent rages and convulsions which syphilis can produce when it reaches the brain. As she lay dying, it's said Ann saw the flames of hell dancing round her bed and even the Devil himself come to collect her soul. If neurosyphilis really was responsible, then her death may have been more agonising than Tom and Laura's put together.

The first version of "Tom Dooley" we have on disc was cut by a duo called Grayson & Whitter in September 1929. The blind Gilliam Grayson, who sings and plays fiddle on the record, was James Grayson's nephew. Henry Whitter accompanies him on guitar. Document Records includes a short biographical note about Grayson in its sleeve notes for the duo's compilation, which tells us Gilliam was born in 1887 on the North Carolina/Tennessee border and that James, his uncle, died in 1901. Grayson and Whitter recorded several other murder ballads too, including "Banks Of The Ohio" and "Omie Wise".

The "Tom Dooley" lyrics they use include many elements from the versions Sutton had already collected, including the familiar tune and chorus, the reference to hiding Laura's clothes and Tom's final session with the instrument – in this case a violin – he'd soon be forced to give up. Most significantly, they give us our earliest evidence that the song now incorporated the Grayson/Tennessee verse describing Tom's near-escape and capture. Given the singer's family ties with the man responsible for that capture, I'm content to assume it was Gilliam Grayson who ensured that verse was included on the recording. Why should Uncle James be left out?

What little music radio there was in 1929 seems to have passed Grayson & Whitter's disc by. In its way, that's a blessing because their version's continuing obscurity allowed many rival sets of "Tom Dooley" lyrics to keep developing alongside it. Unlike, say, Arthur Tanner's 1927 recording of "Knoxville Girl", it never set a single version of the song's tale in stone, driving all variations to the margin. In "Tom Dooley"'s case, that process would have to wait for another 30 years and, by the time The Kingston Trio came along, the song's many variants were established enough to survive their sudden demotion to also-ran status. They may not have been able to compete with the hit version's success, but they weren't erased by it either.

One such variation was collected from a North Carolina woman called Franklin in 1930, who told the song collector Mellinger Henry she'd learned it from her brother. Later reprinted in the *Viking Book Of Folk Ballads*, it includes this verse:

> *I had my trial in Wilkesboro,*
> *Oh what do you reckon they done?*
> *They bound me over to Statesville,*
> *And that's where I'll be hung.* [17]

This stanza appears in recordings by both Sheila Clark in 1986 – a companion to the track of hers I mentioned earlier – and The Great American String Band in 2005. The tone of voice it's written and delivered in always suggests that the move to Statesville was another crafty trick to persecute Tom, when in fact it represented Vance's best chance of saving him.

Doc Watson would have been about seven years old when those Franklin verses were collected and perhaps already familiar with the Tom Dula song his grandmother sang. He was born in 1923 on his poor parents' Watauga County farm and blinded by an eye infection before he was two. Even so, he soon turned out to be the most talented member of what was already a very musical family, playing the harmonica as a child, adding banjo and guitar by the age of 12 and making his first recordings with Clarence Ashley in 1961.

Watson put his own version of "Tom Dooley" to disc on his 1964 debut album, assuring live audiences that it was "a completely different version" to The Kingston Trio's recent hit. It's a rollicking great party of a record, led by Doc's busy, swooping harmonica and driven relentlessly forward with barely a breath between one line and the next. He later wrote that his grandmother had taught him this version of the song, saying it owed its exuberance to the fact that the composer had tried to build a little of Tom Dula's personality as a fiddler into its tune.

Clearly drawing on the same sources Grayson & Whitter used, Watson sings six of the same verses they gave us before adding two fresh ones of his own. The last of these quotes from Tom's supposed declaration of innocence on the gallows platform: "Gentlemen, do you see this hand? Do you see it tremble? Do you see it shake? I never hurt a hair on the girl's head". Many people in Tom's home state still like to believe he was innocent and it may be no coincidence that the only modern bands I've been able to find using this particular verse are The *Elkville* String Band and The *Carolina* Chocolate Drops.

Watson wrote in 1971 that his great-grandparents had been neighbours of the Dula family in the 1860s and that his grandparents knew Tom's mother. In the story passed down to him, it was Ann who plunged the knife into Laura's breast, with Tom's role limited to her burial afterwards.

The Watson family's tale went on to insist that Grayson was the sheriff who arrested Tom, that he did so because he loved Ann himself and that he eventually married her. Hearing her deathbed confession years later, he moved back to Tennessee in disgust. There's so much wrong with that account that I hardly know where to begin, but I think my favourite part is the desperate addendum required to get Grayson packed off back to his real home state before the whole yarn disintegrates. [18]

Doc Watson wasn't the only Watauga County man to have a grandmother tied up in the Dula story, nor to learn his first version of the ballad from her. Frank Proffitt had a granny on the scene too and it's her role in the tale which ultimately gave The Kingston Trio its hit.

According to the family legend that later built up around her, Adeline Perdue was watching in the Statesville crowd as Tom's cart drew past her on its way to the gallows. Telling the story to her children, she described Tom sitting upright in his own coffin, singing the autobiographical ballad he'd just composed. Perdue taught that song to her family and it eventually made its way down to her grandson Frank.

Proffitt grew up to become a farmer at the foot of North Carolina's Stone Mountain, supplementing his family's income by making and repairing traditional musical instruments. One day in 1937, a New York man called Frank Warner turned up with his own family, hoping to buy a dulcimer from Proffitt. Before they left, Warner asked Proffitt to sing him a few of the Appalachian folk ballads he knew and Proffitt obliged, accompanying himself on an old banjo as he sang.

Warner returned to Proffitt's farm the following year, this time with an early battery-driven tape recorder and asked for a repeat performance. "His eyes sparkled as I sang 'Tom Dooley' to him and told him of my grandmaw Proffitt knowing Tom and Laura," Proffitt later recalled. "I walked on air for days after they left." [19]

Assuming that the lyrics Proffitt sang that day were the same ones he uses on his 1962 album, the words Warner heard were an amalgamation of the many traditional verses we've seen so far, with only the few minor tweaks any singer introduces as he gets comfortable with a song. The opening verse is almost identical to Sutton's 1867 version and the remaining five verses cover our familiar material about the mountain, the white oak tree, Grayson, Laura's clothes and the banjo. We can forgive Proffitt his "banjo" reference – which I'm sure he knew was strictly incorrect – for its link to the instrument he himself was playing. Suddenly the banjo player in the song becomes the same man you're listening to right now and even I'm not pedantic enough to deny Proffitt the little bonus that provides.

Let's pause here for a second to get the chronology right. Warner taped Proffitt singing him "Tom Dooley" in 1938, but Proffitt himself wouldn't put it to disc until 1962. Warner recorded his own version a full ten years before that – in 1952 – but first he passed the lyrics Proffitt had given him to the song collector Alan Lomax. The chain this gives us so far is: Proffitt, Warner, Lomax.

When the Lomaxes published their 1946 collection *Folk Song USA*, they included words and music for "Tom Dooley", crediting Warner for adapting and arranging both the words and melody. The accompanying music was a piano arrangement by Charles and Ruth Seeger, parents to the Mike and Peggy Seeger we know today. Now the lyrics appeared cut down to a tight three verses, with the chorus's opening line strategically repeated to add an extra sing-along element. It was this version which The Kingston Trio would use 12 years later. Now the chain ran: Proffitt, Warner, Lomax, Kingston Trio.

The group then comprised Dave Guard, Nick Reynolds and Bob Shane, who sang lead on its "Tom Dooley" recording. I asked Shane – now the only surviving member of that line-up – how they'd first become aware of the song. "We heard someone audition for a gig with that song at The Purple Onion in San Francisco when we were working there in 1957 and we just put it in our show," he told me. "We went in a book and looked up some stuff, which said Tom Dula wrote the song himself while he was in prison." Would that book have been the Lomax one? "Most likely," he replied. [20]

"We were using the song in our show when Capitol Records came up and said 'We'd like to have you on our roster'. Basically, our whole first album was what we were doing in our show."

When that debut album was released in June 1958, "Tom Dooley" was buried half way through side one, with no thought from either the group or their label that it should be released as a single. The break-through came when Paul Colburn and Bill Terry, a pair of radio DJs at Salt Lake City's KLUB, started giving the track heavy airplay and encouraging other radio DJs round the country to pick it up. "In order to get that song, you had to buy the album," Shane said. "The people in Salt Lake City started playing 'Tom Dooley' off it, and it just went crazy overnight. The album sold 27,000 copies in one music store in Salt Lake City."

Even with sales like those, it took Capitol two months to catch on that "Tom Dooley" should be released as a single. They finally put it out in that format on 8 August 1958, it topped the *Billboard* charts in November and had racked up a million sales by Christmas. The album topped *Billboard's* LP charts too and stayed in those charts for an impressive 195 weeks. The group collected gold records for both the single and the album, plus a 1958 Grammy award for "Tom Dooley" as Best Country & Western Performance.

"It did real well for us and gave us a gigantic boost right from the start," Shane said. "We were playing a show in Honolulu and we got a wire from Capitol Records: 'Cancel your date and come back, because you have the number one hit in the country'. Right after that, we had seven gold albums." Had they ever suspected this one song might make the debut album such a huge success? "We didn't know that one song was going to hit from it, no," Shane replied. "That was our first album. We didn't know anything about anything."

The key to their recording of the song, he now believes, was its pared-down nature: "It had three verses, three choruses and two chords on the instruments we were playing – simplicity. The three verses in a row tell pretty much the whole story." Jon Langford of the Waco Brothers, who loves The Kingston Trio's version, points to a second factor in its success. "It's that kind of matter-of-factness in the way they sing it," he told me. "That mis-match between the performance and the lyrics – I really like that about a lot of these songs. It's almost like they're not really listening to what they're saying." [21]

The first Frank Proffitt knew of The Kingston Trio's hit was when he happened to hear the band perform a strangely familiar arrangement of "Tom Dooley" on TV. On The Kingston Trio's own discs, he discovered, the song's composition was credited as "Traditional – Arr: Dave Guard". Shane told me the group credited the song this way on their original release because they'd assumed it must be entirely in the public domain. This was a common habit throughout the music industry at that time, as new groups scoured the folk and blues archives for suitable material. "There were so many old folk songs we had gone through that *were* either anonymous or public domain," Shane pointed out.

In the early 1960s, Proffitt joined with Warner and the Lomaxes' publishers to sue The Kingston Trio over their "Tom Dooley" publishing rights and secure the income those rights could now be expected to generate. The case was settled out of court, but only after an agreement ensuring that the Proffitt, Warner and Lomax families all receive a cut of the record's royalties to this day. Despite the fact that it was Proffitt's 1938 rendition that started this whole chain, even the CD re-issue of his own 1962 album credits the song as "trad./ arr. Lomax/Warner/Proffitt".

The Kingston Trio's hit prompted the American Legion to replace Tom's rudimentary headstone with a much nicer one, though they did get his date of death wrong by two years. Unfortunately, the record also made Tom so famous that souvenir hunters descended on the site almost immediately. They've been chipping fragments off the stone ever since, leaving it, as West says, "incorrect in its information and sad in its mutilation". About 20% of the stone has been stolen in this way now, which may explain why the land's owner discourages visitors.

Most of the "Tom Dooley" recordings since The Kingston Trio's hit follow one or other of the templates we've already discussed. Grayson & Whitter's fans include The New Lost City Ramblers (1959) and Sweeney's Men (1968), while Doc Watson can boast The Elkville String Band (2003) and The Carolina Chocolate Drops (2006). Most popular of all is The Kingston Trio's own Proffitt/Warner/Lomax version, which has inspired Lonnie Donegan (1958), The Frantic Flintstones (1992) and countless foreign language covers.

Others mix and match their chosen verses from whichever predecessors take their fancy. Sheila Clark, for example, faithfully reproduces all The Kingston Trio verses, but tags on Franklin's lines about the change of venue too. Most mongrel of all is Lee Kelly's 2010 recording, which opts for a magpie mix of Grayson & Whitter, Franklin's additions and "Pretty Polly"'s phrase telling us how her "heart blood it did flow". Only Snakefarm can be said to make the song entirely their own, thanks to an imaginative 1999 treatment that recalls a spaghetti western soundtrack more than any bluegrass standard.

Another favourite of mine is Steve Earle's version, which he cut for Jon Langford's benefit CD *The Executioner's Last Songs* in 2002. Langford, a veteran of the 1970s British punk band The Mekons, launched this project after his new band, The Waco Brothers, opened a Chicago show for Earle. The show was raising money for the Illinois Death Penalty Moratorium Project. "We met all these people from the campaign," Langford told me. "I wanted to get involved and Steve just said 'You should do an album'.

"If we were going to make an album, I wanted something coherent to hang it on and the idea came to use death songs against the death penalty. My whole gripe with contemporary country music since I'd moved to the States was that it had abolished all the content that

I enjoyed: the drinking, killing and cheating songs. It seemed like this was a good way to get some of the cheating and killing songs back. I figured we could make something that was really good artistically and make some money for the Moratorium project."

As he began to put the project together, Langford would grab musicians whenever they happened to be in town and record them in his own basement studio at home. Often, he'd wind up playing on the track as well. The result was a couple of CDs pairing alt.country's best artists with some classic murder ballads. There you'll find The Handsome Family's Brett Sparks tackling "Knoxville Girl", Neko Case singing "Poor Ellen Smith" – and Steve Earle's own version of "Tom Dooley".

"Steve brought a big long sheet of all the traditional lyrics to the song, all the different verses and then we sat down and went through them," Langford said. "He just wanted it to be as evil as possible, so we picked out all the right verses for that. He knew quite a bit about the song. We did three or four takes and then he said 'OK, put some of that fucking out-of-tune Mekons guitar on the end', and left. That's the kind of instruction I can obey."

A year before *The Executioner's Last Songs* came out, the USA National Endowment for the Arts placed "Tom Dooley" on its list of 365 Songs of the Century, recognising its role in America's musical and cultural heritage. The Library of Congress admitted The Kingston Trio's disc to its National Recording Preservation Board archives in 2008 on the same grounds.

In 2009, a group of Tom's supporters put together an argument for his pardon on strictly legal grounds. They pointed out that the two deputies sent to retrieve Tom had no authority to arrest him outside their own North Carolina jurisdiction, or to deputise James Grayson either. Tom's constitutional rights were also infringed by imprisoning him before anyone could be sure Laura was dead, they added. This case was presented to North Carolina governor Mike Easley in June 2009, but he rejected it and the campaign's not been revived since.

The new millennium has also brought a handful of songs telling the story from Ann or Laura's perspective. Laura's song comes courtesy of Angela Correa, who calls her 2004 offering "Sunrise Your Hanging Day". She begins in Laura's own voice, mulling over Tom's offer of marriage, but knowing full well what his real intent must be:

And you always say the same thing,
And you're always wearing your smile,
You say "Come on up the hill with me darlin',
And we'll talk for a little while",

And you always ask it the same way,
Your mouth twisted to a crooked grin,
And I always understand your meaning,
Your mind is riddled with sin. [22]

Correa, who released her own murder ballads EP in 2004, first discovered the genre's classic murder songs on a mix tape she was given by a record shop owner in San Diego. She was immediately enthralled by the tales they told, but also struck by how often the victim's voice was left unheard. "I felt there was an entire side of the story missing," she told me. "I felt so much empathy for the gals in the songs, going off with a suitor thinking he was perhaps about to declare his love and instead getting killed to avoid shame, scandal or inconvenience.

"What really drew me to create a response to 'Tom Dooley' was how jolly the version by The Kingston Trio feels. It's bouncy in a really unnerving way considering the subject matter. I got the feeling that the narrator pitied that poor ol' Tom Dooley: he just fell for this gal and she wouldn't have him so he killed her. I started imagining who Laura Foster might be and who this guy that kept asking to go for a walk was. My song's story is very much the voice of Laura Foster singing to Tom Dooley in the verses. I was imagining her letting him know she was wise to him, and playing with that idea." [23]

It's only when she reaches the chorus that Correa steps out of Laura's head to give her own view of Tom:

Tom Dooley you dirty old man,
You took Laura Foster up the hill by the hand,
And folks singing "Hang down your head", man,
But you'll get what you give,
Hanging is too good for you.

The Elkville String Band tackle Ann's story in "Epitaph", a 2003 track which they subtitle "The Ballad Of Anne Melton". In this account, Laura was pregnant with Tom's baby, he planned to leave North Carolina with her and Ann just couldn't bear that thought. Nicole Vidrine starts the song as Ann, mourning Tom's death and recalling the crime they committed together, but then switches to her own voice as she pleads with Ann's ghost to repeat her folklore's deathbed confession. Here's my two favourite verses:

As morning broke upon the hill,
With jagged blade our fates were sealed,
Her body in a shallow grave,
His unborn child not spared nor saved,

So tell me now the secret words,
Your unloved husband finally heard,
As devils moaned beneath your bed,
Your troubled soul the fires it fed. [24]

The "unloved husband" here, of course, is the mythical James Grayson who Doc Watson's family describes above, and the devils are those Ann glimpsed in her syphilis fever. Ann's ghost is left doomed to walk the Earth forever because her soul lacked a cleansing confession.

I made my first trip to North Carolina in September 2010, visiting both the desolate site at Statesville's old railway depot where Tom was hanged and the tiny Wilkesboro jailhouse where he'd been imprisoned. The Statesville depot was as bleak a spot as you could wish to find: a derelict building crouched beneath grey skies, a big patch of scrubby waste ground and a few rusty freight cars parked along the track marking its townside edge. All this was framed against a big, dirty-looking factory in the background. It seemed a fit place for a hanging.

When I got to Wilkesboro, I had to wait a while at the old jailhouse before my own tour could start. That gave me a chance to chat to one of the site's two guides, who mentioned that his great-grandmother had known the Dula, Foster and Melton families in her childhood. He told me she'd lived long enough to hear The Kingston Trio make the song a hit in 1958 and couldn't imagine why anyone would want to sing a song about such dreadful people. "They were just trash," he recalled her croaking at anyone who'd listen. "They were the scum of the Earth."

Jack, the second guide, took over. Hearing my accent, he pointed to a tree just outside the jailhouse and told me it had been grafted from the white oak which stood there in Tom's day. The original tree, he added, had been used by Wilkesboro's townsfolk to hang anyone who'd supported the hated British in the War of Independence. I promised to behave myself, wondering if it was those wartime executions which had led to Tom being "hanged from a white oak tree" in the song. Or perhaps that line was included simply to mention a prominent and characteristic piece of local flora?

Jack led me inside the jailhouse to Tom's old cell, took a quick photo as I paused awkwardly inside its door, then talked me through the collection of Tom's POW release papers displayed opposite. Like everyone else I discussed the case with in North Carolina, he took it for granted that Ann was the real killer – but I'm not so sure. For my money, it was Tom Dula who wielded the knife.

There will be those of you who bridle at that, so let me explain why I say so. Even if we discount the rumours of Tom murdering his Wilmington lover's husband during the war, we know he saw enough battlefield slaughter to risk brutalising any man. *The New York Herald* tells us that the Tom Dula who returned to Happy Valley in 1865 was "reckless, demoralised and a desperado, of whom the people in his vicinity had a terror". As we've seen, his first reaction on hearing local people suggest he might have killed Laura was to threaten them with a beating. Statesville's jailers thought he was dangerous enough to justify the expense of all those extra guards, and some witnesses at his trial feared revenge if they testified against him. "There can be no doubt he was depraved," West writes.

Sending off her "Tom Dooley" lyrics, Maude Sutton recalled hearing the story related in a very different way. "One old lady told me, 'He never told on Ann 'cause he knowed that Ann killed Laura jes' cayse he told a lie on Laura'," she wrote in her letter to Frank Brown. Bob Shane agrees, saying basic male honour in the 1860s would have compelled any man in Tom's position to do the same thing. "A fella said to me once that he took the hit, because that was what men do to save a woman," Shane said. "I started thinking about it and I thought, 'You know, that's very possible'. That's probably what happened, that [Ann Melton] did it."

It's an appealing notion, but there's really nothing to back it up but some rather sentimental folklore. The idea that Tom went willingly to the gallows to protect Ann from hanging instead gives an element of noble romantic sacrifice to his story which some are determined to maintain at all costs. But his speech on the scaffold was a far more rambling, equivocal affair than the folklore's cut-and-dried declaration of innocence suggests and, in any case, he'd just signed a confession accepting his own guilt.

The soft-focus portrait of Tom we're often presented with today also contrasts sharply with the way he was viewed in 1868. "There is everything in his expression to indicate the hardened assassin, a great degree of malignity and a callousness that is revolting," *The New York Herald's* man wrote after meeting Tom in prison. That seems to square with my guide's great-grandmother's view. No wonder those who present Tom as a romantic hero opt for folklore rather than objective evidence when making their case.

Ann may well have helped Tom dig the grave and even to bury the body too, but Occam's razor dictates the truth of Laura's killing itself was probably as simple and as squalid as most murders are: Tom Dula stabbed her and then hanged for his crime.

A Dooley decalogue: 10 great versions of Tom's story.

"Tom Dooley", by Grayson & Whitter (1929). Grayson alternates between sawing fiddle and cheery vocals while his guitarist partner keeps everything rooted. Grayson's uncle was the man who arrested Tom, making him uniquely qualified to handle this debut of the song on disc.

"Tom Dooley", by The Kingston Trio (1958). This six-million selling global hit doesn't stint on the gore, but Bob Shane's smooth-as-honey croon makes the song a lot less frightening. Throw in a clever vocal arrangement for the harmonies, keep the accompaniment simple and you've got a template for the song others still follow today.

"Tom Dooley", by Frank Proffitt (1962). The man who gave The Kingston Trio their arrangement gives us a matchless solo version of his home state's greatest ballad. Proffitt's voice and his slow-picked banjo handle the entire load here and for sheer down-home authenticity, he's unbeatable.

"Tom Dooley", by Doc Watson (1964). Doc gallops through his grandmother's version of the song with a swooping harmonica and some very agile guitar picking. His assertion that its music was inspired by Tom's own exuberant fiddle style is a little fanciful, but when the result's as joyful as this, who cares?

"Tom Dooley", by Juggy's Jass Band (1964). There's more sheer joy on offer here, this time in the form of a jaunty trad jazz instrumental. Banjo, clarinet and trumpet solos take turns at the familiar vocal lines, while a chubby-sounding tuba provides the pulse.

"Tom Dooley", by The Frantic Flintstones (1992). Rockabilly bands always seem to fetishise the Confederate flag, so Tom's story makes a good fit here. It's suitably raucous throughout and boasts a fast, fluid little guitar solo that makes me smile every time I hear it.

"Tom Dula", by Bill Morrissey & Greg Brown (1993). This version's as pretty and gentle as anything Brown's recorded in his exquisite solo work. Morrissey's acoustic guitar teases the tune slowly along as the two men trade vocals. His additional lyrics include the chilling couplet: "If you'd have heard her laughing, / You'd have done the same as me".

"Tom Dooley", by Snakefarm (1999). There's a touch of Ennio Morricone in the tolling church bell and dusty flute sounds opening this eerie, atmospheric version. Anna Domino's matter-of-fact vocals always make me think it's Ann Melton narrating the burial verse, which conjures up Land's "vile guest" in all her callous glory.

"Tom Dooley", by Steve Earle (2002). Earle joined with Jon Langford for this disc to benefit the Illinois Death Penalty Moratorium Project. His performance here is one of the album's highlights, showing all the muscular authority we've come to expect from him. "That sounds like a phonograph record to me," Earle instructs Langford as the take ends. "That one, right there."

"Tom Dooley", by The Elkville String Band (2003). Based on Doc Watson's template, this recording's quickly become one of my favourite traditional treatments of the song. There's nothing fancy or gimmicky about it, but every element serves the whole perfectly. Whenever I find myself singing "Tom Dooley" now, it's this outfit's Herb Key whose phrasing I unconsciously imitate.

6 - Pretty Polly

"America's favorite crime story."
Alan Lomax, **Bad Man Ballads** (1960).

At first glance, "Pretty Polly" is just one more murdered girlfriend song. Like "Knoxville Girl", it has its roots in a very old English ballad telling of a young man who knocks up his girlfriend and then stabs her to death rather than marry her. And, like "Knoxville Girl", the source ballad emigrated to America with British and Irish settlers where it was drastically cut from its original epic length to form a lean, mysterious and brutal folk song.

So far, it's all familiar stuff. But there are two elements which set "Pretty Polly" apart from any other murder ballad I know, and they combine to make its protagonist one of the most chilling the genre has yet produced. To see why that is, let's start with the moment Polly first glimpses the lonely spot Willie – the young man in question – has chosen for her death. As he leads her deeper and deeper into the woods, Polly begins to fear this is not the innocent stroll he promised. One Kentucky version of the lyrics collected in 1908 puts it like this:

He led her over hill and valley so deep,
At last Pretty Polly began for to weep,
"Willie, Oh Willie, I'm afraid of your ways,
I'm afraid you are leading my body astray",

"Polly, Oh Polly, you're guessing just right,
I dug on your grave the biggest part of last night,
Go a little further and see what you spy,
Your grave ready dug and a spade lying by". [1]

Rennie Sparks of US alt.country duo The Handsome Family has long been fascinated by this aspect of the song. "'Pretty Polly' is different from other murder ballads because of that grave that got dug the night before," she told me. "This is a pre-meditated murder, not a crime of passion. There's really no reason to dig the grave ahead of time except to torture the victim a tiny bit more by making her look upon it. It's also a strange reversal of sexual energy. The killer is digging a huge hole and leading the pretty girl into it. He's offering her a dark womb in the woods." [2]

There's more evidence of Willie's sadism in The Stanley Brothers' 1950 recording, which gives him a second, equally psychotic, little speech. Realising that he plans to kill her, Polly falls to her knees, swearing to leave town and raise the child alone. If Willie would only spare her life, she says, he need never set eyes on either of them again. But Willie is unmoved. In this telling, it's not enough for him to show Polly her own grave before he kills her – he has to remind her that everyone in town thinks she's a slut too:

> *Oh Polly, Pretty Polly, that never can be,*
> *Polly, Pretty Polly that never can be,*
> *Your past reputation's been trouble to me.* [3]

All these elements of "Pretty Polly" can be traced directly back to the 18th century ballad which inspired the song, and so can another characteristic which marks Willie as a very modern killer. "Pretty Polly" is rare among murder ballads for the way it constantly switches its narrative point of view, forcing the singer to speak as a neutral witness in one verse, as the killer in another and as Polly herself in a third. To get the most out of the song, performers must constantly be hopping from one persona to the next, and I think the same may be true of the man it depicts.

Many real murderers, including both Jeffrey Dahmer and Ted Bundy, have described stepping outside themselves at the moment they kill, saying that the moment of committing the murder felt like something they were watching themselves do in a movie or a computer game. And that's just what happens in "Pretty Polly" too.

In Dock Boggs' 1927 recording for example, the killer describes his early acquaintance with Polly in frank, first-person terms: "*I used to* be a rambler, *I* stayed around in town". But the moment he consigns her body to a shallow grave is left for the witness to tell: "*He* threw the dirt over her and turned away to go". The same switch of viewpoints appears in many other versions of the song, including Bert Jansch's live 1963 recording at a Glasgow gig. "*I* courted Pretty Polly the live-long night," Jansch sings in his first verse. A few lines later, when the actual killing has to be described, this becomes: "*He* stabbed her to the heart".

One reading of this is to assume that the killer and witness are the same man, but that Willie feels he's watching the murder itself from a vantage point outside his own body. Most recordings give Polly just a single verse of narration, leaving Willie to hop between his two different perspectives for the rest of the tale. Always, it is the goriest passages where he chooses to step back and describe events from the outside.

"'Pretty Polly' is like a little diagnostic manual of mental illness," Sparks said. "There's the OCD of setting up the perfect crime scene and there are the strange transgender switches. The whole thing seems to glow with a hysterical light on the edge of madness."

Polly's bleak little tale has its roots in the English town of Gosport in Hampshire, which lies on the south coast of England just three miles west of Portsmouth. Britain's Royal Navy has been based in Portsmouth ever since 1527 and Gosport has always existed mostly to serve the Navy's needs, supplying that market with meat, bread, timber, rope, beer, iron tools and labour.

"Gosport can claim little that is attractive," one former resident wrote in 1794. "The town has the narrowness and slander of a small country town without its rural simplicity and with a full share of the vice of Portsmouth, polluted by the fortunes of sailors and the extravagances of harlots. To these evils are added the petty pride and sectarian bigotry of a fortified town." [4]

Sailors' tales were a fertile source of material for the printed ballad sheets sold throughout Britain in the 18th and 19th centuries and "Pretty Polly" grew from one of the hardiest examples. Its full title is "The Gosport Tragedy or The Perjured Ship-Carpenter". The oldest copy we have of this song is part of the British Library's Roxburghe Collection, a series of scrapbooks pulling together about 1,500 ballad sheets printed between 1567 and 1790. I'm going to call this copy the Roxburghe "Gosport" to distinguish it from the many later sheets that followed, and the British Library believes it was printed in the first half of the 1700s.

The sheet is about A3 size in our terms, printed at a shop in London's Bow Churchyard and illustrated with a generic woodcut of six people in a rowboat. It takes 34 verses to tell its story – 136 lines in all – separating each stanza from the next with a simple paragraph indent to cram everything in. What happens is this:

A young ship's carpenter called William meets a bright, beautiful Gosport girl named Molly and asks her to marry him. She's reluctant at first, saying she's too young to wed, that she fears William will soon tire of her and that his job means he'd spend half his time at sea anyway. Bubbling beneath all this is Molly's clear suspicion that William's proposed only because he wants to get her into bed and that, once he's achieved this objective, all his promises of marriage will be forgotten. "Young men are so fickle, I see very plain," she reminds him. "If a maid is not coy, they will her disdain."

William persists for the next four verses and eventually talks Molly into a night of what the ballad calls "lewd desire". She discovers she's pregnant in the very next line and reminds William of his promise to marry her. By this time, the king is preparing Portsmouth's fleet to depart on a war mission, but William assures Molly he'll make good on his vow before the Bedford, his own ship, sets sail.

> So, with kind embraces, he parted that night,
> She went to meet him in the morning light,
> He said: "Dear charmer, thou must go with me,
> Before we are wedded, a friend to see",
>
> He led her through valleys and groves so deep,
> At length, this maiden began for to weep,
> Saying: "William, I fancy thou leads't me astray,
> On purpose my innocent life to betray",

PRETTY POLLY

He said: "That is true and none can you save,
For I all this night have been digging a grave",
Poor innocent soul, when she heard him say so,
Her eyes like a fountain began for to flow,

"Oh perjur'd creature, the worst of all men,
Heavens reward thee when I'm dead and gone,
Oh pity the infant and spare my life,
Let me go distress'd if I'm not thy wife",

Her hands white as lilies, in sorrow she wrung,
Beseeching for mercy, saying: "What have I done,
To you, my dear William? What makes you severe?
For to murder one that loves you so dear?"

He said: "There's no time disputing to stand",
And, instantly taking the knife in his hand,
He pierced her body till the blood it did flow,
Then into the grave her body did throw,

He covered her body, then home he did run,
Leaving none but birds her death to mourn,
On board the Bedford, he enter'd straightway,
Which lay at Portsmouth out-bound for the sea. [5]

There are another 56 lines of the Roxburghe "Gosport" to go at this point, but we'll come back to them in a moment. What's clear from the seven verses above is that just about every key element of "Pretty Polly" was already there in "The Gosport Tragedy" over 200 years ago.

The Roxburghe "Gosport" alone gives us the walk to a secluded spot, the passage through hills and valleys, the girl's growing suspicions leading to tears, the grave her killer has already prepared, the knife as his chosen weapon, her blood spilt on the ground and his casual disposal of the body. The English ballad has the same mix of narrators who later appear in "Pretty Polly" too. Willie's given the slightly more formal name of William and his victim is Molly rather than Polly, but these are the tiniest of changes.

147

All that's missing is the striking moment when Polly first sights her "grave ready dug and a spade lying by". That enduring image appears nowhere in the Roxburghe "Gosport" itself, but researchers have traced it back to other English ballad sheets printing the same song just a few years later. Some date the grave-and-spade stanza to between 1750 and 1800, but the earliest example I've been able to find comes from an eight-page chapbook printed by the Paisley bookseller George Caldwell in 1808. He makes "The Gosport Tragedy" his lead song in the book's selection and includes this couplet:

A grave and spade standing by she did see,
And said: "Must this be a bride-bed for me?" [6]

Many early sheets suggest "The Gosport Tragedy"'s lyrics be sung to an old English tune called "Peggy's Gone Over Sea", but the fact that its lyrics follow a ballad's structural rules means many other tunes fit just as well. "Pretty Polly" sticks to ballad rules too, of course, so all we need do to make the original British words fit the American tune we know today is add a few repetitions and tidy up the scansion a bit. The first couple of verses, for example, could easily be rendered like this:

He said: "My dear charmer, thou must go with me,
He said: "My dear charmer, thou must go with me,
Before we are wedded, a friend for to see",

He led her through valleys and groves so deep,
He led her through valleys and groves so deep,
At length, this poor maiden began for to weep.

I doubt if any single version of "Pretty Polly" includes every element in the "Gosport Tragedy" extract I've given here, but all survive somewhere in the American song's tangled branches. "Heavens reward thee when I'm dead and gone" – here used to mean "punish" rather than "reward" in the modern sense – is echoed on "Pretty Polly" discs stretching all the way from B. F. Shelton in 1927 to The Coal Porters in 2010. Peggy Seeger's 1964 version has Willie declare that "killing Pretty Polly will send my soul to hell" and Queenadreena's 2000 recording makes the same point when it reminds us "there's a debt to the Devil that Willie must pay".

Molly's appeal to William that he should "let me go distress'd if I'm not thy wife" has its equivalent in "Pretty Polly" too. The Stanley Brothers were the first artists on disc to have Polly beg "let me be a single girl if I can't be your wife", but that plea's been echoed by Judy Collins in 1968, Patty Loveless in 1997 and many others besides. Molly's "lily-white hands" have never quite gone away either, attaching themselves to Polly's arms in versions by Dock Boggs (1927), The Iron Mountain String Band (1975) and Angela Correa (2004). Molly's astonishment that William could "murder one that loves you so dear" is given to Polly on discs by John Hammond in 1927, Pete Seeger in 1957 and Sweeney's Men in 1969.

The killer's determination to hurry things along – "There's no time disputing to stand" – is dotted through "Pretty Polly"'s whole recording history too. It's book-ended in my own collection by Hammond's "There's no time for talking, there's no time to stand" in 1927 and Beate Sampson's almost identical wording 82 years later. As in "The Gosport Tragedy"'s original couplet, this line is almost invariably followed by one which both mentions the knife and uses "hand" as a convenient closing rhyme. Uncle Sinner's verse from his 2008 recording is just one of many examples:

There's no time for talkin', there's no time to stand,
There's no time for talkin', there's no time to stand,
I drew up a hunting knife in my right hand. [7]

Looking at all the evidence above, only one conclusion is possible: "Pretty Polly" comes from "The Gosport Tragedy". All we have to do now is figure out where "The Gosport Tragedy" came from – and the answer to that question lies in a Florida folklore journal published in 1979.

As soon as Molly's dead and buried, the Roxburghe "Gosport" turns its attention to William's life on board the Bedford. He's lying in his bunk one night, when he hears Molly's ghost calling him:

"Oh, perjur'd villain, awake now and hear,
The voice of your love, that lov'd you so dear,
This ship out of Portsmouth never shall go,
Till I am revenged for this overthrow",

She afterwards vanished, with shrieks and cries,
Flashes of lightning did dart from her eyes,
Which put the ship's crew into great fear,
None saw the ghost, but the voice they did hear.

Molly's spirit seems to hope that William will confess to the murder and turn himself in. When he refuses to do so, the ghost decides to appear directly to the crew as well:

Charles Stuart, a man of courage so bold,
One night was going into the Hold,
A beautiful creature to him did appear,
And she in her arms had a daughter most fair,

The charms of this so glorious a face,
Being merry in drink, he goes to embrace,
But to his surprise, it vanished away,
So he went to the captain without more delay,

And told him the story which, when he did hear,
The captain said "Some of my men, I do fear,
Have done some murder and if it be so,
Our ship in great danger to the sea must go."

This refers to the belief, common among seamen at the time, that sailing with a murderer on board your ship put the whole vessel in great danger. We have evidence of this from other old English and Scottish ballads, including "William Glen", which is set aboard a ship beset by inexplicable storms. Discovering their captain committed murder before leaving port, the crew throws him overboard, at which point the storms instantly subside and they sail safely on. "All young sailors, I pray beware," the ballad concludes. "And never set sail with a murderer."

PRETTY POLLY

"The Gosport Tragedy"'s own supernatural scenes may have been inspired by an 18th century ballad called "The Dreadful Ghost". This tells the story of a girl who hangs herself after being impregnated and abandoned by her boyfriend. He flees to sea in hopes of escaping the girl's vengeful spirit, but she follows him on board and tells the captain to hand him over:

> And if you don't bring him up to me,
> A mighty storm you soon shall see,
> Which will cause your gallant men to weep,
> And leave you slumbering in the deep. [8]

The terrified crew drags her former boyfriend on deck and the ghost forces him into a rowboat which promptly bursts into flames and sinks with him in it. The ghost then ascends to heaven, giving this final warning: "You sailors all who are left behind / Never prove false to young womankind". Many versions of "The Gosport Tragedy" close with a light re-phrasing of exactly that moral.

Returning to our own ballad, the Bedford's captain knows their departure date is drawing near, so he calls all the men into his cabin one by one and confronts them with his suspicions. Soon, it's William's turn:

> Then William, afrighted, did tremble with fear,
> And began by the powers above to swear,
> He nothing at all of the matter did know,
> But as from the captain he went to go,
>
> Unto his surprise, his true love did see,
> With that, he immediately fell on his knee,
> And said "Here's my true love, where shall I run?
> O save me, or else I am surely undone",
>
> Now he the murder confessed out of hand,
> And said "Before me, my Molly doth stand,
> Sweet injur'd ghost, thy pardon I crave,
> And soon I will seek thee in the silent grave",

No-one but this wretch did see this sad sight,
Then, raving distract'd, he died in the night,
As soon as her parents these tidings did hear,
They fought for the body of their daughter dear,

Near a place called Southampton, in a valley so deep,
The body was found, while many did weep,
At the fall of the damsel and her daughter dear,
In Gosport churchyard, they buried her there.

Southampton's just 14 miles northwest of Gosport and only 17 miles from Portsmouth, so all the locations given in the Roxburghe "Gosport" are consistent with one another. It offers a couple of other important clues too, telling us that the ship involved was the Bedford and that it was moored in Portsmouth Harbour when the murder took place. William and Molly are both generic names, used in countless ballads of the time no matter what the real individuals were called, so there's not much to be learned there. Charles Stuart looks a bit more reliable, though, and the ballad is clear the Bedford's crew included someone of that name when the ghost appeared.

Armed with this information, the University of Washington's Professor David Fowler set about researching Royal Navy records to see how many of the Roxburghe "Gosport"'s details he could confirm. The resulting essay, which appeared in a 1979 volume of Florida University's *Southern Folklore Quarterly*, provides our best account of the ballad's background yet. [9]

The British Library's best estimate for the Roxburghe "Gosport"'s printing is sometime between 1720 and 1750 – and Fowler quickly discovered there really was an HMS Bedford moored at Portsmouth for much of this time. Not only that, but the ship's pay books confirm that a man called Charles Stewart joined her crew on 27 January 1726, when the Bedford was acting as a guard ship in Portsmouth Harbour with a skeleton crew of just 80 men on board. Standardised spelling had yet to take hold in the 1720s, so the Stuart/Stewart discrepancy is irrelevant. So far, so good: we've got a man of the right name on the right ship in the right harbour at the right time to support the Roxburghe "Gosport"'s account.

The Bedford was the British Navy's 18th century equivalent of a modern destroyer. She was about 150ft long and 40ft wide, with 70 guns on board and carried a consignment of 440 men when crewed for war. The ship's carpenter when Stewart signed on board is listed as John Billson, who joined the Bedford in that post on 1 May 1723 and remained there till his death on-board in September 1726. His Navy records show his first appointment as any ship's master carpenter was in 1702, suggesting he'd have been somewhere in his mid-forties when he died. He left no widow behind to claim his pay for the Bedford's voyage, so we know he was a single man.

"The existence of the Bedford, and the confirmation that she was indeed in Portsmouth, as the ballad says, provides justification for taking seriously the name of Charles Stewart," Fowler writes in his essay. "Billson's first name is not William, but William and Molly are common names in balladry, enough so at least to justify pursuing Billson a bit further."

Quiet periods, such as the guard ship duty she was now engaged on, were an ideal opportunity for Billson and his gang of about ten junior carpenters to carry out any repairs the ship needed. This would have kept them very busy during the day, but given them fairly regular shore leave to enjoy all the fleshy pleasures Gosport had to offer.

If Billson really was the model for William, these breaks ashore would have been an ideal opportunity to seduce his girlfriend with the promises of marriage the ballad records, and enjoy her to the full when those efforts prevailed. Before the Bedford sailed again, there'd be ample time for the girl to discover her delicate condition and begin reminding Billson of his obligations to her. She'd have known full well that a Navy carpenter had to sail with his ship when hostilities broke out – "in time of war, to the sea you must go" – and that peaceful interludes like these never lasted for long.

And so it proved. On 26 January 1726, Edmund Hook, the Bedford's captain, received orders that he should prepare the ship for active duty. Spain had joined with Austria to threaten the British territory of Gibraltar and was now thought to be plotting with Russia too. King George I ordered the Bedford and 19 other Royal Navy ships to stage a show of force in the Baltic and remind the Russian navy that Britain wasn't to be messed with.

The new orders meant Hook had to get the Bedford's crew up to its full complement of 440 in double-quick time. The Admiralty issued him with warrants giving the Bedford's press gangs the legal powers to force any seamen they found in Portsmouth's pubs and brothels to join the ship whether they liked it or not – a crude form of conscription. In extreme cases, reluctant recruits were simply knocked unconscious and dragged on board against their will. Meanwhile, Hook was pushing Billson and his gang of carpenters to complete the thousand and one jobs needed to get the ship ready for active service.

On 27 January 1726, the day Stewart signed up, Hook's log confirms the Bedford had already begun press-ganging new men and getting them on-board. Stewart's own name in the pay book has the single word "pressing" noted against it, but he does not appear on a separate list of men recruited in this way. Fowler concludes that "pressing" was an indication of Stewart's duties rather than the reason he joined.

Although he gave his signature on 27 January, Stewart did not come aboard the Bedford until two weeks later, and that's probably because he was busy ashore recruiting others. "As a press gang member, he would have been more likely than the average to be known personally to the captain and would spend more time ashore when the ship was in port," Fowler writes. This may help to explain why the Stewart of the ballad was so willing to take his fears to the captain and – as we'll see in a moment – why he's the only crewman the ballad names in full.

Hook had got the Bedford's complement up to 410 men by the time she sailed out of harbour to the Navy's Portsmouth anchorage at Spithead on 26 February, at which point shore leave became very rare. Still he was adding new men every day, finally gathering a crew of 486 against the ship's supposed capacity of 440. The Bedford stayed at Spithead for six weeks as she and the rest of Admiral Sir Charles Wager's fleet completed their preparations, then sailed for the Baltic with everyone else.

All this suggests that any real murder behind "The Gosport Tragedy" – and therefore behind "Pretty Polly" too – most likely happened between 26 January 1726 and February 26 the same year. Any earlier, and the Bedford would still have been months away from sailing. Any later, and its carpenter would have had no opportunity to murder Molly or anyone else in Gosport. Once the Bedford left for Spithead, John Billson would never tread on English soil again.

The six weeks the Bedford spent at Portsmouth's Spithead anchorage trapped the entire crew on their over-crowded ship, but gave them far less work to do than the frantic preparations in harbour. Most likely, this is when gossip about a ghost on-board started circulating. Perhaps this began because someone in the crew noticed the guilt-stricken Billson was having disturbed nights, or perhaps because he'd been foolish enough to confide in one of the other men.

With little to do in their off-time but get drunk, rumours of a ghost swirling through the ship and plenty of time to swap tall stories, the Bedford's crew must have been ready to glimpse spirits in every shadow. It's at this point that a sloshed Charles Stewart stumbles into the dimly-lit hold and sees what he thinks is a beautiful woman holding a baby in her arms. He steps forward to embrace her, but the image instantly vanishes. You or I would conclude this was a trick of the light, remind ourselves how primed we'd been to expect something like this and swear to lay off the rum in future. For an 18th century sailor, though, a very different explanation suggested itself – he'd just seen Molly's ghost!

We know from the Roxburghe "Gosport" ghost's own words that the reported sightings came before the Bedford was ready to set sail: "This ship out of Portsmouth never shall go". The ballad's captain adds that, if there really is a murderer on board, then "our ship in great danger to the sea must go". Clearly, he feared they'd have to sail whether the murderer was found or not, and that implies Charles Stewart's report of the ghost came immediately before their scheduled departure from Spithead on 7 April.

The Bedford reached the Gulf of Finland at the beginning of June and anchored at Naissaar Island off the coast of Estonia. The fleet's job there was simply to park somewhere in the Russians' field of vision and stay put for a bit, radiating a quiet sense of British naval power by its presence alone. After three months in the Baltic, the Admiralty felt Britain's point was made so the fleet set off back to Portsmouth.

There'd been no need for battle on this expedition, but the voyage home presented some genuine danger.

On 22 September, the Bedford had reached a point about 15 miles west of Gotland – placing her smack in the middle of the Baltic Sea – when storms struck the ship. These storms tore up the Baltic for three days and sank no fewer than 17 ships there. Hook's log entry for 22 September records a perilous night as his crew desperately struggled to keep the ship afloat. "At half past 10 p.m., HF topsail," he writes. "At 6 a.m., set fore topsail; broke one of our main shrouds HM topsail. At 8 fixed him again and set main topsail. At 10 saw some breakers bearing NNE 6 or 7 miles; fired a gun being a sign of danger and tacked." [10, 11]

Admiralty Librarian Jennifer Wraight translated this log entry into landlubbers' English for me, explaining that the first section means Hook was hauling in sails on his fore mast and main mast respectively. "Making adjustments to the sails is normally a reaction to weather conditions," she told me. "In stormy conditions, you would normally reduce the amount of sail a ship is carrying, which would be consistent with the log entry. The shrouds are not sails, but part of the rigging: they provide lateral support for the masts. One of the main shrouds breaking would suggest that the mast was under strain. Taking in the main topsail would have reduced strain on the mast while the broken shroud was being repaired." [12]

There was a second threat too, because the breakers Hook sighted told him there was shallow water and rocks near the ship. Wraight believes these rocks carried more potential danger for the Bedford than the weather alone, adding that they would have been all the more difficult to avoid when storms were cutting both visibility and the ship's capacity to manoeuvre. "Tacking – changing direction – would be eminently sensible," she said. "He's taking the ship away from hazard."

Three days later, just as the storms were subsiding, Hook's log tells us that Billson is dead. His 25 September entry gives us the usual long list of times and headings, punctuated by just six words on the carpenter's fate: "At 9 John Bellson, carpenter, died." As with Charles Stewart, there's no consistency in the way Billson's surname gets spelt in the Bedford's records – Bilson, Billson, Bellson – but the "carpenter" addition makes clear it's the same man. The log entry's casual aside looks pretty callous to modern eyes, but Hook would have been well-used to seamen dying of disease during any voyage like this. He lost 40 on the Bedford's Baltic mission alone.

That's probably how Billson died too. Conceivably, he could have met a random accident on the Bedford's storm-tossed decks, but foul play is unlikely. Any suspicion of a murder on board would have required Hook to carry out an official investigation and there's no trace of anything like that in the records. The important thing is that Billson's passing once again matches the facts given in "The Gosport Tragedy" – in this case, its report that the Bedford's carpenter died on board.

Fowler thinks it was probably scurvy that did for him. This disease killed more British sailors than enemy action did in the 18th century and it was not until 1747 that James Lind proved it could be prevented simply by adding citrus fruits to the sailors' very restricted diet. This practice was not adopted by the British Navy until the 1790s and not fully understood even then. The final stages of scurvy produce fits of mad ranting, which seems to match the ballad's description of William's death: "Raving distracted he died in the night". [13]

The Bedford was over 900 miles from Portsmouth when its carpenter died, about 15 miles from the nearest land and with over a month of the voyage home remaining. "Billson would definitely be more likely to be buried at sea than brought home," Wraight said. "Sharing a ship with a decomposing body is not pleasant, nor conducive to health and morale. Cases like Nelson's where they did attempt it, are very rare and they didn't find it easy then."

Almost certainly, then, John Billson's body ended up at the bottom of the Baltic Sea. But his victim, as the ballad tells it, was eventually buried in Gosport churchyard. Molly's parents must have been relieved to lay their lost daughter to rest in sacred ground at last and Fowler concludes it was Charles Stewart who made that possible.

The Bedford's pay books show Stewart on a legitimate absence from the ship between 18 November 1726 and 12 April the following year, a period when no press-gang activity was needed. Fowler thinks Hook may have entrusted him with the task of finding the murdered girl's parents, telling them how she died and passing on whatever information Billson had volunteered to help find her body.

Stewart rejoined the Bedford at her new mooring at the mouth of the Thames on 12 April, and a week later the marks against his name change again to indicate "paid on board". That gives him a spell of nearly five months ashore, during which he may have both contacted the murdered girl's parents and told his story to the London print-shop owner who produced the Roxburghe "Gosport".

Neither "The Gosport Tragedy" nor the Navy's records give us any clue to Molly's real identity – even that Christian name is a fiction, remember – which scuppers any possibility of finding her grave. We do know that Gosport's parish church back in 1726 was St Mary's at Alverstoke, though, so that's almost certainly the place the ballad has in mind when it mentions "Gosport churchyard". Unfortunately, neither Gosport's church records nor the few newspapers which survive from this period can tell us any more. If there was a real murder behind "The Gosport Tragedy", then the ballad itself seems to be our only surviving record of it.

Fowler's 1979 essay is an impressive and meticulous piece of work, which ties "The Gosport Tragedy's" narrative convincingly to the Bedford's 1726 voyage. I'm sure he'd agree, though, that we'd be going a step to far to treat it as conclusive proof of Billson's guilt. For one thing, there were nine or ten other carpenters aboard the Bedford at this time. Only Billson carried the formal rank of "ship's carpenter" which the ballad uses, but we can't rule out the possibility that a little artistic licence has been applied to describe some more junior member of the gang that way. As Wraight points out, Billson's Navy records suggest he was at least 40 years old in 1726, and the ballad paints a picture of a much younger man. [14]

It's equally possible that – whatever the Bedford's crew may have come to believe – the murder ashore existed only in their own imaginations. But even if the song's tale is based on nothing more substantive than the Bedford's prevailing gossip, there's good reason to think Stewart played a role in transmitting it to the wider world.

Stewart's journey from Gosport to rejoin the Bedford on England's east coast would logically have taken him through London and perhaps to one of the many seamen's inns he'd have known there from his work with the Navy's press-gangs. Dives like these were known as "rondys" – short for "rendezvous" – and often included a makeshift jail cell on the premises where press-ganged men could be safely locked away before being taken to the ship. "The oldest rendezvous was at St Katherine's Stairs on Tower Hill, the neighbourhood being frequented by seamen because of the proximity of the Navy Office where pay tickets were cashed," Christopher Lloyd writes in his book *The British Seaman 1200 – 1860*. "A convenient tavern there was The Two Dutch Skippers." [15]

It's less than a mile to Tower Hill from the Bow Churchyard print shop which produced the Roxburghe "Gosport". We know from Henry Plomer's dictionary of 18th century printers that this particular shop was operated by a man called John Cluer from 1726 till 1728, which puts him in charge there when Stewart passed through London. Fowler suggests that Cluer may have frequented pubs like The Two Dutch Skippers hoping to gather material for future ballads, and that Charles Stewart found him there one night on just such an expedition.

That would certainly explain why Stewart is the only man given his real name in the song, why that name is spelt out in full and why he's described in such flattering terms ("a man of courage so bold"). Cluer would have been keen to keep such a useful source of material happy, either because he needed more than one interview to get the Gosport story down in full or because he hoped other lucrative tales might follow.

Just how much of that is true, we'll never know. Someone must have provided the bridge that transformed "The Gosport Tragedy" from a sailors' oral tale to a printed ballad, though, and the details above make Stewart a very tempting candidate. "He is my choice as the mariner who held a London publisher with his glittering eye," Fowler writes, "telling an intriguing story of love, death and the supernatural, which was then turned into one of the most popular broadside ballads of the last 250 years".

Ballad shops all over the UK continued to produce sheets with "The Gosport Tragedy"'s story right through the 19th century, often adding small improvements to the scansion or cutting its length as they went. In some cases, these refinements may have begun in the song's oral tradition, as singers passed it from mouth to mouth and it slowly evolved in response. "This is how diamonds are made from lumps of dull coal," Sparks told me. "The song gets polished by each singer that picks it up and considers it."

Sometimes, the ballad sheet printers could simply transcribe what they'd heard sung in the streets, but in other cases they'd be composing their own verses from scratch. Whatever its source, the most significant change came when someone decided William was getting off rather too easily in the original song. What was needed here, they felt, was for someone to give him a far nastier death.

It's possible that this change appeared as early as 1805, but the first concrete example I've been able to find is a Liverpool sheet produced around 1822. This re-titles the ballad "Love And Murder", cuts it to just 44 lines and sets its action in the English town of Worcester. The story is just as we know it, but the girl's name has now morphed from Molly to Polly. Her killer is called Billy, and his entire life after escaping to the ship is condensed into the ballad's final three verses:

> *One morning before ever it was day,*
> *The captain came up and this he did say:*
> *"There is a murder on board that has lately been done,*
> *Our ship is in mourning, we cannot sail on",*
>
> *Then up stepped one: "Indeed it's not me",*
> *Then up steps another: "Indeed it's not me",*
> *At length up steps Billy and this he did swear:*
> *"Indeed it's not me, I vow and declare",*
>
> *As he was running from the captain with speed,*
> *He met with his Polly which made his heart bleed,*
> *She stripped him and tore him, she tore him in three,*
> *Because that he murdered her baby and she.* [16]

In some versions, Polly is also allowed to taunt her killer as she dispatches him. Mike Waterson's 1977 recording, for example, ends with this couplet:

> *Why, she's snatched him and she's catched him and she's tore him in three,*
> *Saying "That's for the murder of my baby and me".*

There's something very appealing about the dead girl being given this far more active role in her killer's demise. William's old "raving" death simply couldn't compete and was almost instantly replaced by the new scene. Oxford's Bodleian Library has 16 ballad sheets telling "The Gosport Tragedy"'s story in its collection, all produced between 1815 and 1885. Some call the truncated song "Love And Murder", some call it "Polly's Love" and some call it "The Cruel Ship's Carpenter", but every one of them gives the ghost its expanded and more vicious role.

Those sheets' original buyers would have gained an extra little shiver from the number of pieces Polly selects for her lover's corpse. Three was a number often encountered in beliefs about demonology at the time, which presumed the Devil and his agents used it as a means of mocking the Holy Trinity. Satan, it was said, knocked three times on the door before coming to claim your soul, so giving that number a part to play in Billy's death made the ghost more frightening than ever.

It became all the more so once a tidy little internal rhyme was added: "she ripped him and stripped him and tore him in three". This little touch first appeared sometime in the ballad sheets' era, but has survived long enough to appear in recordings by Waterson:Carthy in 2009 and Jon Boden two years later. Boden included the song in his 2011 *A Folk Song A Day* project, applauding the fact that it gives Polly such a satisfying revenge.

As Molly became Polly in Britain, copies of the original ballad were still being produced in America. The earliest version we have printed on that side of the Atlantic is titled "The Gosport Tragedy" and appears in a collection called *The Forget-Me-Not-Songster*, editions of which were produced in Boston, Philadelphia and New York. The particular copy I'm looking at here comes from Leonard Deming's Boston print shop and has been dated to about 1835.

This text for the song – let's call it the Deming "Gosport" – starts by naming its characters William and Molly, then switches to calling the girl Mary half-way through from what seems to be sheer carelessness. It takes a leisurely 108 lines to tell the story in its traditional form, frankly describing Molly's unwanted pregnancy and with William raving himself to death rather than being torn to pieces by the ghost. The ship he flees to is not named, but it's said to be preparing to "set sail from Plymouth to plough the salt sea". Plymouth is another British naval city, about 160 miles west along the coast from Portsmouth, and I imagine it's just the similarity of the two names which accounts for this confusion.

The Deming "Gosport"'s main contribution to "Pretty Polly"'s development comes in the new details it introduces for some key scenes, many of which would remain in place for well over a century. As William's lining Molly up for her fatal walk in the woods, for example, the Boston sheet makes his promise of marriage more explicit than ever:

> *And if that tomorrow, my love will ride down,*
> *The ring I can buy our fond union to crown.*

That ring's still appearing as late as 1962, when the Canadian singer Leo Spencer gives it a mention. When everything goes haywire and Molly's begging for her life, it's not her the Deming "Gosport" describes as "so comely and fair", but her assassin – and that idea appears again in a 1957 recording of "Pretty Polly" by the Kentucky banjo player Pete Steele.

The Deming "Gosport"'s re-imagining of William's confrontation on board ship is particularly striking, swapping the English ballad's somewhat stilted language for a far more conversational tone. Stewart reports his own ghost sighting to the captain and then:

> *The captain soon summoned the jovial ship's crew,*
> *And said "My brave fellows, I fear some of you,*
> *Have murdered some damsel 'ere you came away,*
> *Whose injured ghost haunts you now on the sea,*
>
> *"Whoever you be, if the truth you deny,*
> *When found out, you'll be hung on the yard-arm so high,*
> *But he who confesses, his life we'll not take,*
> *But leave him upon the first island we make",*
>
> *Then William immediately fell on his knees,*
> *The blood in his veins quick with horror did freeze,*
> *He cried "Cruel murder! Oh, what have I done?*
> *God help me, I fear my poor soul is undone."* [17]

The traditional verses resume at this point, explaining that William's the only one glimpsing the ghost this time, describing his lonely death and getting Molly's remains properly interred at Gosport in just 12 swift lines.

By 1850, after a century or more in print, "The Gosport Tragedy" was familiar enough to make it worth parodying in London's music halls. A version called "Molly The Betrayed or The Fog Bound Vessel" was produced for the comic singer Sam Cowell. The ballad shops quickly printed up sheets using Cowell's lyrics, hoping to capitalise on the popularity of his performance, and by 1855 there was some official sheet music too.

Cowell began his stage career as a child, touring America in various Shakespeare plays with his actor father. Sometimes, he would perform "coon" songs front of curtain to keep the audience entertained while scenery was being changed behind him. Returning to England in about 1840 and still just 20 years old, he decided there was more money in this burlesque side of his act and ditched the Bard to make room for more comic songs. "By 1850, he had abandoned the legitimate stage entirely in favour of the songs and supper rooms of the West End," *The Cambridge Guide To American Theatre* tells us. "An ugly little man with a lugubrious expression, he specialised in cockney song-and-patter acts." [18]

And that's exactly what "Molly The Betrayed" is. Spelling out its words phonetically in an attempt to mimic Cowell's bizarre stage accent, the parody tells the same core story as "The Gosport Tragedy" but mixes its narrative passages with a string of silly jokes. Its targets include the ballad sheets' sometimes rather strained rhymes, their reliance on highly melodramatic plots and the conventions of rural folk songs at the time.

This last element suggests audiences in 1850 were just as likely to have encountered the original tale in its folk song form as they were to have found it on a printed ballad. Certainly, "Molly The Betrayed" would have meant nothing to anyone who didn't already know the original song in one form or another, which testifies again to how popular it had become.

What emerges from all this is something very like the comic monologues Stanley Holloway made famous in the 1930s. A couple of brief extracts will give you its flavour:

In a kitchen in Portsmouth, a fair maid did dwell,
For grammar and grace none could her excel,
Young Villiam, he courted her to be his dear,
And he by his trade was a ship's carpen – tier,
Singing doodle, doodle chop, chum, chow choral li la.

And a few verses later:

Then he calls up his men with a shout and a whoop,
And he orders young Villiam to stand on the poop,
"There's summat not right," he says, "'mongst this here crew,
And blow'd if I don't think, young Villiam, it's you". [16]

This version added a fifth title to the song's growing collection. The first evidence we have of it taking the name we know today comes in another parody, which seems to have been current in the 1890s. That's when a woman identified only as Mrs M. M. said she learned the song she performed for collectors at her Missouri home in August 1938. She called this song "Pretty Polly" and its four verses form a bawdy parody of our own ballad. Here's a taste:

"Pretty Polly, Pretty Polly, oh won't you come to me,
Pretty Polly, Pretty Polly, oh won't you come to me,"
"Oh no, my young man, I'm afraid you'll undo me,
Oh lay your leg over me do",

Her drawers they was tied and he couldn't undo 'em,
Her drawers they was tied and he couldn't undo 'em,
She snorted and cried "Just take your knife to 'em,
Oh lay your leg over me, do." [19]

The structure there is very much like "Pretty Polly"'s and the opening lines are almost identical. Both songs include a knife, both have Polly weeping at some point along the way and both give her an unwanted pregnancy. The fact that Mrs M. M. knew her song as "Pretty Polly", coupled with the very prominent use of that phrase in its opening lines, suggests the real ballad may already have adopted that name when the parody was produced. If so, no printed copy seems to have survived.

More reliable evidence emerged around 1917, when the English song collector Cecil Sharp heard an unusual version in North Carolina. Sharp had already expressed some interest in "The Gosport Tragedy", saying ten years earlier that it was one of the few supernatural folk ballads still popular among the rural singers he interviewed. His North Carolina find was titled "The Cruel Ship's Carpenter" and sung with a new twist to William's death:

> He entered his ship on the salt sea so wide,
> And swore by his maker he'd see the other side,
> While he was a-sailing in his heart's content,
> The ship sprang a leak: to the bottom she went,
>
> While he was a-lying there, all in sad surprise,
> He saw Pretty Polly appear before his eyes,
> "Oh William, oh William, you've no time to stay,
> There's a debt to the devil that you're bound to pay". [20]

William's victim had first been called Polly almost a century before and retained that name on and off ever since. If you discount the Missouri parody, then Sharp's is the earliest version I've seen to call her "Pretty Polly" in full. Once Molly became Polly on that 1822 Liverpool sheet, the temptation to attach "Pretty" in this way was always going to prove irresistible. The fact that several unconnected folk songs sometimes called themselves "Pretty Polly" already did not prevent our own ballad being re-titled in her honour.

Song collectors still find the odd American version calling the girl Molly rather than Polly today – another reminder of the song's roots – but these are very much the exception rather than the rule. Less than a decade after Sharp noted down the lyrics above, the song's first commercial discs appeared. In 1927, John Hammond, B.F. Shelton and Dock Boggs all released recordings of the song they called "Pretty Polly" and its earlier names dropped away.

The first man to put "Pretty Polly" on disc was John Hammond, who cut it for Gennett Records at a Richmond, Indiana session in April 1925. Gennett stressed his roots as an East Kentucky banjo player by calling the song "Purty Polly" on the label of its 1927 release. In this version, Willie not only tells Polly he's dug her grave already, but also exactly how long the job took: "six long hours".

Hammond's lyrics show that the process of Americanising "Pretty Polly" still had some way to go. He sets the story in London for a start, and allows himself a leisurely 11 verses to get it told. No trace of the maritime setting remains, but there's still the odd line which retains a flavour of English folk songs, such as his description of Polly "with her rings on her fingers and lily-white hands". Others carry a distinct whiff of American puritanism: here, it's Polly's sinful love of her own body which sends her soul to hell.

This last element is characteristic of many American adaptations of British songs, which often erase their source ballads' frank acknowledgement that an unwanted pregnancy caused all the trouble. Hammond comes as close as he dares to suggesting Polly's indiscretion with a line pointing out that, even for people who are not yet married, "there's pleasure to see". In the English ballads, which spell out the nature of that pleasure elsewhere, Willie needs only to tell Polly that he wants them to visit some friends. The much shorter American song has to make each verse work that bit harder, though, and this coinage is a clever way of nodding towards sex while also allowing the singer to insist that wasn't what he had in mind at all.

Two other banjo players released their own versions of "Pretty Polly" in 1927 and both were as careful as Hammond to skirt around this sensitive issue. B. F. Shelton, another Kentucky native, and Dock Boggs from the next-door state of Virginia both use the "pleasure to see" verse, but only Shelton has Willie confess that he's "courted" Polly right through the night.

For all its careful evasions, though, it's still the Dock Boggs' "Pretty Polly" which Sparks selects as the song's single greatest rendition. "I just can't get a handle on his creepiness," she said. "I don't think he intended to be creepy. I think he just wanted to sing these songs and play them to the best of his ability. But 'Pretty Polly' may be a kind of

Rorschach test in which the singer reveals more than he or she wants to reveal. I can hear the dark thunderbolt-smoting God of American puritanism in Dock Boggs' voice: we are all doomed sinners."

We've come a long way from "The Gosport Tragedy"'s unblinking gaze: "At length with his cunning he did her betray / And to lewd desire he led her away". It takes quite a determined search of "Pretty Polly"'s lyrics to reveal even a hint of that idea in the American song, and for most casual listeners the result is that Polly herself emerges as a rather baffled virgin. Far from concealing the song's sexual content, though, Sparks believes this piety just highlights it all the more.

"The more we cover up what we find frightening to sing about, the more these things pop out from unexpected symbols and signs," she said. "It's kind of like a poker tell – when people have a great hand or a terrible hand they often unconsciously give themselves away, even though they're doing their darndest to keep it all hidden."

In 1938, The Coon Creek Girls became the first women to record "Pretty Polly". They were a string band led by Lily May and Rosie Ledford, a pair of Kentucky sisters recruited to provide music for an Ohio country music station. Their rendition sticks closely to their male predecessors' lyrics, showing no greater empathy with Polly than any of the male performers had managed. It was this recording which introduced Sparks to the song. "I was in my twenties when I heard The Coon Creek Girls sing it on some compilation," she said. "It was creepy – a chorus of girls singing about a guy who is leading his lover to her grave. Horrifying, but those girls had such lovely harmonies."

Interviewed in 1997, Lilly May's grand-daughter Cari Norris suggested her grandmother may have seen the song partly as a commentary on her relationship with the band's domineering manager. "It expressed her own feelings about her career under John Lair in a way," Norris said. "Because she was controlled in many ways. And I think she felt powerless. [...] That's what art does: you say things in metaphors, which are more powerful anyway." [21]

The song's next significant recording came from The Stanley Brothers in 1950, underpinning Ralph Stanley's high lonesome vocals with a stately stand-up bass to fatten out the sound. It's notable not only for its slurs on Polly's past reputation, but also for a masterly bit of misdirection in the opening verses, which depict Willie as a rather gentle figure:

> *Oh Polly, Pretty Polly, would you take me unkind,*
> *Polly, Pretty Polly, would you take me unkind,*
> *Let me sit down beside you and tell you my mind,*
>
> *Oh my mind is to marry and never to part,*
> *My mind is to marry and never to part,*
> *The first time I saw you, it wounded my heart.* [3]

Butter wouldn't melt. Even as he's giving Polly these loving assurances, though, Willie knows full well that the grave he's just dug for her is waiting and that it won't be empty for long. The Stanley Brothers skip both the "spade lying by" verse and any description of Polly's murder itself, perhaps fearing they'd put off the record buyers of the day, but Ralph Stanley re-instated both these scenes when he returned to the song in 1997 for a duet with Patty Loveless.

Until the mid-fifties, the musicians recording "Pretty Polly" had all come from the adjoining bluegrass states of Kentucky and Virginia, with even The Coon Creek Girls' radio career taking them no further than neighbouring Ohio. Pete Seeger, a New Yorker, broke that regional monopoly in 1957, edging the song across a genre boundary too, from country into folk. Seeger used a canny selection of Shelton's and Boggs' verses which helped confirm a clear trend in the song's development so far.

Taking the period from 1927 to 1960 as a convenient snapshot of "Pretty Polly"'s first third of a century on disc gives us seven different performers to consider: John Hammond, B. F. Shelton, Dock Boggs, The Coon Creek Girls, The Stanley Brothers, Pete Seeger and Estil C. Ball. The first three of these average out at 11 verses each, the middle three at nine verses and the final three at eight. We've seen already that the more you distil "Pretty Polly", the stronger its liquor becomes, so it's no coincidence that Ball's version is both the shortest recording of the song so far and one of the best.

Ball, who often performed with his wife Orna, was a white gospel singer whose rich baritone voice and unhurried guitar playing contrasts sharply with the keening vocals of many bluegrass singers and the frantic picking they rely on. He's best-known for his song "Tribulations", a hair-raising catalogue of what we sinners can expect when the *Book Of Revelations* plays out. He peoples that song with angels pouring their wrath on humanity's head, men begging fruitlessly to die and Christ resolutely turning His back on anyone marked for damnation. Like the merciless deity Sparks detects in Dock Boggs' recording, this is a very vengeful God indeed – and Ball takes some relish in acting as His prophet.

There's a touch of the same Old Testament fervour in the Library of Congress recording Alan Lomax made of Ball in 1959. Performing solo this time, Ball distills "Pretty Polly" down to six stark verses. Strip out the repetitions and he requires just 12 lines to have Willie collect Polly, take her to the grave he'd already prepared, kill her, throw her into the ground and accept his own damnation. He doesn't even have the decency to give Polly a quick end, leaving her instead to choke slowly to death on the dirt of her own shallow grave. She's still moaning there as he walks calmly away.

Ball's lyrics mark one of the best uses of the song's shifting perspective too. One opening quote from Willie aside, he tells the whole story in the third person, whipping back the curtain only in his final verse to reveals it's the killer who's been speaking all along. At half the length of Shelton or Hammond's versions, this is the tale's most brutal telling yet and made all the more so by its refusal to offer any hint of the killer's motives. "Don't ask for the comfort of an explanation," Willie seems to sneer as he strolls away. "There isn't one."

"**P**retty Polly"'s American career moved into overdrive with the folk revival of the 1960s, adding the first really famous names to her list of biographers and reaching a global audience for the first time as a result. Bob Dylan, Bert Jansch, Sandy Denny, The Byrds and Judy Collins would all perform the song before the 1960s were out and only Bob failed to find it a place on one of his albums.

Dylan did include "Pretty Polly" in his early New York sets, though and also borrowed its melody for his own 1962 composition "The Ballad

Of Hollis Brown". His hero Woody Guthrie had already used the tune to fuel his own "Pastures Of Plenty" in 1941, so we know it was well-established in America's national folk canon by then. Peggy Seeger and Tom Paley teamed up for their own recording of "Pretty Polly" itself in 1964, followed by both The Byrds and Judy Collins four years later. Perhaps because of Dylan's interest, the song soon started to make itself felt in Britain too. The Scottish guitarist Bert Jansch included it in his set at a 1963 Glasgow folk club gig which later surfaced on a live album and Sandy Denny cut a studio version in 1967. Sweeney's Men, a Dublin band, and Leicestershire's Davy Graham both put mournful versions of the song on their 1969 albums.

Of all these artists, none outshine Denny and Collins. Both women start the story gently but build to full-throated anger and pain as Polly meets her death. Although both versions include snatches of direct narration from Willie and Polly themselves, the singers come across as quoting these characters rather than choosing to inhabit either one. Instead of speaking directly for Polly's killer in the final verse, Collins consigns Willie to hell with these words:

> A debt to the devil Willie must pay,
> A debt to the devil Willie must pay,
> For killing Pretty Polly and running away. [3]

Crispin Gray discovered "Pretty Polly" in the Collins recording, introducing it to singer Katie Jane Garside when they put their own band, Queenadreena, together in 1999. "I've heard recordings of the song by women that sound remarkably close to male versions in terms of attitude," he told me. "But not so with the Judy Collins version or Katie Jane's rendition, which I think are both very female. I don't mean just because they're obviously female voices. As the song portrays violence done to a woman by a man, I'm not sure a man could ever approach or understand it in quite the same way.

"That's not to say Judy Collins and Katie Jane sound the same either, because they don't. To my ears, Judy Collins' delivery is pure and wistful while Katie Jane, particularly in our later live versions, is more wild, unhinged and traumatised – although I think they both manage to inject a certain ghostliness." Video footage of Garside performing the song certainly suggests a woman possessed by its strange magic. "Polly takes over and shows you how it's done," she told me, "Some nights, the song comes with a rage so blissfully pure my mouth is 100 miles wide, crashing through forests, armies and deserts." [22]

Other female singers take a more distanced approach. Kristin Hersh of the rock band Throwing Muses has recorded "Pretty Polly" too, so I asked her to what extent a female performer must channel Polly herself as the song progresses. "I find I can avoid an empathy stomach ache if I divorce myself from the meaning of the words when I sing it," she replied. "I guess it's more like reporting, which would bring it into the realm of myth. That's nice. Myth is important." [23]

Sparks makes a similar point. "That's the beauty of art: it's not real," she said, "We don't have to worry about Pretty Polly after the song is over, because she is so stylised, so symbolic a figure that there is no real woman there to mourn or fret over.

"I don't think the gender of the singer is that important. In a way, I think it's a bit of misogyny to suppose that women don't have thoughts just as dark and inexpressible as men. 'Pretty Polly' isn't really about a murder at all: it's about our fear of sexual abandon and our fascination with our own mortality. It feels good to listen to the song because it lets a little air out of the volcano of our unconsciousness."

The Byrds reclaimed "Pretty Polly" from the folk singers who'd made it their own when they included it on the band's classic 1968 country-rock album *Sweetheart Of The Rodeo*. Garlanded with the outfit's trademark chiming guitars, this was one of the first male versions to completely avoid calling the killer "I". Roger McGuinn quotes Willie and Polly both, just as Denny and Collins did, and imports Collins' third-person damnation stanza verbatim, but never quite steps into the killer's head. The result is less sinister than many earlier versions, but it's a gloriously pretty record and that's made it an enduring template for the song.

For Hersh, the mismatch between a happy tune and sinister content in a version like this only strengthens the song's appeal. "It's the dark lyrics in contrast to that bright melody," she said. "I always like to hear inherent sadness beneath a brave front." Jon Boden agrees. "Of all the girlfriend murdering songs, this must be the one with the most inappropriate tune," he writes in *AFSAD's* online sleeve notes. "Somehow, that makes it all the more horrific."

By 1970, the folk revival was just a distant memory and "Pretty Polly" found few takers in the rock scene that replaced it. The song remained as popular as ever among bluegrass musicians and their fans, but dropped out of sight for almost everyone else. If you ever did hear it on the radio at that time, it was likely to be on a programme devoted to music for toddlers.

"Pretty Polly" has always had this odd parallel life as a children's song. Posting to the folk music board Mudcat in September 2001, one woman recalled hearing a version called "Little Molly" during her own childhood. "When I was little, the woman who took care of us when my parents were at work used to sing it," she writes. "She was an older lady and we kids were all terrified of her, but she was the only woman around who would babysit that many kids until midnight every night." [24]

The lyrics she recalls from those occasions include all of the song's goriest details, complete with the waiting grave, the stabbing and the heart's blood. In her babysitters' telling, throwing a little dirt over the girl is not callous enough for Willie, so he strews the grave with thorns as well.

"My feeling is that we all still have a strange urge to scare children," Sparks said. "We perhaps don't tell them the unedited version of Grimms' fairy tales, but we do sing them 'My Darling Clementine' or 'Rock A-Bye Baby' with a strange excitement. It's on a very unconscious level, but somewhere we have a need to let children know they're going to die. These songs give us a way to hint at that."

Bluegrass music returned to mass attention when the Coen Brothers released their movie *O Brother Where Art Thou?* in 2000. Its accompanying soundtrack album sparked a brief craze for any vintage recording with a banjo and a fiddle on it, but also helped to fuel the growing Americana/alt.country movement and its fascination with murder ballads. "I've spoken to many happy listeners who thought they didn't like folk music because they only knew protest songs," Hersh said. "Songs like 'Pretty Polly' are so creepy and cool in comparison."

One young musician who discovered "Pretty Polly" at about this time was Jake Speed, whose Cincinnati band The Freddies included the song on their 2002 debut CD. "I put 'Pretty Polly' on the first album to show people the tradition my original music was attempting to emerge from – the dark, ballad-based storytelling tradition," Speed told me. "There's a desperation to the song that I always liked. Maybe the killer in the song is just so pathetic and desperate that I wanted to feel a little of that." [25]

Other Americana musicians of Speed's generation felt the same way, coalescing into a whole new sub-genre called Hillbilly Noir. In the early noughties, bands playing every level of venue from a neighbourhood bar to the local sports stadium realised that bringing an old murder ballad into their set could add that crucial whiff of sulphur mainstream rock had long since lost.

And audiences responded well. Queenadreena's fans were a good 30 years younger than most Ralph Stanley listeners, but the reception they give "Pretty Polly" on the band's 2005 live album marks it as a crowd favourite. "It never failed to get a great response," Gray said. "We often used it as the last song in the set or as an encore – the song the whole gig would build up to. It was one of the very few songs that we played right from the outset to the last Queenadreena performance in 2009."

A few songwriters have taken this process a step further, by penning their own response to "Pretty Polly" rather than simply covering the original track. Perhaps the best of these answer songs comes from Fred Burns, who recorded his own "Pretty Polly's Revenge" in 2011. "What if the seemingly helpless Polly had been packing heat that fateful day?" he asks. It doesn't take long to find out:

> Well, Willie pulled his dagger, but Polly grabbed her gun,
> He pulled his dagger to kill her, but Polly grabbed her gun,
> She shot him through the heart, Lord, the bullet pierced his heart,
> And his evil blood did run,
>
> In the grave he dug for Polly is where Willie fell,
> In the grave he dug for Polly is where Willie fell,
> Now he lies in Polly's grave, Lord, he lies in Polly's grave,
> He's dead in Polly's grave, but his soul burns in hell. [26]

It's a neat twist and one which returns "Pretty Polly" to the vengeance her older sister's ghost wrought on Willie three centuries ago. It took us 100 years from those beginnings to give the murdered girl a hands-on role in Willie's death and another 200 after that to produce a version of the song she's allowed to survive all the way through. Just this once though, thanks to Fred Burns, it's Willie who ends up in a shallow grave and Polly who gets to walk away. Whisper that news to the mud of a Gosport churchyard – as I did when researching this chapter – and your answer will be Molly's sigh of gratitude from far below: "That's for the murder of my baby and me".

Pretty perfect: 10 great versions of Polly's story

"Purty Polly", by John Hammond (1927). This Kentucky banjo player, the first man to put the song on disc, sets his coldly matter-of-fact vocals against a growing frenzy of banjo playing. The more evil Willie becomes, the more Hammond's picking threatens to spiral beyond control. The second his tale's done, he snaps the music to a halt as sudden and irrevocable as Polly's death itself.

"Pretty Polly", by Hobart Smith (1956). Liam Clancy recorded this fiddle instrumental during a song-collecting trip to Virginia. Smith, a veteran of his local community's square dance celebrations, was mostly a banjo player but proves equally proficient on the fiddle here. He saws up a storm, conjuring up a picture of happy dancers whirling merrily around him to the steady beat of Smith's own stamping foot.

"Pretty Polly", by The Stanley Brothers (1950). Ralph Stanley's keening, high lonesome vocals join with banjo, fiddle and stand-up bass for the song's single most essential recording. In just two-and-a-half chilling minutes, Willie moves from an apparently sincere marriage proposal to calmly stabbing Polly because he thinks she's put it about a bit. "You can't beat that mountain sound," Ralph Stanley said when he revisited the song 50 years later. This record is the living proof.

"Pretty Polly", by Sandy Denny (1967). The Fairport Convention singer's piercingly clear voice starts gently, but builds steadily in force throughout. She stares the song's violence straight in the eye, relishing the tale it has to tell, but her grim tone as Willie walks away makes it clear his damnation is utterly inescapable. Each line is decorated with a little flourish of Spanish guitar at its close as the other acoustic instruments drive things on beneath.

"Pretty Polly", by Judy Collins (1968). Collins' voice is every bit as lovely and powerful as Denny's. She takes the song much more slowly, however, lingering over its every development with a haunting sense of regret. Stephen Stills and James Burton share guitar duties, edging the track subtly towards rock territory. It's very much a full-band treatment, so folkaphobics will find nothing to scare them off here.

"Pretty Polly", by The Byrds (1968). The song's never been a chart hit, but if The Byrds had released this version as a single, it surely would have been. Packed with the band's trademark chiming guitars, it's a gloriously pretty record. Like The Kingston Trio's "Tom Dooley", McGuinn & Co's take pulls off the tricky task of including all the gore without offending even the most timid listener.

"Pretty Polly", by The Iron Mountain String Band (1975). Using rare lyrics uncovered during the band's own Virginia field research, this makes a great addition to the song's hardcore bluegrass recordings. Eric Davidson's quick, snaky banjo is the highlight, aided by reedy mountain vocals and what sounds like someone slapping their legs to serve as percussion. It's unusually frank for an American version too, allowing Willie to boast he's "going to have Pretty Polly before she gets too old".

"The Death Of Polly", by Mick Harris and Martyn Bates (1994). Hailing from Napalm Death and Eyeless in Gaza respectively, Harris & Bates offer one of the song's most original readings yet. Dotting eight of its standard verses over a generous 14 minutes, they fill the rest of their time with doomy atmospherics and wordless groans. Something of an acquired taste, perhaps, but true to the song's spirit and an intriguing glimpse into Willie's mental landscape as he leads Polly off into the woods.

"Pretty Polly": Gillian Welch & David Rawlings (1996). Rawlings takes lead vocals on this encore filmed at Johnson City's Down Home club in Tennessee – and provides a tidy little solo on his trademark Epiphone guitar too. Welch, her head bent in concentration, adds second guitar and some wonderfully eerie vocal harmonies. Here, the Stanley Brother's charge becomes even more vehement: "Your *bad* reputation is *ruining* me," Willie snarls.

"Polly's Love", by Waterson:Carthy (2009). The first family of English folk give "Pretty Polly"'s 18th century source song a rare outing.

Norma Waterson drips melancholy with every word of her vocals, while Martin Carthy's acoustic guitar provides slow and understated backing. After William's killed Polly, we get a full account of his fate on-board ship, including the "ripped him and stripped him and tore him in three" verse as Polly's ghost takes revenge.

7 - Poor Ellen Smith

"He told me there was a woman dead down there in the woods.
He said she was dead and said for me to go and see. [...] We went down
and I saw a white apron hanging on a bush and, a few yards behind it,
a woman's feet which were turned towards me. I didn't go very close,
but I saw from the blood on her that she had been shot and was dead."
Harriet Pratt, quoted in the
Twin-City Daily Sentinel of 21 July 1892.

There were two Peter DeGraffs.

Bad Peter pushed the besotted Ellen Smith away, refused to wed after making her pregnant and beat her when she pursued him. Good Peter begged Ellen to stay with him, suggested names for their child and protested his love for her even on the gallows. Bad Peter shot Ellen dead at a secluded spot on the outskirts of Winston and blackened her name in court to try and save his own skin. Good Peter took extraordinary risks to ensure her dead body was quickly found, and later tried to rescue her soul from damnation with a sunset ritual at the murder scene.

Fam Brownlee, a local historian in Winston-Salem who's studied the case, sees DeGraff's dual nature as central to its story. "I don't get the feeling that he planned to kill her," he told me when we met at Forsyth County Library. "Cold-blooded murder does not sound like Peter at all. Look what he did – he took her apron off and hung it on a branch. And then he put her body on some greenery like a bed. That doesn't square with this cold-blooded thing. I think he was probably pretty horrified." [1]

The killer and the remorseful penitent: two Peter DeGraffs. So perhaps it's only fitting that we also have two ballads telling his story. In the older of these two songs – properly called "Ellen Smith" – he's presented as an innocent man, unjustly executed for a murder he didn't commit:

178

I know they will hang me at last if they can,
But God knows I'll die as an innocent man. [2]

But in "Poor Ellen Smith" itself, which followed rather later, there's a frank acknowledgement from DeGraff that he's still got Ellen's murder on his conscience:

My days in this prison are ending at last,
But I'll never be free from my sins of the past. [3]

Ellen is treated very differently in rival versions of the song too. The two main ballads are entirely sympathetic to her, never allowing her name to appear without the adjective "poor" or "sweet" prefixing it, but there is another set of lyrics which takes a much harsher view. It's very seldom put to disc – I've found just two recordings in the past 90 years – and that's because its message to Ellen is one of Old Testament condemnation:

The men they will mourn you, the wives will be glad,
Such is the endin' of a girl that is bad,
Perhaps you're in heaven, God only knows,
But the Bible plainly tells us you've gone down below. [3]

The title "Poor Ellen Smith" now tends to be used for all these ballads, no matter which set of lyrics it's attached to. The two core songs' identical metre – chosen to fit the popular old hymn tune "How Firm A Foundation" – has allowed their lyrics to migrate freely back and forth for at least 65 years. Asking which of the two strands any particular post-war version of the song descended from almost always produces the answer that it's a mixture of both.

The truth of the killing itself is no picnic to unravel either. First, there's the fact that DeGraff was a congenital liar, contradicting himself almost from one minute to the next in whatever he told police, reporters and the jury at his trial. Winston's newspapers lapped up every word of the swashbuckling self-portrait he gave them, but even they felt obliged to add a disclaimer. "DeGraff does not tell the same story to everybody that goes to see him," the *Western Sentinel* warned. "DeGraff talks freely and leaves the impression he is a pretty big liar," added the *Union Republican.* [4, 5]

Even the court papers from DeGraff's trial can't be entirely trusted. A careless mistake on his arrest warrant, dating Ellen's murder a month earlier than it actually occurred, was slavishly copied on several later documents, including the jury's official verdict. The result is a set of trial records which cannot agree whether she died in June 1892 or July the same year.

Another complication springs from the way Ellen's story became embroiled in Winston's party politics. The *Twin-City Daily Sentinel*, which supported the Democrats, had a long-standing grudge against Forsyth County's Republican sheriff, Milton Teague. DeGraff remained at large for almost a year after killing Ellen, and the *T-CDS* used this as a stick to beat Teague at every opportunity. Unfortunately, the paper was so rabid in this campaign that it often dressed up the most casual item of local gossip as if it were concrete fact, creating a whole new layer of distortion for our own age to stumble over.

"After the initial report of the murder, they just took off after the sheriff," Brownlee said. "Every week they had an article saying, 'Peter DeGraff has been seen here, here and here in the city, and the sheriff has done nothing'. That wasn't true, because nobody had seen him and he wasn't here." The *Union Republican* – a GOP paper, of course – defended Teague by calling the *T-CDS* coverage "incessant bosh" and soon both papers were devoting as many column inches to attacking one another as they were to reporting the case. [6]

Then there's the folklore to contend with. Many accounts of Ellen's death will tell you she was mixed-race, simple-minded or pregnant when she died, but there's not a scrap of evidence for any of these assertions. The idea that her song was once banned by law for fear it would provoke a riot is equally unfounded. Because Winston is only 55 miles from Tom Dula's Wilkesboro, many myths about his execution have attached themselves to Peter DeGraff too. These were untrue even in their original form, and become all the more so when people graft them to the wrong case.

Take all these elements together, and you'll see why the story behind "Poor Ellen Smith" has become one of the most confused and misreported in the whole murder ballads genre. Let's see if we can straighten it out a bit, shall we?

Ellen Smith was just 15 years old when she left her parent's farm in North Carolina's Yadkin County for a new life in Winston. Her parents, Julius and Julia Smith, worked a patch of land owned by Julia's brother. "At that time, there's a good chance they were growing tobacco," Brownlee told me. "They're farmers, but they don't own a farm. They're poor people. Typically, if you're a girl and you're born on a farm, you at some point marry a neighbour's boy and become a farm wife. That's what your prospect was, that's what your history was, and your children did the same thing."

In the North Carolina of the 1880s, a farm girl of 15 was considered quite old enough to marry off. For poor tenant farmers like Ellen's parents, a daughter was a double liability, giving them one more mouth to feed without matching the heavy physical workload they could expect from a son.

Ellen was pretty enough to attract suitors from the neighbouring farms, but knew that marrying one of them would merely exchange one life of heavy labour for another. "Anybody that's ever been around farm life knows that it's hard work," Brownlee said. "Hard and dirty and uncomfortable and dangerous. So there's always a few that didn't want to live on the farm, and Ellen was one of those. She left and she came to the big town of Winston – the bright lights and the big city."

Winston was then a tobacco boomtown. Pleasant Hanes built his first processing plant there in 1872, followed by R. J. Reynolds founder Richard Reynolds three years later. The tobacco industry brought Winston its first railway line in 1873, helping to drive a ninefold increase in the town's population during that decade. By the time Ellen got to town in 1889, there were over 30 competing tobacco plants in Winston, which Hanes and Reynolds vied to buy up as each man struggled to outstrip his rival. With every new spurt of growth, another tranche of workers arrived in town, eager to get jobs with either the tobacco industry itself or the many satellite industries which had sprung up to serve it.

All these new people meant Winston's leisure industries were booming too. The prestigious new Zinzendorf Hotel opened a quarter mile outside the city limits in 1891, along with a host of bars and theatres in the middle of town. These were filled not only by the new workers still flooding in to Winston's factories, but also by revellers from the surrounding townships and farms who wanted a little excitement on Saturday night. Whatever your tastes – high or low – Winston could cater for them.

"In those days, virtually every important opera singer or travelling theatre company stopped in Winston," Brownlee explained. "I doubt there was ever a weekend where there wasn't some kind of vaudeville act performing here. And we had plenty of saloons too: there were five consecutive buildings on Third Street that were nothing but saloons. There would have been all these country boys cutting it up."

All this was a heady prospect for a girl who'd so far seen little but the mud and toil of Yadkin County. Ellen found a job right in the middle of town, persuading a merchant called Kenny Rose to take her on as a live-in cook at his Fifth Street home. "Her employer was obviously a young, ambitious guy because, by the time DeGraff is hanged in 1894, he has his own store," Brownlee said. "She landed a good job. She's in a respectable house, right in the heart of everything."

Ellen was so small at the time Rose hired her that he guessed her age was only 13. "The girl was not bright intellectually," he'd later recall. "She was a good hand to work but did not have good sense." Some have interpreted this as indicating Ellen had what we'd today call learning difficulties, but I'm not so sure. The language of the 1890s was far harsher than our own when discussing mental disabilities, and quite happy to speak of those affected as "idiots" or "lunatics". If that were really what Rose had in mind, I doubt he'd have expressed it with such a mild phrase as "did not have good sense".[7]

Like most farm girls at the time, Ellen would have had very little formal education. She seems to have been able to read, but still relied on others to write out her letters for her. Rather than meaning she was mentally handicapped, it's equally possible Rose meant only to convey she was naïve when she first arrived in Winston, and ill-equipped for the dangers a lone girl must face in the big city. "By 1890, Winston was a fairly sophisticated town and it was growing fast," Brownlee reminded me. "She didn't have a clue. How could she?"

It's also worth remembering that Rose didn't make his remark until 1893, which means he'd have been thinking as much of the 19-year-old Ellen as the 15-year-old he'd first hired. By 1893, the older Ellen had given him ample proof she liked the worst possible men, and that the same adventurous streak which had brought her to Winston often made her rather reckless when she got there. For a serious-minded fellow like Kenny Rose, a girl could hardly show worse sense than that.

Antoine and Ellen DeGraff brought their family from Elizabeth City to settle on Winston's western edge in 1875, when their son Peter was just six years old. He was the third of the family's four children, the others being Joseph, Mary and Lee.

Antoine and Joseph both worked as labourers, and Antoine would later set himself up as a basket maker, but Peter was already determined to find something more exciting for himself. "From boyhood he led a reckless life, drinking, gambling, carousing, sporting deadly weapons and bad habits generally," the *Union Republican* tells us. "[He had] an especial fondness for the opposite sex, and generally to their sorrow."

Taking a cue from his father's claim that the family was related to French nobility, DeGraff began dressing and behaving as if he were a roguish young aristocrat. He was not physically imposing – rather short in fact – and had quite a prominent nose, but he made up for these defects by growing a fussy little French moustache and adopting a dandyish wardrobe of sharp suits and hats. He could be both charming and eloquent when he wanted to, always seemed to have money to throw around, and liked to present himself as a bad boy. That was a mixture which many of the local girls found hard to resist, and which DeGraff was happy to exploit.

The main job he held as a young man was tending bar at a lowlife joint called Pitts' Store, where much of the alcohol he sold seems to have evaded duty. Slinging suds in a dive like that wouldn't have paid enough to fund his jack-the-lad habits, which begs the question of where the rest of his money was coming from. Aside from a few shifts at another establishment called Brindle's, there's no mention of DeGraff holding any other job in these years, so whatever extra cash he did manage to accumulate likely came from some pretty shadowy sources. Perhaps that's why he took to carrying a pair of pistols with him wherever he went.

DeGraff's first serious run-in with the law came at 17, when the police picked him up in Winston. "He was arrested for carrying a gun in town which was a serious offence in those days," Brownlee told me. "This was just like Dodge City: you check your guns at the city limits." DeGraff was convicted of carrying concealed weapons within the city's boundary and thrown in jail for 60 days – but decided to leave a little early.

On 20 March 1886, the jailer Henry Burke made a routine check of DeGraff's cell, only to discover that he'd escaped overnight by digging a hole in the wall. This had meant making his way through the cell's interior wall of bars, the plank partition behind that and finally the building's exterior brick wall. The two cellmates he'd left behind – who were both too big to squeeze through the hole themselves – had then lowered him to the ground on a rope made from knotted blankets.

"The hole was made with a small piece of timber, with which he prised out the spikes at the end of the bars and then broke them off at the next fastening," the following week's *Western Sentinel* explained. "It was found that three bars were broken and that a hole through the south side of the building was made just large enough to let a small body through. DeGraff has left for parts unknown." [8]

Where DeGraff went after breaking jail, I don't know. But by 1890 he was back in Winston – and that's where Kenny Rose's cook caught his eye.

A photo of Ellen, taken in the summer of 1890, shows a buxom, confident young woman, modestly dressed and staring directly into the camera's eye. Contemporary descriptions mention her dark curly hair, blue eyes, pretty white teeth and, as the *T-CDS* noted, "a rather sharp nose". She was "not bad looking," the same paper grudgingly conceded, "but had a rather bold countenance". [9]

Jennifer Bean Bower of Old Salem Museums puts DeGraff and Ellen's first meeting at January 1890, though DeGraff himself claimed it took place a year later. Bower's estimate is backed by Wiley Lashmit, who testified at DeGraff's trial that he'd seen DeGraff and Ellen together as early as October 1890 and that, even then, their relationship was a pretty volatile one.

Lashmit and DeGraff had been drinking together at Winkler's Saloon near the railroad tracks when they saw Ellen approaching. "She walked up and caught hold of his arm," Lashmit recalled. "He told her he would shoot her damn brains out if she did not leave. They went off [down the tracks] together and when he returned DeGraff told me he had given the damn bitch a good whipping." DeGraff himself insisted the altercation had never gone beyond a few harsh words.

One thing we know for sure is that, by July 1891 at the latest, DeGraff and Ellen were sleeping together. No matter how he blew hot and cold at Ellen, she always seemed willing to welcome him into her bed, and that's something DeGraff would not have discarded lightly. For Ellen, though, Brownlee's convinced their affair was far more than just a casual fling. "She's one of those women who sees a bad boy and decides that she can tame him," he said. "She's trying to get him to marry her at the same time she was trying to get him to quit drinking so much, gambling and chasing other women. She's got a full reform movement going on, where she's going to fix him and marry him. Except he ain't the marrying type."

It wasn't long till DeGraff was under scrutiny from the police again, this time for a double murder. John Smith and Mary Goins had both been shot dead in a drunken altercation near a Winston whorehouse called Lee Wilson's. The killer escaped, but all the survivors' descriptions of him agreed he looked a lot like Peter DeGraff.

Smith and his friend Wilburn Walker, out for a night's drinking in June 1891, tried to enter Wilson's at about 10.30 p.m., but were told to get lost. Smith hurled a few boozy insults at the place as Walker tried to steer him away, and a group of men appeared from Wilson's shouting threats to kill Smith if he didn't shut up. Their ringleader, a small, nattily-dressed man wearing a white straw hat, was waving a pistol around.

Walker and Smith tried to take refuge at the nearby home of a black couple called Henry and Mary Goins. The small man from Wilson's caught up with them as Walker hammered at the Goins' door, pushed his gun into Smith's face and snarled, "I'm going to shoot you". If Walker dared to step inside, he added, then he'd shoot his brains out too. That's when Mary Goins opened her front door to see what all the noise was about.

"Mr Walker came in and, as he did, a small man with a light suit and a hat on pressed open the door and came in also," Henry Goins told the coroner. "A big man [Smith] came in front of him. As the small man came in, he commenced shooting. When the first shot was fired, I heard my wife cry out, 'Oh!'. I looked and saw she was trembling and then I knew she was shot. At this time, Mr Walker commenced shooting too, as fast as he could pull the trigger. [...] The little man ran out of one of the two doors." When the dust settled, Walker could see that both Mary Goins and John Smith were dead. "After I saw that Mrs Goins was shot, I began to shoot at the little man," he confirmed. "The little man shot Mrs Goins." [10]

Walker never faced any charges in the affair. The small man's two companions, Will Fansler and Charles Crutchfield, were arrested as accomplices to murder, but dismissed for lack of evidence against them. That left only the small man at large. Everyone the police questioned – including the madam Lee Wilson and her girls – insisted they'd seen nothing of the incident and could not put a name to the small man's face, so he was never found. As far as the courts were concerned, the murderer remained unidentified, but no-one else was in any doubt. "Everybody in town knew it was Peter DeGraff," Brownlee told me. "The shooter was described as slight and small and dandy and quick with the gun. That's Peter DeGraff."

Three months after Mary Goins' death, Ellen discovered she was pregnant with DeGraff's child, and he began feeling the pressure to wed even more. He stalled, sometimes admitting to friends that he was the child's father and sometimes denying it. "He said her mother wanted him to marry her as it was his child, but he had not made up his mind to do it," the storekeeper D. H. Hudson recalled.

Told of his cook's delicate condition, Kenny Rose allowed her to stay on until December 1891, and then colluded with Ellen in a lie that she was leaving simply to take up a better job with a Winston railway conductor called Captain Stagg. It appears she really did live and work at Stagg's house for a while, because it was not until March 1892 that

DeGraff escorted her out of town to Mike Davis's place. "She stayed at my house for three weeks," Davis later testified. "Peter DeGraff asked my wife to let Ellen stay there while she was in a critical condition. DeGraff visited her nearly every night."

Davis, like many of the people DeGraff hung around with in Winston, was both poor and black. Both men spent their time in the parts of town where poverty and petty crime met, and I dare say DeGraff was no more welcome in white Winston's polite society than Davis himself would have been. Whether they were genuine friends is another matter. In many of his dealings with Davis, DeGraff seems to have treated him as someone whose race meant he could be bullied into any favour required.

It was also in March of 1892 that DeGraff visited Morganton, about 90 miles west of Winston, and posted Ellen several letters from there. In one of these, he asked her to name the child after him if it turned out to be a boy, or after herself if a girl. The couple's plan seems to have been for Ellen to have the baby in secret at her parents' farm in Yadkin County, and then hand it over to her mother. This was a common practice at the time: the child's grandmother would pretend it was her own, the real mother would behave as its big sister, and everyone was spared disgrace. Most important of all from DeGraff's point of view, there would be no need for him and Ellen to marry.

As things turned out, Ellen's sickly baby died very soon after birth, so none of this subterfuge with her mother proved necessary. A few weeks after the delivery, she was well enough to resume her job in Winston as Kenny Rose's cook. She was keen to pick up with DeGraff where they'd left off, but now he just wanted out.

When the semi-literate Ellen wanted to send a letter to DeGraff, she'd dictate what she had to say to a friend called Albert Van Eaton and have him write the words out on paper for her. He remembered Ellen sending DeGraff a gift of two pears and a small book at around this time, together with a note prepared in this way. In her message, Van Eaton said, Ellen had begged DeGraff not to be mad with her, but he treated this olive branch with scorn. "I still have her damn little book yet,' he remarked to Van Eaton a few weeks later.

One point of contention between the couple seems to have been that Ellen was telling people DeGraff was her dead baby's father, and he resented this information getting out. His claims around this time that Ellen had other lovers may simply have been an attempt to muddy the water over this issue of the baby's paternity. Witness after witness lined up at DeGraff's trial to describe how his attitude to Ellen soured after her return to Winston. One of these accounts came from the owners of Hudson's grocery store, where DeGraff had once allowed Ellen to pick up a few modest items on his tab. Somewhere around the beginning of June, he called in at the store and told the owners he was no longer willing to settle Ellen's bills. W. J. Hudson testified that, during this visit, DeGraff had said if Ellen didn't stop following him around, he was going to "slap her down".

A few weeks later, D. H. Hudson happened to meet DeGraff alone in the street and innocently asked where his girl was. "DeGraff said 'his girl' had gone back on him," Hudson testified. "She had been going around talking about him and he would get even with her, and if she did not stop it he would shoot her." Most of the other people who heard DeGraff utter threats like these shrugged them off as foolish posturing, but Hudson was not so sure. "Peter did not seem to be mad or bragging when he said he would shoot his girl's heart out," he said. "This was about three or four weeks before the murder." Day by day, DeGraff's resentment grew. A week or so into July, he told a bartender called C. Penry that, if Ellen ever spoke to him or meddled in his business again, he would kill her. He showed Penry a pistol which he boasted "would do the work", but the barkeep just told him to put the gun away and not to say such stupid things again.

The final threat described in court came on Saturday 16 July, when Albert Van Eaton bumped into DeGraff loitering by the side of the road with a half-pint bottle of bourbon. "He called me to go with him to the spring and take a drink of whiskey," Van Eaton recalled. "He said that his girl had gone back on him and he was going to shoot her damned heart out. He had two pistols in his pockets. He said he'd pulled out his pistol that day to shoot her, but she did not believe he would do it, and he didn't." Van Eaton acknowledged in court that DeGraff often behaved thuggishly, but said he'd still found it hard to believe he actually meant to murder Ellen. Indeed, as the two men parted that day, DeGraff made one remark which could easily have been taken as a plan to patch their relationship up. "He said he was going to write her a note," Van Eaton recalled.

At 2 p.m. the following Wednesday, 20 July 1892, Ellen closed the door of Kenny Rose's house behind her and set off for what would be her last afternoon on Earth. She stopped off at Rose's store and bought a yellow silk handkerchief, then caught the westbound streetcar along Fifth Street towards the Zinzendorf Hotel.

By this time, she may finally have had enough of DeGraff's callous behaviour towards her. One *T-CDS* story claims she'd spent the morning dictating a letter to DeGraff, getting a male friend – probably Van Eaton – to write it out for her. "She stated that she never wanted to see him again, and enclosed a handkerchief for him, which was to return a gift of one to her by him," the paper reported. I'd be inclined to dismiss this as one more example of the *T-CDS* inflating rumour into fact, were it not for Rose's confirmation that she bought that replacement handkerchief a few hours later.

DeGraff was sighted early that afternoon too. "Wednesday afternoon, about 2 o'clock, he was at Pitts' bar and purchased liquor, leaving there and going across the Hanes Field," the *Union Republican* later reported. A journey in that direction, as the paper also pointed out, would have taken DeGraff directly to the Zinzendorf's spring. [11]

Ellen was next seen by a lady called Pink McCanless, who passed by the Zinzendorf's spring at about 3 p.m. on her way into town from Salem. "I saw a man and woman lying down in the bushes," she said. "The man had his head lying in the woman's lap. The woman laughed. The man had his arms thrown up on the shoulders of the woman." McCanless was sure the woman she'd seen was Ellen. She had not seen the man's face, but was quite clear about his clothes. "The man I saw lying in Ellen's lap had on a light suit and a broad-brimmed hat," she said.

Returning home by the same route early that evening, she saw the same man again, this time walking alone from the area of pine trees where she'd first spotted him towards the spring itself. Now that he was standing up, she could get some idea of his stature, which she described as "medium-sized".

A young man called Bob Brewer, who'd come out for an evening stroll to help his supper go down, was standing at the spring just after 7 p.m. when he saw DeGraff approaching from a thicket of pine trees about 150 yards away. Brewer, who was 17, knew Peter through Lee DeGraff, his younger brother, so he stopped to chat for a while. "I sat down on a rock and he washed his hands in the spring and then in the branch," Brewer later told Sheriff Teague. "He asked me to lend him my handkerchief to wipe them. As I handed it to him, I noticed a silk handkerchief sticking out of his coat pocket, but said nothing to him about it.

"As DeGraff wiped his hands, he stood looking into the pine thickets and said, 'Bob, I have an engagement with a girl to meet her in this pine thicket tonight, and I tell you now, any girl that would meet a fellow in a place like this ought to be shot'." DeGraff was wearing a check brown suit and a straw hat that evening, Brewer continued, and when he stooped down to dunk his hands in the spring, two pistol handgrips poked into view from beneath his jacket. He told Brewer he had been drunk all day and asked with concern how he looked in the face.

A couple of hours later, just as the sun was setting, Brewer was out near the spring again when he saw DeGraff walking towards the same pine thicket he'd seemed so fascinated by earlier. Assuming he was simply on the way there to keep his date, Brewer thought no more of it.

Later than night DeGraff turned up at Mike Davis's place. He blurted out that he had killed Ellen, but said he would do anything to undo the deed now if he could. DeGraff had been drinking bourbon for three solid days now, and was swinging wildly between tearful declarations of love for Ellen and half-baked plans to dump her body in a local well. "When DeGraff came to me, he seemed scared," Davis recalled. "As we were good friends, he told me he had shot her – that first he was going to whip her and that his reason for killing her was that she had been following him about." Davis urged him to leave town, but DeGraff was adamant he would not.

Harriet Pratt, a black laundry maid at the Zinzendorf Hotel, was walking by the spring about 8 the next morning when a young white man approached her. "He was dressed in a solid brown suit of clothes with a black derby hat on," she told reporters later that morning. "He told me there was a woman dead down there in the woods. He said she was dead, and said for me to go and see, and I told him, if he would go with me, I would.

"We went down, and I saw a white apron hanging on a bush and, a few yards behind it, a woman's feet, which were turned towards me. I didn't go very close, but I saw from the blood on her that she had been shot and was dead." The woman's hat had been laid over her face, and Pratt told the white man he should remove it so they could try to identify her. "He took a small cane he had in his hand and hoisted the hat," she said. "Looked at her face good. He told me he knew the woman. He seemed uneasy and told me to put my hand on his bosom and feel how his heart beat."Pratt raised the alarm, presumably by running up to the hotel and telling someone there what she'd found. C. C. Halliard, one of the men she summoned, was next on the scene, where the same white man Pratt had seen pointed him towards the body. As he drew closer, Halliard saw the apron, flapping from its perch right by the path every passer-by would take. As one of the papers would later confirm, whoever tied it there seemed to intend it as a flag drawing attention to where the woman's body lay. Halliard untied it from the branch where it had been fixed and draped it across the girl's face to protect her from the gathering flies.

Word of the find was already spreading, and soon the *T-CDS* had a reporter there. "The woman was lying flat on her back, with her white apron spread over her head," he wrote in that afternoon's edition. "Her hands were lying by her side, her fingers slightly clutching her dress. On removing the apron, the features of a girl about 19 years old were discovered. The face was much swollen and disfigured, not apparently from any struggle but from laying on the ground a long time. The green flies had gotten in their horrible work. [...] Her dress waist was profusely stained with blood. She was lying in a patch of thick, bushy undergrowth, about ten steps from the path which divided the woods where she lay from an open field on the left."

The *Union Republican* confirmed all this in its own report, adding: "A bullet hole, plainly visible by the clothing being powder-burned, showed that the weapon that sent the fatal ball was in close proximity to her person when discharged." There was no sign of a pistol anywhere near the body, so suicide could be immediately ruled out.

The fact that the body was found outside Winston's city limits made it a Forsyth County matter, so word of the discovery was sent to Sheriff Teague. By then, someone must have already put a name to the dead girl's face and raised her links with DeGraff, because Teague immediately mentioned him as the most likely killer when he received this first message from the scene. When that afternoon's edition of the *T-CDS* went to press, the paper knew enough to use Ellen's full name in its headline, report she had been Kenny Rose's cook, mention her family background in Yadkin County and name DeGraff as the man she'd been seen with on Wednesday afternoon. Almost certainly, it added, he had been Pratt's mystery man in the brown suit too. The same story called Ellen a girl of "questionable character", which probably means they'd got wind of her illegitimate child.

Teague arrived at the crime scene with Augustus Fogle, the local coroner, at about noon. Fogle swore in a coroner's jury immediately from the dozens of onlookers already swarming round. "They had the inquest right on the spot," Brownlee told me. "Fogle takes one look, 'She's dead – we're going to have ourselves a coroner's inquest right here'. So he just corrals six guys, swears them in and they have the inquest." Pratt, Halliard and the other witnesses were still hanging around, so Fogle was able to begin questioning them right away.

Ellen's body was taken first to a nearby barn on Fourth Street, and then to Winston Town Hall for the county medical examiner Dr Dalton and his colleague Dr Galloway to carry out a formal post-mortem. This seems to have been done in an open yard, with dozens of curious spectators straining to see as the two doctors stripped Ellen's remaining clothes away and began to cut her open. None of the press accounts of what they found mention any indication that Ellen was pregnant when she died. The two doctors could hardly have failed to notice this if it were true, and the scandal-hungry *T-CDS* would certainly have fallen on any evidence of pregnancy with glee. This idea is never even hinted at anywhere in the three years of press coverage Ellen's case received, and I'm confident it entered the folklore only as a confused reference to her earlier child by DeGraff.

Dalton and Galloway concluded that Ellen had been killed by a bullet fired at point-blank range into her left side. It had passed right through her body, cutting the large blood vessel beneath her heart before exiting on the right. It was that severed blood vessel that caused her to bleed to death. Their post-mortem also provided a vital clue to finding Ellen's killer. As he cut her clothes away to examine the wounds beneath, Galloway discovered this note tucked into the front of her blouse:

> July 18th, 1892:– Dear Miss Ellen, i write this to you to see if you are mad with me. If you are let me know. Please Don't think hard of me for i have loved you all my life and can't love nobody but you, so please let me prove your love. Peter DeGraff. So I want you to come tomorrow to the spring, if you will please come and don't fail for i want you to come good by love. Want to kiss for you xxxxx as you have done before. P.D.A.f.

Galloway passed the note to Winston's chief of police John Bradford, who gave it in turn to Fogle for his coroner's jury to consider. With DeGraff's long history of petty crime in Winston, his notoriously volatile relationship with Ellen and his known fondness for guns, no-one had any difficulty believing he was the shooter. A warrant for his arrest was issued that afternoon and Teague recruited a posse of deputies to begin searching for him next day.

Just one task remained before Thursday was done. At 6 p.m., Ellen's body was bundled into a cheap pine coffin and given a pauper's burial in the town's poorhouse cemetery on North Liberty Street. Given that both Ellen's name and her family connections in Yadkin County were common knowledge by then, it's not clear why the authorities wanted to dispose of her body with such indecent haste. I can only speculate that they feared Winston's anger at DeGraff's crime may reach a point where it threatened public order, and hoped a swift burial for Ellen would help to dampen the fires.

The next few days' newspapers all named DeGraff as both the man McCanless had seen with Ellen on Wednesday afternoon and the one who guided Pratt and Halliard to her body. They reminded their readers what a bad lot Peter DeGraff was, set out his troubled history with Ellen and stressed he seemed in no hurry to discuss the matter with police. Most forthright of all was the *Union Republican*:

> It is evident from the facts, circumstantial though they be, that Peter DeGraff is the murderer of Ellen Smith. They have been intimate for a

long while. Three months ago, Ellen suffered confinement at her home in Yadkin and became a mother, the offspring living but a short while, and DeGraff was the father of the child.

The Sunday night prior to the murder, DeGraff visited Ellen at Mr Rose's and a quarrel ensued and a threat was heard on his part that he would shoot her. The note upon her person is also evidence that deeply implicates him.

DeGraff remained in Winston for four days, sleeping first in a tobacco barn, then at his parents' house and finally in Pitts' Store. Jane Pitts, the owner, later insisted she'd let him hide there only because he'd assured her he was innocent. "He said he loved her and he did not kill her," Pitts testified. "My stepdaughter asked DeGraff if he did not kill the girl. He said he did not."

Teague's men were searching for him all this time, but DeGraff seems to have had little difficulty evading them. "I saw several of the officers and my reason for shunning them was that I had heard they proposed to take me dead or alive," he later claimed. "At one time they were right on me, but I walked away unmolested. [...] The officers were nearby and I took refuge behind a pile of wood. They passed on and I got up and went in another direction."

It was only when DeGraff heard rumours that Winston's citizens were talking of organising a vigilante squad to find him and lynch him that he decided the town was getting a little too hot for comfort. He fled Winston, spending two days in Danbury before deciding to move on again. On the Tuesday or Wednesday following Ellen's death, he arrived in the small town of Mount Airy, about 35 miles to Winston's north. He would not set foot in his home town again for almost a year.

As we've seen, the Winston papers began sniping at Ellen's character from the moment her body was found. It didn't take long for that attitude to appear in ballads about her too.

The "girl that is bad" verse I quoted above first appeared on disc in 1962, but can be traced right back to the West Virginia coalfields of the 1920s. Frank Proffitt used these lyrics on his 1962 Folkways album, which has some useful sleevenotes from Anne and Frank Warner. These begin with a few basic facts about the murder, pointing out that most versions of the song centre round DeGraff protesting his innocence. "Frank's version seems more concerned with reaching a verdict on the morals of the victim!" the Warners add. [12]

Proffitt, a North Carolina native born in 1913, first knew "Poor Ellen Smith" as an instrumental. "I heard all the old folks, including my father, play it on the banjo," he says. "But I never heard the words till some boys from this country went to the coal mines of West Virginia in 1923 and came back a-singing it." Those are the lyrics Proffitt uses in his own recording, backing them with the traditional tune played on his home-made dulcimer.

Even in our own age, there's no shortage of people prepared to dismiss any female murder victim as a loose woman who'd brought about her own downfall. In the 30 years following Ellen's death, that attitude would have been even more prevalent, and it's exactly the view Proffitt's West Virginia lyrics conjure up here:

> *Many hearts she has broken, many lies she has told,*
> *It all now is ended in her bed in the snow,*
> *Poor Ellen, poor Ellen, you've wasted your life,*
> *You could have made some man a very good wife.*

Quite why somewhere at Winston-Salem's latitude would have had a July snowfall, I don't know, so let's dismiss that simply as a convenient rhyme. Whoever coined these lyrics clearly didn't know when or where the real murder took place, and probably didn't care much either. Proffitt's recording is the only trace I've been able to find of these particular lyrics – written or audio – in the 116 years following Ellen's death.

They did not surface again until the modern bluegrass band Crooked Still revived them on their 2008 album *Still Crooked*. The fact that this version's lyrics are so sparse – just 16 lines in all – creates space for the band to show off their instrumental skills. It's Brittany Haas and Tristan Clarridge's twin fiddles which come across most prominently, though banjo player Gregory Liszt gets a brief solo too. Aoife O'Donovan's sweet, pure vocals take the song at a rapid clip, while Clarridge's overdubbed cello part adds an undercurrent of melancholy. This emphasis on the song as a musical showcase pushes its narrative content well into the background – and with lyrics as judgemental as these, perhaps that's just as well.

On the day after our interview at the library, Fam Brownlee and I met in the middle of Winston to retrace Ellen's steps on her final day. We started outside the tiny tailor's shop on Fifth Street which now occupies the spot where Kenny Rose's house used to stand, and then followed the old streetcar route out towards the Zinzendorf Hotel.

I'd spent the previous evening mulling over the case in a Trade Street bar, trying to make sense of the often contradictory evidence it presented. There's no doubt DeGraff killed Ellen – he repeatedly confessed as much – but working out what transpired between them on that Wednesday afternoon in July 1892 was far more difficult.

The idea that DeGraff's note to Ellen was an entirely cynical ploy to lure her out of town so he could kill her just didn't ring true to me. Instead, the note seemed to bear a tone of desperate affection – alcohol-fuelled affection, I'm sure, and no doubt pretty transitory too, but affection nonetheless. Had Ellen really been intending to break up with him that day, as reports of the note she'd dictated suggest? How would DeGraff have reacted to that? Relief? Or anger that *she'd* had the cheek to dump *him*? I began to think of DeGraff as an extreme version of the hard-drinking, abusive husband who beats his wife one day and begs her to take him back the next. Factor in a bellyful of cheap hooch, plus the two pistols in his waistband, and it wouldn't take much for their rendezvous to end in tragedy.

As we walked along Fifth Street next morning, I asked Brownlee for his own take on DeGraff's contradictory character, and how he thought those crucial two days had played out. He began by reminding me that, although the spot DeGraff summoned Ellen to was more secluded than anywhere in Winston itself, it was far from being completely isolated. The path from the Zinzendorf ran past just ten paces away, and the spring itself was a popular picnic site for everyone in town.

"I don't see him just sitting down and cold-bloodedly saying, 'I'm going to lure Ellen out there'," Brownlee told me. "If that was what he wanted, I think he would have lured her further out. I think he was probably determined this meeting's going to be the last one: 'She is going to understand that she has to leave me alone. She's interfering with my fun!' But Ellen was a pretty stubborn person. I suspect she just dug in and said, 'No, uh uh, you have abused me. You got me pregnant. I had your baby and that baby died, and you owe me. I love you and I'm never going to leave you.'

"That 'never' is a word that a guy like Peter don't want to hear. And, of course, he always had a gun on him. Once that gun comes out, anything can happen. But I don't see him as a psychopath: I see him as a ne'er do well guy who now and again gets into a situation where a gun is the worst thing he could have on him."

This presents DeGraff as a man who was happy to talk big with his mates about planning to slaughter an inconvenient girlfriend, and stupid enough to wave a gun around in half-serious threats too – but also one who was utterly appalled when he saw that he'd actually killed her. "If he'd been that cold-blooded killer, he would have tried to hide the body," said Brownlee. "Instead, he puts it on this bed of greenery – and then he goes home, assuming there'd be a huge hue and cry because someone had found her. He thought somebody would find the body right away.

"When he got up next morning and found nobody knew she was dead, I think he felt bad about it. So he goes back and says to this laundry maid from the hotel, 'There's a dead woman back there, you need to go look'. I think he felt bad about her laying out there in the woods dead, and all he wanted was for her body to be found."

By now, we were approaching Fifth Street's western end, and found the steep incline of Glade Street cutting straight across our path. Brownlee pointed to the modern concrete offices across the street from where we were standing, and told me that was once the site of the Zinzendorf Hotel. Turning right down Glade Street, he led me to a new condominium development on the outer edge of its sharp, climbing curve. Next to the single building completed so far stretched the land earmarked for its next phase, dotted with bare-limbed trees and unkempt bushes.

Back in the 1950s, Brownlee explained, that field had been home to the YWCA's tennis courts, and as a child he'd often ridden past them with his parents in the family car. "My grandmother Estelle was a farm

197

woman and she did not drive, so now and again we would pick her up and take her into Winston-Salem to shop," he said. "Whenever our route took us up here past the YWCA, she would always point and say, 'That's where they found poor Ellen's body – right there'."

As I stood drinking it all in, I began to understand what Brownlee had meant by describing this as a spot which was both secluded and semi-public at the same time. Even though Glade Street would have been little more than a narrow cart track back in 1892, it still ran very close to the murder scene. The Zinzendorf's spot on the crest of the hill behind us looked directly down on the sidewalk where we now stood. And yet, in the fading light of evening, with all the trees and bushes here in their full July bloom, how easy it must have been to pass within yards of an innocent girl's dead body and never think for a moment that anything was amiss.

DeGraff spent the next year living quietly in Mount Airy, where he called himself H. C. Hendricks and took a job in Yokely's Sawmill. He was safely out of Sheriff Teague's Forsyth County jurisdiction there and, as no likeness of him had ever appeared in the newspapers, no-one in Mount Airy had the faintest idea who he was.

With the real DeGraff laying low, there was little genuine news to report about the case. The *T-CDS*, which supported the Democrats, responded by concocting a string of stories claiming he'd been spotted all around Winston, always behaving in a way that suggested he held Sheriff Teague in utter contempt. The paper was determined to oust the Republican Teague from office. This campaign provided the means to do so, and its thrust was always to depict DeGraff as a swaggering, romantic figure whom the paper dubbed "Winston's Jesse James".

The stories this produced never gave any specifics allowing them to be challenged or disproved, relying instead on the reporter's own imagination and whatever bit of gossip about DeGraff he'd happened to pick up in a Winston bar. What they all had in common was that they made Teague look like a fool, and often a coward too. The *T-CDS* hinted also that he was corrupt, saying DeGraff held damaging information about the sheriff and that Teague feared this information would come to light if he arrested him. Once again, they gave no supporting evidence for this, but only a steady drip of innuendo.

All this time, remember, DeGraff was actually 35 miles away, keeping his head down at Yokely's Sawmill. A man named Alredge who'd worked with him there later came forward to confirm that DeGraff had arrived in Mount Airy by 27 July at the latest, which means none of the *T-CDS*'s reported sightings of him in Winston could possibly be true.

As its name suggests, the *Union Republican* had a party political interest in Teague's future too. It wanted people to understand its brash, amoral rival was printing stuff that was simply untrue. "The sensational accounts daily appearing in the *Sentinel* to the effect that DeGraff has been seen at various places in the community drinking to the health of the sheriff in a bar-room, buying cigars at a drug store and the like are simply written, we take it, for the past-time of the editor – possibly to test the gullibility of his readers," the *Union Republican* wrote. "Certainly the statements cannot be accepted as true by reasoning people." The *T-CDS* answered this by reproducing a paragraph from the *Union Republican's* defence of Teague under the headline "Our Humorous Contemporary". [13, 14]

And so it went on. Both sides knew that the sheriff's post next came up for election in November and that the Democrats had a strong challenger called Bob McArthur standing, so neither was going to let up till the votes were counted.

The most serious condemnation of Teague came at a 22 October hustings meeting, where both he and McArthur spoke. One of the criticisms Teague faced was that he failed to go after DeGraff in person as soon as he heard Ellen was dead. He'd tried to answer this by pointing out that he was giving evidence in court that morning, and claimed Judge Armfield had denied him permission to leave. He was still holding to that story at the hustings meeting when McArthur sprang a surprise.

Producing a letter from the judge, McArthur read it aloud to the entire gathering – and it was strong stuff. Armfield's account of what had happened that morning differed very sharply from Teague's, and came within an ace of calling the sheriff both a coward and a liar. "Sheriff Teague approached me as I sat upon the bench and informed me that a woman had been killed the evening before, and that a man named DeGraff was charged with the murder," he wrote. "I told him the man must be arrested at once, and that if he wanted to go to arrest him, I would excuse him from the court. He replied that he would rather stay in court and send a deputy." [15]

Teague never recovered from this and, when the election came on 11 November, McArthur beat him by 2,857 votes to 2,496. Everyone agreed that it was his failure to capture DeGraff which cost the sheriff his job.

In his first six months of office, McArthur made no more progress finding DeGraff than Teague had done but, because he was a Democrat, the *T-CDS* was no longer inclined to criticise. All its stories about DeGraff being sighted in Winston disappeared, but by then it was too late to scrape away the layer of glamour its earlier campaign had given him. In March 1893, a Winston pawnbroker decided to capitalise on this by placing a pistol and a long knife in his window with a placard reading "Property of Peter DeGraff". Whether or not these weapons were the real thing is beside the point – the lesson here is that DeGraff was now notorious enough for even his discarded property to have celebrity value.

I began my quest to find "Poor Ellen Smith"'s original lyrics over a pot of camomile tea in Midtown Manhattan. My companion across the coffee shop table was Laura Cantrell, a former DJ on New York's WFMU and one of the best country singers America's produced in the past 15 years. Her cover of "Poor Ellen Smith" on 2005's *Humming By The Flowered Vine* is a favourite of mine, so I was keen to find out what she knew of the song's history and how she'd approached the job of making it her own.

"It was my idea to bring the song in," she explained as our waitress retreated. "I knew Molly O'Day's version of it from 1949, and I was a big fan of hers. I'd written a song about her – 'Mountain Fern' – and I found her an interesting character. She was a very traditional performer, but she was young and energetic and a woman fronting a band. There's a Henry Whitter version of 'Poor Ellen Smith' from the 1920s, and it seems like Molly's mostly comes from that – though she makes it a much more driving and up-tempo song. Her version just takes off and *goes*." [16]

O'Day was a banjo player as well as a singer, and one of such formidable skill that she's said to have once bested the great Earl Scruggs in a Kentucky banjo contest. Her music career took off in 1940 when she joined Lynn Davis & His Forty-Niners, later marrying Davis and making him a member of her own Cumberland Mountain Folks. "Molly would get out and she'd just about go berserk pickin' the banjo," Davis told an interviewer in 1997. "She really put on a show." That's borne out by O'Day's turbo-charged recording of "Poor Ellen Smith", which must have rendered her fingers a frantic blur for anyone watching in the studio. [17]

The lyrics she uses for the song start with the couplet almost every recording since has used for its own opening:

> *Poor Ellen Smith, how she was found,*
> *Shot through the heart, lying cold on the ground.*

Despite her interest in O'Day, it was not her lyrics Cantrell chose to use. Instead, she wanted to pay tribute to a different woman altogether, and this meant looking back to the song's older, original form. Versions from this older strand can be easily distinguished by their opening lines, which use the old ballad sheet trick of reminding people they need to shut up and pay attention before the story begins. One Kentucky version, collected in 1911, puts it like this:

> *Come all you kind people, my story to hear,*
> *I'll tell you what happened in June of last year.* [18]

Folklorists refer to the first of these two ballads as "Poor Ellen Smith" and the second simply as "Ellen Smith". O'Day's 1949 lyrics are the oldest version of "Poor Ellen Smith" – written or audio – which I've been able to find, but Cantrell's choice leads us all the way back to 1893. When "Ellen Smith"'s lyrics first appeared, the real Ellen had been dead for only 14 months and DeGraff was still alive.

As I said earlier, the fact that both ballads have exactly the same metre has encouraged singers to swap lines from one to the other at will. The "Poor Ellen Smith" title now tends to be applied to both ballads, no matter which set of lyrics is attached. Fortunately, we've still got that opening couplet to help tell the two strands apart. Another dead giveaway is that "Ellen Smith" often names her accused killer too:

> *I choked back my tears for the people all said*
> *That Peter DeGraff had shot Ellen Smith dead.* [2]

I said "accused killer" there, because "Ellen Smith" is also quite clear that DeGraff was not the guilty man:

> *My soul will be free when I stand at the bar,*
> *Where God tries his cases, and there like a star,*
> *That shines in the night shall my innocence shine,*
> *O Lord, I appeal to this justice of thine.*

The "Poor Ellen Smith" lyrics, on the other hand, give their narrator no name at all – but they are clear he has something terrible on his conscience:

> *My days in this prison are ending at last,*
> *But I'll never be free from my sins of the past.*

It's pretty clear from context that the sins he has in mind are Ellen's betrayal and subsequent murder.

So, let's recap. If you're looking at a set of lyrics which open by calling the audience to attention, which name Peter DeGraff and insist he's an innocent man, that's "Ellen Smith". If your version of the song opens with that "found / ground' couplet, leaves its narrator anonymous and hints pretty strongly at his guilt, it's "Poor Ellen Smith". Any version that won't slot neatly into one of those categories is either an anomaly like Proffitt's West Virginia ballad or – more likely – an intertwining of the song's two main strands. Clear? Good.

Cantrell first came across the "Ellen Smith" lyrics she used in Ethel Park Richardson's 1927 book *American Mountain Songs*. She didn't know it at the time, but Richardson actually turned out to be a relative of hers – her grandfather's great aunt to be precise – and one whose interests and career were eerily similar to her own. "She was an amateur song collector in the 1920s, when there was a big wave of interest in publishing authentic American songs from the oral tradition," Cantrell explained. "She started writing little skits using folk-related material and they were used on the radio in Chattanooga. Someone from NBC heard one of them and invited her to come here and write a programme for the network. She came and lived in New York for several years and she had a couple of different programmes here. I was definitely tipping my hat to an old relative by using those lyrics."

The other element in Richardson's verses which caught Cantrell's eye was what seemed to be a more polished "written" quality than the folk process alone can usually produce. "They're not the standard lyrics," she said. "Because she was a budding writer, I think she re-wrote it. That's my feeling, because it's done out in a more formal way than actual spoken language. If she were here to ask, I would say 'OK, now where did you actually get your version?'"

In fact, it's only our own hindsight which now makes us see "Ellen Smith" as the unusual song and "Poor Ellen Smith" as the norm. I've found nine sets of lyrics for Ellen's ballad which predate O'Day's recording, and all but one follow the "Ellen Smith" template. Even the exception – a 1915 North Carolina version called "Poor Little Ellen" – mixes some garbled "Ellen Smith" couplets with the new verses of its own. We don't know when "Poor Ellen Smith" first appeared, but its emergence as the song's dominant strand is a relatively recent phenomenon.

Back in London, I found that trying to answer Cantrell's question about the source of Richardson's lyrics led me first to a dead end. The only commercial disc of the ballad Richardson could possibly have heard is Henry Whitter's 1924 recording, but the fact that he cuts the song down to a mere ten lines (against Richardson's 40) rules him out as her source. Of the various early "Ellen Smith" lyrics song collectors have contributed, that 1911 Kentucky version is closest, but not so close we can establish a definite link.

None of the reference books or websites I consulted could push the ballad's history back past 1911, and neither could the bulging envelope of 1890s press clippings I'd brought back with me from Forsyth County's library. An online search in the Library of Congress's vintage newspaper files gave me several interesting snippets about Ellen's murder, but nothing I hadn't already known about the lyrics. It seemed the best I was going to be able to do was speculate that Richardson had transcribed a set of lyrics she'd heard sung somewhere in Tennessee and – perhaps – polished them up a little before publication. And that's what I was getting ready to write.

Then I decided to give the newspaper archives one last try.

It was starting to get dark as Peter DeGraff and John Russell picked their way through the pine trees where Ellen had died 11 months earlier. They were only ten yards from the path, but already the woods were closing in around them. DeGraff found the spot he wanted, signalled Russell to wait and then stepped forward alone. He turned his face solemnly to the sky and made the incantation in loud, clear tones. "Ellen Smith! Ellen Smith! Ellen Smith!" he cried. "If you are in Heaven, stay there! If in Hell – arise!"

They waited in silence for a moment or two and then, when it became clear nothing was going to happen, made their way back out of the woods and set off for Russell's father's house, where DeGraff planned to spend the night. They got there at about 10 p.m.

The date of this expedition was 23 June 1893, and DeGraff had been back in Winston for only a few days. Why he'd decided to risk entering the town again after nearly a year safe in Mount Airy is anybody's guess, but it may be simply that he had grown bored with the stiflingly quiet life he'd been leading at the sawmill. "If he had stayed there and kept his mouth shut, he would have been fine," Brownlee told me. "But I have a feeling that working in a sawmill anonymously just didn't suit him. Mount Airy was not a rockin' town – and he wasn't even in Mount Airy, the sawmill was about two miles outside there."

Whatever his reasons, DeGraff was back. He'd been careful, taking the southbound train from Mount Airy on 20 June, but getting off at the intermediate stop of Rural Hall so he could walk the remaining 12 miles and sneak into Winston on foot. Unluckily for him, though, someone at Rural Hall recognised him as he left the train, and sent a telegram to Sheriff McArthur saying DeGraff seemed set on returning home. At first, McArthur dismissed this telegram as just one more false lead and did nothing to follow it up. Three days later, on 23 June, a man called Frank Hines burst into his office and delivered the breathless news that DeGraff had just been seen walking through Salem's Old Town, heading north into Winston itself. Most likely, he'd arrived in town on the evening of the 20th and found somewhere to hole up undetected for the intervening three days.

Milton Livengood, a friend of DeGraff's, later testified that the two had eaten dinner together at Livengood's house on 22 June, when DeGraff insisted he was innocent of Ellen's murder. His explanation this time was that she'd been accidentally killed in the crossfire when he and a rival boyfriend began exchanging shots near the spring. How this battle could have resulted in Ellen taking a bullet at point blank range, he was unable to explain.

Frank Hines' tip convinced McArthur he should take DeGraff's return seriously, so that evening he borrowed a couple of officers from Winston's police department and the three men set off to question DeGraff's known associates and search their homes. The two officers were named Adams and Cofer. Their first break came at Charles Russell's place, where Charles admitted DeGraff had just been there. He and John Russell, Charles' brother, had left the house about 7.30 that evening on their way to visit DeGraff's parents, he said. I suspect Charles must also have let slip that DeGraff planned to spend the night at his father Gideon Russell's house, because that's where McArthur decided they should search next.

"Adams knocked at the door," the *Western Sentinel* later reported. "The house was dark. Russell asked who was at the door. 'McArthur,' said Adams. 'Come to the door, old man'. [...] After fumbling around for some time, the old man arose and made a light. At this time, Adams peeped through the window and saw DeGraff lying on the floor. The latter jumped up and ran into another room and secreted himself in a bed by covering himself up with a feather tick."

Gideon, having stalled for as long as he could, finally let the men in. Adams snatched Gideon's lamp from him and rushed past into the back room where he'd seen DeGraff go. He was in such a hurry that the rush of air blew the lamp's flame out, leaving everyone in confused darkness for the few seconds it took McArthur to relight it. Adams drew his pistol, pointed it squarely at the bed, and pulled away the skimpy mattress DeGraff had used to conceal himself. "Get up!" he demanded. "We've got you." DeGraff, who'd had both arms folded over his face, replied: "All right, Mr Adams, I'll give up. I want you to treat me like a gentleman, though!" Adams assured him: "We will not hurt a hair on your head if you act right."

"While dressing, DeGraff joked [with] the officers," the *Western Sentinel* continued. "He asked them if they came out there to arrest him with the little pistols they exhibited. 'Let me show you some,' he said, addressing the sheriff. Going to his belt, DeGraff pulled out three, two of which were about a foot long and shot .44s. The third was a .38. The officers agreed they were fine weapons and dangerous to 'monkey' with". Adams gave a fuller account of this conversation when later testifying in court. "The first thing DeGraff said was to make fun of our pistols, which he called little pop guns," he recalled. "He said 'Let me show you some pistols'. He told the sheriff to look down the barrel of one [but] this the sheriff refused to do. DeGraff said he could have gotten us if he had wanted to as he had 57 rounds. He was not frightened."

In the event, DeGraff came quietly enough. He rode into town, mounted behind Adams on the officer's horse and was locked up at Winston jail in the early hours of Saturday morning. By Monday, he had already obtained a makeshift file of some kind, and was caught trying to saw through one of his cell's iron bars with it.

DeGraff's preliminary hearing was held at Winston's courthouse on 27 June. Justice T. H. Pegram presided over the hearing, which drew a crowd of over 500 spectators to catch a glimpse of the notorious Peter DeGraff. They were "packed like sardines in a box," the *Union Republican* said. DeGraff gave every sign of enjoying this attention, and seemed to relish the prospect of speaking before such a big audience. So confident was he of his eloquence that he decided to represent himself.

"The prisoner was dressed in a bright-colored suit of clothing, sported a heavy watch chain and deported himself as if he were on pleasure bent," the *Union Republican* reported. "He appears unconcerned, laughs, winks, and seems eager to talk." The *Western Sentinel* agreed: "DeGraff's countenance was bright, his hair combed smoothly and his shoes blacked. He looked dignified and smiled frequently at his friends."

DeGraff entered a plea of "Not Guilty" and the hearing began. Dr Galloway, Pink McCanless and Albert Van Eaton all gave their testimony as I've outlined it above, establishing in turn Ellen's cause of death, the fact that DeGraff had been with her on her final afternoon and that he'd often threatened her life in the preceding weeks. Police Chief Bradford confirmed the note found on Ellen's body during her post-mortem matched other samples of DeGraff's handwriting which he'd been shown. DeGraff allowed all this evidence to pass without comment, but did not remain so sanguine when Mike Davis took the stand.

Davis described his meeting with DeGraff on the night of Ellen's death, and his evidence proved the most damning yet. "DeGraff said he killed her, and had a great mind to drag the body and throw it in Brindle's old well," Davis said. DeGraff sprang to his feet at this, and immediately began trying to browbeat the elderly Davis into recanting his statement. Evidently Davis had misunderstood their entire conversation, DeGraff claimed. All he'd really told him was that Ellen had been murdered, and that he (DeGraff) would almost certainly be blamed. Far from suggesting that he hoped to dump her body in Brindle's well, he continued, he had merely invited Davis to join him for a pleasant drink there. Wasn't that how their chat had really gone?

Davis – a black man in a white man's court remember – briefly allowed himself to be bullied into saying he may have misunderstood what DeGraff had said. This recantation, the *Union Republican* said, was made simply from fear of DeGraff. As soon as Pegram intervened to assure Davis no harm would come to him, he returned to his original account and refused all efforts to make him drop it again.

When DeGraff's turn came to speak, he said he had no witnesses to call on his own behalf, but would simply make a statement to the court. Even though Ellen was a girl of bad character, he said, he supposed they were sweethearts – but they were not engaged. He denied not only that he had written the note found on Ellen's body, but that he had ever written her any notes at all. He also denied ever having hit Ellen and said he was not the man who'd helped Harriet Pratt find the body.

"I was at home drunk when the murder occurred," DeGraff declared in court. "I went to Mosstown the night the crime was committed to get some medicine from an old coloured woman. I never heard anything about the murder until informed by a negro whom I met on the road. I went and told Mr Brindle about it. I also went over to see the woman. A large crowd was present and, immediately after I arrived, someone said Peter DeGraff did it. I turned around and went back to Brindle's."

Pegram decided there was quite enough evidence against DeGraff to justify a Grand Jury hearing, and returned him to jail until that could be arranged. He also refused to grant him bail. Back in his cell, DeGraff continued to protest his innocence to jailer James Ziglar and anyone else who'd listen. Once again, though, he never told his story the same way twice, and people quickly concluded he wasn't to be trusted. "DeGraff's evidence at the preliminary hearing and his rattle-brain assertions to those who visit him do not coincide," the *Union Republican* warned. "He babbles much and his ideas are scattering."

Soon after the hearing, the *Western Sentinel* dispatched a reporter to interview DeGraff in jail. "I am as clear of that murder as you are," DeGraff told him. "Of course, they may find me guilty and put a rope around my neck and hang me, but that will not make me guilty in the sight of God."

It was around this time that DeGraff first spun his extraordinary Men's Adventure tale about the year he'd spent away from Winston. In this, he claimed he'd roamed the US from Virginia to New Mexico in those 11 months, bedding beautiful young women, outwitting roadside vagabonds and palling around with unsuspecting lawmen the whole time. The *Sentinel* lapped up this account, printing every word for its readers' drooling enjoyment, but DeGraff later admitted the whole thing was pure fiction. "The *Sentinel* reporter came to the jail and asked me where I had been," he said. "He asked for a lie and I told him lies."

As DeGraff's trial approached, his brothers and friends set about trying to intimidate the witnesses against him. Lee DeGraff had already told Bob Brewer Peter would shoot him if he ever recounted their conversation at the spring again, but now it was Mike Davis who came under most pressure. Winston's authorities were so concerned he'd flee town that they decided to lock him up.

Nearly a month before the trial was ready to begin, Davis was thrown in jail and told he'd have to remain there till his testimony was complete. There's no suggestion he committed any offence to justify this, but the papers simply sniggered at his accommodation in "Hotel Ziglar". Davis, who insisted he'd never had any intention of leaving town, took his 26 days imprisonment philosophically. No doubt he was so used to this cavalier treatment from Winston's white establishment that it barely even surprised him anymore.

The Grand Jury's indictment against DeGraff came down in the first week of August, and Forsyth County's Superior Court scheduled his murder trial to begin on 11 August. Judge Robert Winston, who was assigned the case, knew how hard it would be to find 12 jurors who had not already made up their minds about DeGraff's guilt, so he ordered McArthur to assemble a special panel of 150 men to draw from.

When 11 August dawned, the panel and witnesses found they had to fight through a huge throng of spectators just to reach the tiny courtroom's entrance. Even with every seat in the public gallery filled, over 200 people were left crammed into the courtyard outside, devouring whatever scraps of gossip they could glean at the door and passing it back to those behind them. DeGraff's defence team, Thomas Sutton and Frank Baldwin, made a bid to forestall the trial before it had even begun. They'd discovered that John Speas, a member of the Grand Jury indicting DeGraff, was a relative of Ellen's, and argued this meant the indictment should be quashed. No indictment would have meant no murder trial either, but Winston over-ruled their motion and said the proceedings could go ahead.

Jury selection was so hotly contested that only 11 men acceptable to both sides could be found in the whole of McArthur's 150-strong panel. At lunchtime on the trial's first day, Winston ordered the sheriff to bring in another 25 potential recruits, and it was only when they'd been added to the pool that the jury's final seat could be filled. At last, the trial proper was ready to begin.

The prosecution was handled by W. W. Barber and the two partners in the private law firm Glenn & Manly. The firm was hired to aid in DeGraff's prosecution by Rosa Smith, Ellen's aunt, who'd organised a campaign to raise money for their fees. It was then thought improper for white women to attend anything as squalid as a murder trial, but Rosa insisted on being there every single day.

Kenny Rose, the Hudson brothers, Albert Van Eaton, Dr Dalton, Pink McCanless, Wiley Lashmit and Bob Brewer all gave their evidence for the prosecution on the first day, and all testified just as I've described above. John Russell was called for the prosecution too, and told the court about his recent trip to the woods with DeGraff and the necromantic ceremony they'd attempted there. DeGraff, fearing that Ellen's sins of the flesh might have sent her soul to Hell, had hoped to rescue her from that fate by casting his little spell, Russell explained.

Day two brought Mike Davis to the stand, who once again described how DeGraff had confessed to killing Ellen and talked about throwing her body down Brindle's well. Southern courts in those days considered any black person's testimony next to worthless unless supported by a character reference from someone white. The prosecution team had prepared for this, and produced two white witnesses who swore Davis was "a good honest negro". One of these witnesses was Pleasant Hanes, the tobacco baron who'd driven so much of the town's recent growth. The defence countered with its own white witnesses, who gave the opposite verdict on Davis's character, but could produce no-one who matched Hanes' authority on the other side. He was a big gun for the prosecution to pull out, and a measure of just how important Davis's testimony was thought to be.

Joseph DeGraff, Peter's brother, and John Russell both claimed Davis had admitted in private that he intended to "swear a lie" when he reached the courtroom, but neither could produce any evidence to support this. DeGraff's defence team tried to undermine Davis's credibility by reminding the jury that he had recanted his testimony – however briefly – at the preliminary hearing. Frank Baldwin snidely added that Davis had "come into court with the odour of the jail on his clothes". Glenn angrily countered: "But why was he put in jail? Because he would have been chased out of the country and prevented from giving testimony here." [19]

Harriet Pratt, who hadn't been present at the preliminary hearing, was called to the witness stand too. Finding herself in a room with Peter DeGraff for the first time, she had no hesitation in identifying him as the man who'd guided her to Ellen's body. The city's treasurer and a former registrar of deeds, called on for their experience in verifying signatures, both confirmed the note found in Ellen's blouse matched other samples of his handwriting.

DeGraff's defence team tried to muddy the water with suggestions Ellen had had other boyfriends besides DeGraff, implying it may have been one of those men who killed her. The leading candidate they produced was a man called Mr Ray, who Julia Fulton said she'd seen accompanying Ellen to a joint called Hundley's Bar on the Wednesday she died. "I have not seen him since the murder," she added. Officer Adams gave the lie to this account when he returned to the witness box and testified that Ray had actually disappeared from Winston nearly two weeks before Ellen died.

DeGraff himself did not take the stand until the trial reached its third day. This time, he admitted he'd written the note found in Ellen's blouse (having denied it before) and said he'd last seen her alive on the Monday preceding her death (as opposed to the Saturday or the Sunday, both of which he'd said before). He denied ever having told Livengood the story about Ellen being shot accidentally in crossfire, said he'd never seen Pratt before in his life and claimed he hadn't known Ellen was pregnant when he visited her in Yadkin County. Davis and Brewer both had grudges against him, so they were simply lying.

Confronted with his threats against Ellen, DeGraff replied vaguely that he "might" have said such things. The most help Baldwin could offer his client on that score was to urge the jury to view such threats as "the vapourings of an ignorant and boastful man".

"I was drinking on the Monday and Tuesday before the murder and on Wednesday was drunk," DeGraff admitted. "[But] I did not kill Ellen Smith. God in Heaven knows it. I love her to this day. I loved her as a sweetheart. I had sexual intercourse with her, but cannot say I was the only man that had similar privileges."

So far, this was just the same confused, often self-contradictory account he'd offered many times before. But the case took a dramatic turn when DeGraff was asked to describe his trip to the woods with Russell and exactly what he'd hoped to achieve there. He replied that he'd gone there in observance of an old superstition he'd picked up in Winston's black neighbourhoods. "I had always heard that, if a murderer would go to the scene of the crime, they could see their victim," DeGraff said.

There must surely have been a stunned silence in court when he uttered these words. DeGraff seemed not to realise at first that, by describing himself as Ellen's murderer, he'd undone all his earlier denials, and given the court what amounted to a straightforward confession. He'd begun his account of visiting the woods meaning only to show the jury how concerned he was that Ellen should not be unjustly damned, but ended it by placing his own head squarely in the noose.

All that remained of any substance was the two sides' closing statements, which filled all that afternoon. Glenn reminded the jury of DeGraff's note to Ellen, and compared DeGraff's washing of his hands in the spring with Lady Macbeth's "out damn spot" scene. "On Wednesday, this poor girl dressed herself in her best," he said. "She started with joy in her heart, little dreaming that in a few hours she would be cold in death. It was the blood of this poor girl that sent him to the spring." Turning directly to DeGraff, he added: "You are not so much convicted by the witnesses for the state as by your own testimony."

In his summing-up for the defence, Sutton did what he could to counter the note's damning impact on his client by pointing out that it had actually proposed a meeting on Tuesday 19 July – the day before Ellen's death – rather than on the fatal day itself. "The note was dated Monday and the appointment was for Tuesday," he reminded the jurors. "Can you jump to the conclusion that he met her on Wednesday?" This argument might have carried more force if DeGraff had not already told three different stories about when he'd last seen Ellen alive. That had created quite enough confusion to be going on with, so you can see why the jurors might not have felt like fretting over the exact dates the note carried too.

The defence closed its case by reminding jurors that all the evidence against DeGraff was circumstantial, and that they must find him guilty only if they believed the prosecution had removed all reasonable doubt. Both those things were true, but also an indication of how few other cards Sutton and Baldwin had to play. All Winston's newspapers agreed they'd represented DeGraff as well as any lawyers could, given the weight of evidence against him.

Above left: Tom Dula, shown here in his Confederate army uniform, was handsome enough to bed Wilkes County's reigning beauty. (*Unknown*)

Top right: Laura Foster's dead body, as portrayed by The Wilkes County Playmakers. (*Karen Reynolds*)

Above: Souvenir hunters have taken pieces of Tom's grave home with them. (*Author's Photo*)

Left: Laura Foster's grave prefers not to say whether it was Tom Dula who killed her. (*Author's Photo*)

Above left: Tom Dula has his own Historical Marker sign alongside North Carolina's Highway 268. (*Jason O Watson Historical/Alamy Stock Photo*)

Above right: Paul Slade visits the Wilkesboro jail cell where Tom Dula was held in 1866. (*Author's Collection*)

Middle left: Tom Dula was hanged here, at Statesville's old railway depot. "As bleak a spot as you could wish to find." (*Author's Photo*)

Left; Steve Earle recorded "Tom Dooley" for Jon Langford's *The Executioner's Last Songs* project. "He wanted it to be as evil as possible," Langford recalls. (*Manny Moss*)

Top left: "Pretty Polly" descends from an 18ᵗʰ century English song called "The Gosport Tragedy". All the trouble started with a sailor and his girl. (*Source: unidentified ballad sheet*)

Top right: Sam Cowell sang a cheeky parody of "Pretty Polly" in Victorian London's music halls. (*Unknown*)

Above: The Handsome Family at a 2010 Halloween gig. "'Pretty Polly' is like a little diagnostic manual of mental illness," says the band's Rennie Sparks. (*Greg Willis*)

Above: Kristin Hersh loves the contrast between "Pretty Polly"'s dark lyrics and its bright melody. "I like to hear inherent sadness behind a brave front," she says. (*Audrey_Sel*)

Right: St Mary's in Alverstoke. The real "Polly" was probably buried at this Hampshire church. (*Author's Photo*)

PETER DEGRAFF.

Top left: Winston-Salem brickmaker George Black was just a teenager when he joined the crowd watching Peter DeGraff's execution. (*Author's Photo*)

Top right: Laura Cantrell at New York's Radisson Martinique Hotel in March 2015. "Murder ballads give singers a meaty task to tackle," she says. (*Author's Photo*)

Above: North Carolina's Forsyth County Library has a wealth of information on the "Poor Ellen Smith" case. (*Author's Photo*)

Top left: This Lawson family portrait was taken just days before the massacre. Clockwise from top left: Arthur, Marie, Charlie, Fannie, Mary Lou, Carrie, Raymond, Maybell and James. (*Unknown*)

Top right: Marie, James, Raymond and Mary Lou Lawson all died in this room of the family's cabin. "There was blood everywhere," said one neighbour. (*Unknown*)

Above: Charlie Lawson's Christmas killing spree made front-page news throughout the US. (*Author's Photo*)

Top left: Paul Slade interviewing Lawson family expert Richard Miller in the Madison building where the family was embalmed in 1929. (*Lisa O'Donnell*)

Top right: The Lawson family's crowded grave in Browder Cemetery, North Carolina. (*Author's Photo*)

Above left: Lawson family researcher Patrick Boyles with his copy of The Carolina Buddies' 78rpm disc. "Marion and Arthur showed the crib at county fairs," he says. (*Author's Photo*)

Above right: Dave Alvin cut "Murder Of The Lawson Family" for his 2001 album *Public Domain*. "These songs served a purpose for their community," he says. (*Eric Frommer*)

Judge Winston handed the case over to the jury for their deliberations to begin at about 8.30 p.m. on day three, and DeGraff was returned to his cell to await their verdict. All his former *sang froid* had now melted away. "When carried back to the jail Monday, DeGraff cursed the witnesses and said they had sworn lies against him," the *Western Sentinel* reported. "He remarked that he 'guessed people were satisfied now'."

The jury was already seated in court when McArthur and Adams led DeGraff in to learn their verdict at 9 o'clock on Tuesday morning. Judge Winston called the proceedings to order, told DeGraff to stand, and asked the jury's foreman to announce its decision: guilty of wilful and malicious murder. Winston thanked them for their work, sentenced DeGraff to death and set his hanging day for 21 October 1893. Sutton immediately announced plans for an appeal.

Later reports in the *Western Sentinel* revealed the jury's vote had stood at eight guilty to four undecided in their first Monday evening ballot. None of the four dissenting voters had wanted DeGraff to go free, but they weren't yet fully convinced of his guilt either. By the time the jurors retired that night, two of those dissenters had switched sides, making the vote 10-2. Their 6.30 meeting the following morning made it unanimous: DeGraff was guilty of murder, and all 12 jurors said so. "I was convinced in my mind that he was the man who committed the crime," one juror later said. "DeGraff's own story about why he went to the spring with John Russell on the evening of his arrest was a bad give-away for him." The *Western Sentinel* headlined its trial report with exactly that conclusion: "HE GAVE HIMSELF AWAY".

DeGraff took the news of his fate stoically as he sat in court. "Although thousands of eyes scrutinised his every movement, he received the fatal word without a tremor," the *Union Republican* reported. "DeGraff received the sentence as he did the verdict, with seeming indifference. If affected, he did not show it." Already, the paper was looking forward to the entertainment DeGraff's hanging looked likely to provide. "He bids fair to die game," it said.

My return to the newspaper archives, this time via an online subscription service, produced a stack of over 80 Ellen Smith stories from the Winston newspapers which had escaped Forsyth County Library's rather spotty microfilm files. I always prefer to read stuff on paper, so I printed them all out and began working through the 1890-1895 time period I'd selected in chronological order. Most of the clippings added no more than a single additional fact or a dash of enlivening colour to what I knew already, but I ploughed on regardless.

I was about two-thirds of my way through the stack and just starting to slip into autopilot when I spotted a three-line announcement hidden away at the bottom of page 2 of the *Western Sentinel's* 7 September 1893 edition. "In a few days, the *Sentinel* will publish some verses by Peter DeGraff on the death of Ellen Smith," it promised. Verses by DeGraff himself which had escaped the attention of every other researcher? Suddenly I was wide awake.

My guess is that the paper's using the word "*Sentinel*" there as a collective term to cover both itself and its sister paper the *Twin-City Daily Sentinel*. The *Western Sentinel* was a weekly, so saying the verses would run "in a few days" suggests the daily *T-CDS* was where they'd first appear. I've been unable to confirm that, however, because no newspaper archive I've found has issues of the *T-CDS* from that particular month.

Fortunately, the *Western Sentinel* often recycled *T-CDS* copy in its own pages, and I found the verses reprinted in its 14 September edition. But I also discovered that the paper's hurried teaser had slightly misunderstood what was coming up – perhaps because of some minor confusion between the two different titles. The verses, it turned out, were not credited to DeGraff, but to a man called Charles Pepper who was locked in Winston jail with him while DeGraff awaited trial. The *Western Sentinel* ran them in full, and here they are:

THE SONG OF PETER DEGRAFF
Come all you kind people my story to hear,
And what happened to me in June of last year,
Of poor Ellen Smith and how she was found,
Shot through the heart lying cold on the ground,

'Tis true I'm in jail a prisoner now,
But God is here with me and hears every vow,

POOR ELLEN SMITH

Before him I promise the truth to relate,
And tell all I know of Ellen's sad fate,

The world of my story has long known a part,
And knows I was Ellen's own loving sweetheart,
And while I would never have made her my wife,
I loved her too well to take her sweet life,

I saw her on Monday before the sad day,
They found her poor body and took it away,
My heart was quite broken, I bitterly cried,
When friends gently told me how Ellen had died,

That she had been killed never entered my mind,
Till the ball through her heart they happened to find,
O, who was so cruel, so heartless and base,
As to murder sweet Ellen in that lonesome place,

I saw her that morning so still and so cold,
And heard the wild stories the witnesses told,
I choked back my tears when the people all said,
That Peter DeGraff had shot Ellen Smith dead,

Half crazy with sorrow I wandered away,
And lonely I've wandered for many a day,
My love in her grave, her hands on her breast,
While blood-hounds and sheriffs would give me no rest,

They said I was guilty and ought to be hung,
The tale of my crime was on every tongue,
They got their Winchesters and hunted me down,
But I was away in Mount Airy town,

I stayed off a year and prayed all the time,
The man might be found who committed the crime,
So I could come back and my character save,
'Ere the flowers had faded on poor Ellen's grave,

I came back to Winston my trial to stand,
To live or to die as the law may demand,
McArthur may hang me – my fate I don't know,
But I'm clear of the charge that is laid at my door,

Ellen sleeps calmly now in the lonely graveyard,
I look through the bars and God knows it's hard,
I know they will hang me at last if they can,
But God knows I'll die as an innocent man,

My soul will be free when I stand at the bar,
Where God tries his cases, and there like a star,
That shines in the night shall my innocence shine,
O, Lord, I appeal to this justice of thine.

The paper added an editor's note saying its verses had been "composed and written in jail by Charles Pepper, for his friend, Peter DeGraff". Pepper, I learned after yet another dive into the archive, was arrested in July 1893 for stealing an elderly mule from a Kernersville man named W. W. Fulp. DeGraff and Pepper were in Winston jail together for about a month – perhaps even in the same cell. In its next edition, the *Western Sentinel* revealed that one of its reporters had just visited DeGraff in jail and given him a copy of the paper containing this song. "He returned thanks for them and began reading the verses written by his friend Charles Pepper," the paper's man crowed.

Whether DeGraff had any hand in writing these lyrics is something we'll never know. He was certainly smart enough to use the newspapers to try and win public sympathy for himself, and may have hoped a song like this would advance his cause. Even if we assume Pepper was the sole author, though, the verses' origins make it very clear why this "Ellen Smith" strand views DeGraff so kindly. It would be only natural for Pepper to take DeGraff's version of events at face value and base his verses on that alone. Many of the song's lines are very close to DeGraff's own words, as these two examples demonstrate:

DeGraff

"I also went over to see the woman. A large crowd was present and immediately after I arrived someone said that Peter DeGraff did it."

Pepper

"I saw her that morning so still and so cold / And heard the wild stories the witnesses told / I choked back my tears when the people all said / That Peter DeGraff had shot Ellen Smith dead."

DeGraff

"Of course, they may find me guilty and put a rope around my neck and hang me, but that will not make me guilty in the sight of God."

Pepper

"I know they will hang me at last if they can / But God knows I'll die as an innocent man."

Both those DeGraff quotes appeared in the *Western Sentinel*, which suggests that Pepper was using the paper's coverage as one of his sources. I wouldn't put it past the rag to commission a song like this at its own initiative and supply Pepper with the clippings he needed to write it. The *Union Republican* later complained that the *Sentinel* titles had turned DeGraff into "a martyr rather than a criminal", so it's no surprise to see that attitude leaking into Pepper's verses too.

Beyond the odd minor rephrasing, there's nothing in any version of "Ellen Smith" which doesn't ultimately derive from Pepper's composition. Many of its lines made their way directly into the earliest versions of "Poor Ellen Smith" too, where they remain a fixture to this day. Cantrell was evidently right to detect a more formal "written" quality in these lyrics – though now it seems we have Pepper rather than Richardson to thank for this.

It's very rare to be able to say you've found the single original version of a folk ballad dating back this far – let alone one which still has its author's name attached – but I think that's a reasonable enough claim to make here. Pepper's lyrics were already in print just 14 months after Ellen was killed, and widely circulated long before DeGraff's execution. It's fair to conclude his verses were the spring from which all later ballads about the case have flowed, and this book's publication marks the first time they've been unearthed in over a century.

"What a score!" Cantrell said when I e-mailed her a copy of Pepper's song. "Ethel's lyrics most certainly come from this version, almost verbatim, and make me wonder if there was actually a performed version of this song that hewed to these lyrics. It would be very unlikely that Ethel would have seen this article, unless the lyrics were reprinted regionally, which I guess is possible." [20]

It's certainly true that DeGraff's trial and punishment was reported from coast to coast in the US – I have clippings about his execution from both the New York *Sun* and San Francisco's *Morning Call* – so there's no reason ballads about him couldn't have travelled just as far. The "Ellen Smith" verses found by Kentucky song collectors in 1911 contain several verses which are almost identical to Pepper's, and others composed simply by swapping his couplets around into new combinations.

There's good evidence the 1911 Kentucky singer learned the words by hearing them rather than reading them. He or she sings "Mount Assy" for "Mount Airy" and "Macaulches" for "McArthur". These mistakes could easily have been avoided if transcribing a set of written lyrics, but arise far more easily when trying to remember a song you know only from someone else's performance. Most likely, it's this oral transmission of Pepper's written verses which brought the lyrics to Richardson's ears – and hence to Cantrell for her 2005 recording.

She tackles it as a train-beat shuffle, her own bell-clear vocals backed by Jon Graboff's mandolin and Kenny Kosek's fiddle. "I'd got Neko Case's version and Molly O'Day's in mind when we recorded it," she told me. "But somehow I twisted round the melodies. It's a familiar tune that's not quite a standard, which gives you a little freedom to adapt it. I felt I wanted to do it as a traditional song, but if we ended up with some little corners that were bent differently than in other versions, that would be OK. It can be a living thing."

For Cantrell, the element that distinguishes Ellen's ballad from many of the other songs in this book is its matter-of-fact tone. "It's not as interior as some of the other murder ballads can be," she said. "The character of the murderer is talking about the fact of what happened: there's a plainness to it. There's some remorse, but not quite a total acknowledgement. It's more: 'This is what happened'.

"As a singer, you get to convey many different things in a murder ballad that you don't get to do in a love song or any other kind of song. There's this touchstone of deep, ugly stuff. To sing about that can be an interesting, exciting thing to do because you're conveying a lot of that information just with the voice. It's a meaty task for a singer to tackle."

It follows that, no matter how beautiful the musical backing is on any murder ballad recording, the song itself must retain the ability to unsettle its audience. Cantrell's version certainly had that effect on one member of her own family. "My daughter is 8½, and she loves the *Humming By The Flowered Vine* album," she told me. "When I was on tour, my husband would put it on iTunes so she could listen to it at bedtime when Mom wasn't there. She was doing that quite contentedly until she finally digested the lyrics to 'Poor Ellen Smith', then she brought in the iPad and said, 'Daddy, I don't like that song! Take it off.' It's about something quite brutal, so I understand how that can be a tough thing."

DeGraff's application for a new trial went in at the beginning of October 1893, meaning his 21 October execution could no longer go ahead. Quite a few people missed the news of this postponement and turned up in Winston for the hanging on the 21st anyway, only to go home disappointed.

On 26 November, McArthur brought DeGraff news that the state's Supreme Court had refused to consider his appeal. "As soon as the words fell from the sheriff's lips, the prisoner began cursing everybody who was in any way connected with his trial," the *Western Sentinel* reported. "He acted like a wild man and said he hoped a cyclone would pass over the town and kill all his enemies. He used horrible oaths and said that witnesses were employed at the trial to swear his life away. The sheriff and the jailer were horrified at DeGraff's language." DeGraff continued his uproar all night, quieting down only when Ziglar threatened to chain him to the floor with a gag in his mouth. [21]

When DeGraff's mother came to visit him a few days later, he told her he planned to cheat the gallows by killing himself before he could be hanged. Ziglar responded by confiscating DeGraff's razor and hiring a man called Vickers to stand suicide watch over him every night. The *Union Republican* reminded Ziglar to watch out for anyone smuggling a dose of poison into DeGraff's cage, in case he was allowed to kill himself that way. Later rumours that he'd succeeded in poisoning himself turned out to be a misunderstanding about the sleeping draught Ziglar had been giving him each night since the murder trial's conclusion. "Peter is as far from committing suicide as I am," Ziglar assured reporters. [22]

Even Antoine DeGraff now accepted his son was guilty of Ellen's murder, but clung to hopes that the boy had been so drunk when he pulled the trigger that he'd barely known what he was doing. Joseph and Lee DeGraff, Peter's two brothers, organised a petition asking state governor Elias Carr to commute his death sentence to life imprisonment. They found there was very little public support for this idea, however, and Carr remained unmoved. Dalton and two other doctors examined DeGraff in his cell and pronounced him sound in both mind and body, ruling out any chance of using what one paper called "the insanity dodge" to avoid execution. Sutton wrote to his client saying they had now exhausted every measure possible and telling him he must simply accept his fate. [23]

On 2 January 1894, Carr signed DeGraff's death warrant and announced the hanging would take place on Thursday, 8 February. DeGraff responded with an open letter to Winston's people, which he sent to the papers for publication about a week after Carr's announcement. This extract will give you its flavour:

> I know I have got to die sometime, but to die for the murder of Ellen Smith, God knows I will die an innocent man, and some bright day the people will find my words to come true, when you will grieve over the days you treated me so cruel, but my blood will be on your hands and in that great day of accounts you will have to stand before the great judge of heaven and earth to answer for all you did to me.

Even DeGraff himself, it seems, was now recycling lines from Pepper's ballad – "God knows I will die an innocent man" – but this bid to win public sympathy did him no more good than the petition campaign had done.

By 25 January, anticipation of DeGraff's hanging had reached such a pitch that even the arrival of his gallows rope from Richmond made a page 3 story for the *Western Sentinel*. "It is 25 feet in length and a little over one half-inch in size," the paper breathlessly reported. "The knot is already tied and greased ready for use." The same issue reported that DeGraff had told an anonymous visitor that he now blamed no-one but himself for his fate. "I have forgiven everybody and do not fear to die at all," the paper quoted him saying. "But I am sorry I didn't draw my pistol and shoot the officers down." Asked by reporters what had become of his vow to kill himself before reaching the scaffold, DeGraff replied: "I may have said something of the kind when I was excited. To tell the truth, I hardly know what I have said or done". [24, 25]

He'd turned down every previous offer to have a clergyman visit him but now, with the gallows just two weeks away, asked to see the Baptist minister H. A. Brown. Reverend Brown agreed to accompany DeGraff on his walk to the scaffold, but refused to baptise him on the grounds this sacrament was not needed for salvation. I wonder if his real objection may have been that DeGraff was still refusing to admit he'd killed Ellen. Without that admission, how could Brown accept his professed repentance was genuine?

A barber called at the jail to give DeGraff a haircut and shave on the evening before his death, and he was given a new black suit at the county's expense. A group of four or five religious young men visited his cell at about 8 p.m., praying and singing hymns with him there. For the sake of his own soul, they urged DeGraff to make a clean breast of killing Ellen before he died, but once again he refused. "Death has no more horror for me," he assured them. "I am going straight to my God."

When the time came for bed, Ziglar offered DeGraff a second dose of his usual sleeping powders, thinking the first might not be enough to help him doze off on such a terrible night. "Peter replied that the powders were quite strong and he was afraid they would put him to sleep so he would never awake," the *Western Sentinel* reported. "He added that he was not ready to die: that he wanted to live as long as he could."

Next morning, the weather was appropriately grim, shrouding the whole of Winston in dark clouds and rain. DeGraff got up at about 8 a.m. and picked at his breakfast as best he could. The execution was not scheduled till noon, but already big crowds were gathering outside the jail to catch a glimpse of him as he left for his final ride. Every road around Winston was clogged with wagons, buggies and carts carrying eager spectators towards the roped-off scaffold in Liberty Field.

DeGraff was dressed and ready when his parents and younger brother Lee arrived at the jail for their last visit. He told them he was resigned to his fate, and the whole family reassured each other they'd one day meet again in heaven. Better a quick death today than a lifetime rotting away in prison, Antoine said. Ziglar refused Ellen DeGraff's request to enter her son's cell, but did allow her to kneel and pray in the hallway outside its bars. There were many tears.

McArthur arrived to escort DeGraff to the gallows at 11.10 a.m., and he emerged from his cell with a Bible clutched in his hand. "Peter was perfectly cool, and walked down the prison hall shaking hands with each inmate, both white and colored," the *Western Sentinel* reported. "He urged them to live as to meet him in Heaven. [...] Tears trickled down the cheeks of the hardest criminals as they shook hands with him for the last time." DeGraff himself broke down only when he reached George Brown, who had recently been arrested with Lee DeGraff on charges that the two of them robbed a Stokes County farmer.

Pausing at the jail's exit, McArthur and DeGraff were joined by Ziglar, Winston's Mayor Garland Webb and the *Sentinel* reporter. Drawing a deep breath, the five men threw open the jail doors and stepped outside towards the waiting carriage. I imagine a sudden surge of noise as the doors flew open, two lines of hard-pressed coppers struggling to keep a clear corridor through the raucous mob outside and a ten-yard sprint to safety. McArthur had chosen a closed carriage to conceal DeGraff from sight during the journey, but few people can have been in any doubt who it contained. The dozens of jeering spectators who followed it as it pulled away from the jailhouse took care of that.

Among the crowd already waiting at the roped-off scaffold was a 14-year-old boy called S. S. Kinney, who lived near the Winston railway yards on Belew's Creek Road. "I was a curious boy and took it all in," he told a reporter in 1975. "They built a scaffold especially for the hanging. I wanted to see it. I don't think there was anyone there with me, but I walked all the way out there. It was a long way, and I recall it was a rather cool day. I guess I was about 30 feet from the scaffold. Really I was just a kid in the crowd." [26]

George Black, who went on to become one of Winston's biggest brick manufacturers, would then have been about 17. He was in the crowd at DeGraff's hanging too, and later shared his memories of it in an interview with Brownlee. "He and his brother were among the first to arrive," Brownlee wrote in 2015. "A deputy told them to stay behind the rope. 'If we catch you on the wrong side,' the deputy said, 'we'll put you up there with him'. George called the gallows 'the stage' because this was a show, like Old John's Circus, or Buffalo Bill's Wild West. Not far from the 'stage', and not far from where Ellen Smith was buried, was a freshly-dug grave and, next to it, a coffin covered by a quilt." [27]

Most newspapers put the crowd that day at about 6,000 people. "A number of the library's blog readers have commented on the size of the crowd at the hanging and the fact that people brought picnic lunches," Brownlee told me. "The *Union Republican* mentions that the conduct of the spectators was reprehensible. They were laughing, and clowning around."

DeGraff climbed the scaffold steps shortly after noon. He was joined on the crowded platform by McArthur, Ziglar, Police Chief Bradford, Officer Adams and two clergymen: Reverend Brown and Reverend Lutz. "The rope was around his neck," the *Western Sentinel* reported. "DeGraff looked rather pale, but appeared remarkably calm. He raised his hat and bowed to the crowd. He took a seat between the sheriff and Reverend H. A. Brown. He held a small Bible with his hat in one hand."

McArthur was first to address the crowd. He read DeGraff's death warrant aloud, with the condemned man attending closely to every word. Reporters noticed DeGraff nervously twitching his fingers as McArthur spoke, but could detect no emotion on his face. After reading the warrant, McArthur reminded everyone attending that this was supposed to be a solemn occasion. "Those who have come out here through mere curiosity should take it as a warning," he said, adding that anyone who caused a disturbance would certainly be arrested and thrown in the county jail. He was forced to repeat that threat several times before the day's events were done.

After a brief religious service from Brown and Lutz, DeGraff himself stepped forward. The crowd fell into silent anticipation. Speaking rapidly, but still showing no sign of nerves, he began with a reminder these would be his last words on Earth, and urged everyone listening to follow a more virtuous path than he himself had trod. Then he got to the meat:

> That thing you call corn liquor, cards, dice and other games of chance, pistols and bad women are the things that have brought me to this place – to stand on this scaffold. White and coloured, I pray you to hear my words. I have kept back for months what I am going to tell you. God told me to keep it back. Yes, I shot that woman. I was drunk at the time. I put the pistol to her breast and fired.
>
> The only words she said after I shot her were: "Lord have mercy on me". I stand here today to receive my just reward. I again say to the people here, beware of bad women and whiskey.

There was more, but I doubt most people were listening. "I can still recall the crowd gasping when he said: 'I killed Ellen Smith'," Kinney told his interviewer 81 years later. DeGraff, who had dramatised his own story all his life, timed this final reveal to perfection, delivering it to the largest, most attentive audience he could wish for. When I mentioned to Brownlee that it sounded almost as if DeGraff was enjoying himself at that moment, he replied: "That's what George Black said too. He said it was like watching an actor up there."

DeGraff stepped back to let Brown deliver a final blessing, shook hands with everyone on the platform, and then handed the hat and Bible he'd been carrying to Lee. The black hood was pulled over his head, the rope secured and, at precisely 12.52, McArthur pulled the trap. DeGraff's neck was broken by the drop and brain death would have followed two or three minutes later. Someone must have been measuring his zig-zagging heartrate as he died, because next morning's *Western Sentinel* was able to give a minute-by-minute breakdown: 48 beats in his first minute after the drop, 90 in the second, 68 in the third, 92 in the fourth and so on. The paper was so proud of having these figures that it carried them in the story's third paragraph, adding that DeGraff's heart took seven minutes to stop altogether. If you wanted to be sure he'd suffered, here was your proof.

POOR ELLEN SMITH

DeGraff's body was taken down, placed in the waiting coffin and buried in the same paupers' ground where Ellen had been laid to rest 18 months earlier. A few days later, DeGraff's mother revealed that he'd given her a private note two days before the hanging, and that this had also contained a confession of Ellen's murder. "Dear mother," he wrote. "I can't fool you any longer. I did kill that girl but I was drunk when I did it."

The version of "Poor Ellen Smith" we know today has its roots in Molly O'Day's 1949 recording of the song, which everyone from The Country Gentlemen to Mac Wiseman and Laura Cantrell have acknowledged as a key influence. Several versions in this strand had established themselves in the tradition long before O'Day came along, but these are the five stanzas she chose to use:

> Poor Ellen Smith how was she found,
> Shot through the heart lying cold on the ground,
> Her clothes were all scattered and thrown on the ground,
> The blood marks the spot where poor Ellen was found,
>
> They picked up their rifles and hunted me down,
> They found me a-loafing all around the town,
> They picked up her body and carried it away,
> And now she is sleeping in some lonesome old grave,
>
> I got a letter yesterday I read it today,
> The flowers on her grave have all faded away,
> Some day I'll go home and stay when I go,
> On poor Ellen's grave pretty flowers I'll sow,
>
> I've been in this prison for 20 long years,
> Each night I see Ellen through my bitter tears,
> The warden just told me that soon I'll be free,
> To go to her graveside 'neath that old willow tree,

My days in this prison are ending at last,
I'll never be free from my sins of the past,
Poor Ellen Smith how was she found,
Shot through the heart lying cold on the ground.

I'm not suggesting she actually wrote these words – her own discs credit them simply to "Trad" – but I am going to call them O'Day's verses just for the sake of convenience. By my reckoning, nine of the 20 lines are taken from Pepper's "Ellen Smith" lyrics, sometimes with a light rephrasing, but always keeping his ideas and images intact. The new elements include the hint of sexual violence in verse one, the killer's desire to visit Ellen's grave and that "sins of the past" couplet I mentioned earlier. By distilling Pepper's 48 lines to less than half that length, the new song gains the same mystery and concision "Knoxville Girl" and "Pretty Polly" achieved in cutting their own source ballads.

It's also careful to eliminate any place names in the song which listeners outside North Carolina might find confusing. Pepper's mention of "Mount Airy town", for example, is cannily replaced by a generic reference allowing listeners to imagine the tale playing out anywhere they please. A Kentucky strain of the song, dating back at least as far as 1911, tackles the same issue by inserting a reference to the state's most brutal prison:

Oh they sent me to Frankfort, I've been there before,
I wore the ball and chain till it made my ankles sore.

I've also heard a version which replaces "Mount Airy" with "Wilkesboro town", a reference which seem to have muscled its way into the song from "Tom Dooley". Folklore from the Tom Dula story often clings to DeGraff too, including the notion that he composed and performed his own ballad while sitting upright in a coffin on his way to the gallows. Pete Steele, a Kentucky banjo player of the 1940s, would introduce "Poor Ellen Smith" by calling DeGraff "a boy that took the punishment for some other man's crime", and that idea's imported from myths about Tom Dula too. [28]

O'Day's strand of the song has produced recordings by The Stanley Brothers, Flatt & Scruggs, The Kossoy Sisters, Wilma Lee, The Kingston

Trio, Neko Case and a host of others. Some sneak in Pepper's "innocent man" couplet as a crafty addition, but even then it's clear they're working to the O'Day template. "It's a cool song," Brownlee said of this version. "'Poor Ellen Smith, how was she found? / Shot through the heart laying cold on the ground' – they've got you hooked right there. The thing about her clothes being scattered around, that's sort of true because of the apron Peter took off her. But it was hung neatly on a branch – he didn't just take it off and throw it."

Although the apron gives these lines a technical justification, their real job is to suggest that Ellen was found not only dead but half-naked too, and hence bring a touch of sexual titillation to the song. It serves also as an oblique reminder that Ellen's body really was stripped in public during her post-mortem, and that the *T-CDS* tried to stir up a minor scandal over this. Similarly, I can never hear verse four's reference to DeGraff visiting Ellen's grave without wondering if it began as a nod to his attempted necromancy in the woods. Both trips demonstrate his concern for the murdered girl, after all, and both require him to return home so he can visit a spot associated with her death.

No two performers phrase the latter half of "Poor Ellen Smith"'s opening verse in quite the same way, and it's interesting to see how each navigates the mixture of sex and violence it presents. Wilma Lee goes for the same frank combination O'Day uses. Both The Stanley Brothers and Flatt & Scruggs are happy to mention the blood, but soften the couplet's sexual innuendo by saying Ellen's clothes were "ragged" rather than "scattered". For the latter, it's only her curls that are on the ground. The Kossoy Sisters' 1956 recording with banjo player Erik Darling drops the sexual element altogether, replacing it with an extra measure of violence:

> *Her body was mangled and all cast around,*
> *And blood marks the spot where poor Ellen was found.*

When The Kingston Trio came to cover "Poor Ellen Smith" in 1962, it was a selection of The Kossoy Sisters' verses they used. They had no problems singing about Ellen's body being inexpertly chopped up and distributed throughout the surrounding area, but prissily removed the mention of blood in the next line. In their version it's "X marks the spot". As with their earlier recording of "Tom Dooley", the group's relentlessly cheerful delivery sits oddly with the song's gruesome content. Neko Case closed this 50-year circle with her own 2002 recording of The Kossoy Sisters' lyrics, which restores the "blood" reference in its full glory.

Irene and Ellen Kossoy's own background belies the hillbilly performance they give the song. "I love them," Brownlee said. "You listen to it and it sounds like they're up in the mountains somewhere, but nothing could be further from the truth. They were born in New York City, lived in Greenwich Village. There's not an authentic bone in their bodies, but they got the sound! And Erik Darling? He ain't no Tennessee boy neither."

It's only fitting that this pivotal recording of the song should have been made by three people with entirely urban backgrounds. Ellen's real story played out in the big city, not in the mountains and hollows its musical setting suggests. It was Winston's role as an 1890s Gomorrah which made her and DeGraff the people they were, and ensured their collision was inevitable. Who better to document a hard-boiled tale like that than a couple of dames from New York and their Baltimore henchman?

The Bible which DeGraff handed to his brother Lee on the scaffold disappeared from view after the hanging, and did not surface again till 2009. The trail to its discovery began with Randy Furches, a Winston-Salem musician who also happens to be DeGraff's great great nephew.

Furches is related to his city's most notorious killer through Mary DeGraff, Peter's sister. She was Randy's great grandmother on his mother's side, which makes DeGraff his great great uncle. Furches first learnt of these family links in 1979, when the *Western Sentinel* ran an 85th anniversary piece on DeGraff's hanging. Furches' mother, Mildred, showed him the story and told him DeGraff was his relative. Then just 24, Furches took little interest in the revelation. "At that age, I was not interested in history," he told me. "I was interested in girls and college and drinking and whatever else I could get into." [29]

That 1979 conversation was the only time Furches had heard any of his relatives mention the case. "It was never, ever talked about," he said.

"The DeGraff side of the family vacated Winston after Peter's hanging, and moved the entire family to an area outside Winston called Colfax. My Mom mentioned that, on some Sundays, her father would put all the kids in the car and take them out to Colfax to see their DeGraff relatives. She remembers playing with them, but nothing was ever said about Peter DeGraff or why the DeGraffs lived in Colfax now."

That's how things stayed till 2007 when Furches, by then a keen amateur musician, first discovered that his ancestor's story had been told in song. "I came across a version of 'Poor Ellen Smith' by Peggy Seeger," he said. "I listened to it and it started coming together for me – how the story related to me and what needed to be done. I was filled with a desire to research it, to find out more about it."

Another thing Furches uncovered by questioning his family was that Antoine DeGraff, a first-generation immigrant, had insisted his children spoke only French in the family home. "No-one else spoke French," he said. "Peter's family was isolated, separated from the start. I'm sure he had problems learning in a bi-lingual way." When he came to record his own version of Ellen's ballad in 2009, Furches was able to build details like this into the new spoken-word verses he added to the traditional lyrics.

I asked Furches if he'd emerged from his research feeling a kind of responsibility to speak on DeGraff's behalf. "Yes, because his song was a fraud," he replied. "It was designed as a ruse to get him out of jail. It told a bunch of lies. I thought, 'To make things right, he's going to have to tell the truth'. So, after each verse of the song that was a lie, I spoke a verse of truth: Lie, truth, lie, truth, that was the set-up of the song."

Here's how Furches' new lyrics have DeGraff sum up the couple's last few days and his final words from the gallows:

Ellen and I grew closer but I was a failure because,
I chose not to leave behind the scoundrel I always was,
Something must have happened, I guess I wasn't good enough,
We parted in bitter anger and I walked out on that love,

I had to see her again, but I feared that she'd say no,
So I sent her a pleading letter and off to Hanes Park we did go,
I shot her dead, I admit it, hear my dying plea,
Drinking and friends can't save you, love's the only source of liberty. [30]

Furches posted the song online, added it to his live set, and performed it one night at a Winston-Salem rock venue called The Garage. Ellen's story, he discovered, still had enough juice for the *Winston-Salem Journal* to print a piece about this new addition to her canon. Earsley Fulton, another descendent of Mary DeGraff, read that story and phoned Furches' mother to say she now owned Peter's Bible, which had made its way to her via Lee DeGraff's grand-daughter Edith. Furches visited Fulton at her home near Winston-Salem to see it for himself.

Holding the Bible in his hand, he saw Peter DeGraff's pencilled signature on its flyleaf, dated 1893, and a handwritten inscription reading, "This is for God that sav my sol". The mis-spellings there echo the ones on DeGraff's note to Ellen, and provide one more bit of evidence the Bible really was his.

For Furches, the Bible's inscription was heartening confirmation that even a man like DeGraff could find salvation on the very brink of death. "I felt vindicated," he said. "I saw my great great uncle's writing and I knew what had happened. He accepted Christ, and wrote in this Bible which he carried to the gallows. Then he preached a sermon to the 6,000 people watching – preached a sermon with a noose round his neck! Can you imagine?"

Hunting them down: 10 great versions of Ellen's story.

"Poor Ellen Smith", by Dykes' Magic City Trio (1927). Not the song's first recording – Henry Whitter cut that three years earlier – but easily my favourite of the three 1920s versions that survive. John Dykes' toe-tapping fiddle pattern alternates with vocals from Hubert Mahaffey, who parcels out the lyrics in a series of two-line bulletins. You can almost see the barn dance spinning around them.

"Poor Ellen Smith", by Molly O'Day (1949). There's plenty of fiddle on this version too, though it's kept well in the background by O'Day's driving banjo and the country yelp in her voice. She had a fondness for maudlin material like Matty O'Neil's "Don't Sell Daddy Any More Whiskey" elsewhere in her set, but here it's good times all the way. Irresistible.

"Poor Ellen Smith", by The Kossoy Sisters (1956). Irene and Ellen Kossoy's sisterly harmonies won their version of "I'll Fly Away" a spot on the *O Brother, Where Art Thou?* soundtrack, and they're deployed to equally good effect here. Erik Darling (soon to replace Pete Seeger in The Weavers) does the girls proud with the banjo breaks he inserts after every verse.

"Ellen Smith", by Flatt & Scruggs (1962). Lester and Earl take it slow on this gently mournful version, easing the tune along with some carefully restrained picking from both of them. Despite that truncated title, it's the standard "Poor Ellen Smith" lyrics they use, delivered in flawless high lonesome style by Lester Flatt. Everyone else keeps it simple, and the song's all the more powerful as a result.

"Poor Ellen Smith", by Frank Proffitt (1962). A rare recording of what I call the song's "bad girl Ellen" lyrics. Proffitt's solo performance – voice and dulcimer only – is stark in both its production and the certainty with which it condemns Ellen to hell: "Such is the endin' of a girl that is bad". But there's an edge of sadness in his voice too, and perhaps it's that which redeems the song.

"Poor Ellen Smith", by Tommy Jarrell (1973). Jarrell, born in 1901, was the real deal: a working man from DeGraff's own Mount Airy who won a big reputation for his banjo and fiddle playing after hours. I've chosen his banjo version here, but his fiddle rendition's pretty damn good too. It's said Tommy's father Ben learned the song after an 1894 visit to DeGraff's cell in Winston jail.

"Poor Ellen Smith", by Wilma Lee & Stoney Cooper (1976). A full-blown Nashville country production, complete with brief solos from the fiddle, banjo and lap steel guitar. It's fast and full of energy, very much in the Molly O'Day mould, and also the only performance I know that refers to DeGraff in the third person throughout. "He'll never be free from his sins of the past," Lee confides.

"Poor Ellen Smith", by Kristin Hersh (1998). Accompanying herself both on guitar and (I think) autoharp, the Throwing Muses singer boils the story down to an economical ten lines. Arguably, the music's a little busy, but that's more than made up for by the harmonised choruses she shares with her young son Ryder. It's always a pleasure to hear blood relatives singing together, and this track's no exception.

"Poor Ellen Smith", by Neko Case & The Pine Valley Cosmonauts (2002). Case sticks closely to The Kossoy Sisters' lyrics for this contribution to Jon Langford's *Executioner's Last Songs* project. Her voice is as clear, sharp and strong as ever, supported by Steve Goulding's metronome-steady drums and the mighty Jon Rauhouse on banjo. Two minutes and seven seconds was never better spent.

"Poor Ellen Smith", by Randy Furches (2009). Furches' maternal grandfather was Peter DeGraff's nephew. He tackles Ellen's song by interspersing five of its traditional verses with spoken-word stanzas from DeGraff himself, declaring his love for Ellen but also confessing he shot her dead in a moment of anger. The killer's anguish is given voice by Hank Johnson's strangled blues licks on electric guitar.

8 - Murder Of The Lawson Family

"Believed to have become suddenly insane, Charles Lawson, 42, who lived near Germanton in Stokes County, Christmas Day killed his wife, Fannie, 38, and six of his seven children and then committed suicide."
Twin-City Sentinel, 26 December 1929.

"Immersed in the clotted blood on the living room floor, where the five bodies were found, was a little Christmas poem. Most of its words had been blotted out by the red stain oozing over it but the large number of curiosity seekers who passed through the death chamber today could plainly make out the words 'Santa Claus'."
Statesville Record & Landmark, 30 December 1929.

The Lawson family massacre of 1929 left enough blood on Charlie Lawson's cabin floor for neighbours to scoop it up with a coal shovel. Sixty years later, the author Trudy Smith, who's produced two books about the case, met a reader whose ancestor had visited the cabin soon after the killings. "Their family still had a jar which contained Fannie's blood, scooped up from the edge of the porch as a souvenir," she recalled. [1]

People have always wanted to take a little of the Lawson murders home with them. Even the dogwood tree Charlie leaned against as he took his own life was stripped bare within a few hours of his body's discovery. "They wanted a piece of this terrible event," local historian Chad Tucker said in 2006. "They wanted something from this farm to keep. To say, 'I've been there'." Charlie's guns, the bricks from his demolished cabin's old chimney, even the raisins from a cake Marie Lawson baked a few hours before her death, have all become collector's items for those with an interest in the case. Like that jar of Fannie's blood, these items are passed from one generation to the next in parts of North Carolina and treated as treasured family heirlooms. [2]

It's easy to see why these particular murders sparked such fascination. First, there's the fact that Charlie Lawson slaughtered his family on Christmas Day, a date guaranteed to add extra poignancy to any murder. He was a father killing his own children, which takes things up another notch, and did so when three of those children were under five years old – the youngest just four months. Then there's the odd mixture of brutality and tenderness he showed, bludgeoning the infants to death one minute and lovingly placing pillows beneath their shattered skulls the next. Although incest, poverty and a brain injury have all been put forward as possible explanations for the slaughter, we'll never really know what made Charlie do it.

Songwriters and poets fell on the story with glee. The most significant was Walter "Kid" Smith, a singer in the same North Carolina musical scene which produced the banjo legend Charlie Poole and his fiddle player Posey Rorer. Smith crafted the Boxing Day press reports into the ballad verses we know today and recorded them with Rorer's new band The Carolina Buddies in March 1930. "Murder Of The Lawson Family", as Smith called his ballad, gave Columbia Records a big topical hit. When Arthur Lawson, Charlie's one surviving child, found grief overwhelming him in later life, it's said he would lock himself away with a bottle of whiskey and play that record over and over again.

Dave Alvin, late of The Blasters and now one of our greatest Americana songwriters, included "Murder Of The Lawson Family" on his 2000 album *Public Domain*, putting a melody he borrowed from an old English folk song to Smith's original lyrics. "Most murder ballads tend to be about one person killing another, or maybe one person killing two other people," Alvin told me. "In this case, it's a whole family. There's usually an innocent in a murder ballad, but this was an innocent *family*. And there's little justification given for it. It's left to the listener to decide. Was it economics? Was it insanity? Why did this guy kill his family? So that mystery gives it some power.

"It's the murder of innocent children, which is pretty intense. And then it has that final verse, which is kind of sentimentally sweet but at the same time gives the whole scene some kind of redemption." [3]

I knew just the verse he had in mind:

They all were buried in a crowded grave,
While the angels watched above,
"Come home, come home, my little ones.
To a land of peace and love". [4]

Everyone the Lawsons had known came to see their seven coffins lowered into that crowded grave at Germanton's Browder Cemetery on 27 December 1929. Their grief was both genuine and deeply-felt, but we can't say the same for the 5,000 outsiders who also packed the cemetery that day. Photographs from the occasion show a crowd as tightly packed as that at any rock festival and we have reports of people clambering into the trees surrounding the tiny graveyard to secure a better view. These people were drawn by nothing more than a prurient curiosity about the case, which had filled front pages in North Carolina and the surrounding states since the first reports emerged on Boxing Day morning. Now they wanted to see the bodies for themselves.

"From hillside and valley, from hamlet and city they gathered," the *Winston-Salem Journal* reported. "For three miles along the road, cars were parked, while men and women, many with babies in their arms, made their way through the mud to the cemetery. There they crammed and jammed to get a glimpse of the seven caskets and tuned their ears to hear the tributes paid." [5]

Many of those visiting the graveyard also took the opportunity to call at the Lawsons' cabin a mile away and gawp at the blood still coating its floorboards. Charlie's brother Marion knew that Arthur, then just 16, would need money to keep up the mortgage payments on Charlie's land and these ghoulish visitors gave him an idea. Within ten days of the massacre, he had the cabin securely fenced off and began running newspaper ads for the 25c tours he planned to offer there.

At their peak, these tours pulled in as many as 500 people a day – many of whom pocketed a raisin from the surface of Marie's cake or some other small keepsake before leaving. Tucker believes that, if Marion had allowed people to visit the cabin without the fence and the guides to keep them in some kind of order, there wouldn't have been a

235

stick of furniture left behind. "You'd have started to see anything that could be removed quickly gone," he told the film-maker Matt Hodges.

When the family's belongings were auctioned at the end of January 1930, it was the murder weapons themselves which ignited the crowd. "The shotguns used to slay the seven members of his family attracted the greatest interest and went under rapid-fire bidding," the *SR&L* reported. "Other articles that held intimate connection with the Christmas Day tragedy also brought favorable prices under the bidding of curiosity-seekers."

Later that year, Arthur joined the tent show exhibition of Lawson family memorabilia which Marion had put together for Mount Airy's county show. "They took the crib and pieces of furniture out and exhibited it at the fairs for people to see," Lawson family researcher Patrick Boyles told me. Other accounts say Marie's cake, the stove it was baked in and at least one of Charlie's guns were also exhibited at the tent shows, with a barker stationed out front to summon in the crowds. [6, 7]

The song's history is intertwined with the case's early tourist trade too. Walter Smith would sometimes lecture to tour groups at the cabin, topping off his talk with a solo performance of The Carolina Buddies' hit song. Both Wesley Wall's poem "The Lawson Tragedy" and Elbert Puckett's "Song Of The Lawson Family Murders" – recently given an excellent musical setting by Lauren Myers – started life on the souvenir leaflets sold on Lawson cabin tours and at the tent show's county fair appearances.

For all this frantic commercial activity, however, the most striking souvenir of all remains the one Charlie himself provided a week before the murders. That's when he took the whole family for an outing to Winston-Salem, bought them all new clothes and insisted they have a family portrait taken by the town photographer. A few days later, that photo would be on the front page of newspapers all over America, showing Charlie flanked by Fannie and Marie as he stares down the camera with a firm, patriarchal glare. "He left a message for everybody," Fannie's great niece Evelyn Hicks told Hodges. "'It's my family and I can do what I want with them.'"

Eleven years before he killed his family, Charlie Lawson had a run-in with a black worker at a Winston-Salem tobacco warehouse which nearly cost him his own life. Charlie was visiting the Piedmont warehouse on Trade Street in November 1918 when Jesse McNeal clipped his leg while pushing a tobacco cart past. Charlie spat an angry warning at McNeal to look where he was going and the next thing anyone knew, the two men were rolling round on the floor in a vicious fight.

McNeal produced a knife and plunged it first into Charlie's head and then his chest. "One stab was just behind the ear, penetrating the mastoid, while the second was in the lung," *The Charlotte Observer* reported. "The wounded man was rushed to the hospital and his condition is regarded as serious, little hope being entertained for his recovery. After a lively race, McNeal was arrested and locked up." [8]

On 5 December, the *Twin-City Sentinel* added that Charlie ("a well-known farmer of Stokes County") had been discharged from Winston-Salem's City Hospital and was now back at home. "Jesse McNeal, the negro who assaulted him, is still in jail awaiting trial for the offence," the paper went on. "The case will be called for trial in the municipal court and Mr Lawson was notified to return here Monday to testify." McNeal's trial concluded on 20 December, when he was found guilty of assaulting Charlie with a deadly weapon and sentenced to 18 months on Forsyth County's road gang. [9]

By the time of the stabbing, Charlie and Fannie had been married for seven years and already had four children: Marie, Arthur, William and Carrie. William died of pneumonia in November 1920 and was buried in the Browder Cemetery plot where everyone but Arthur would join him nine years later. They added Maybell to the family in May 1922, James in April 1925 and Raymond in February 1927.

Charlie bought the Brook Cove cabin and the 128 acres that went with it just two months after Raymond's birth. He borrowed $3,200 from the Wachovia Bank for the purchase, striking a deal which set his mortgage payments at $500 a year (nearly $7,000 a year in today's money). The family set about making the primitive wooden cabin as comfortable as they could and soon Charlie's tobacco crop was doing well enough for him to start thinking of replacing the cabin with a modern home on the same site. He was well-respected among his neighbours, who all described him as a hard-working, sober and scrupulously honest man.

It was in the summer of 1928 that Charlie's luck turned sour again. He was digging a trench to drain water out of his tobacco packhouse's basement, using a mattock. At the end of its long handle, the mattock had a large flat blade on one side and a spiked one behind. Tom Manring, Charlie's brother-in-law, told the folklorist Donald Nelson what happened next. "He marked off the area to be dug up, which was next to a wire fence and proceeded to take a mattock and begin work," Nelson wrote in a 1973 essay. "He was concentrating on where the tool was to strike, momentarily forgetting the fence. His mattock blade struck on a strand of taut wire and sprang back, striking Lawson forcefully across the head. A few days later, he encountered his brother-in-law Tom Manring and related the story, saying that he had nearly killed himself." [10]

The mattock injury left Charlie with a nasty cut on his scalp and two fairly spectacular black eyes. He complained of severe headaches for months afterwards, saying the "misery in my head" was almost too much to bear. "I think it affected his brain," Charlie's nephew Claude Lawson told the *Danbury Reporter*. "His wife said he would be sitting there at night and suddenly jump up to see if all his guns were loaded." Chester Helsabeck, the Lawsons' family doctor, later confirmed Charlie had suffered "some sort of nervous trouble" all through the rest of 1928 and Charlie's sister-in-law added he'd seemed unable to either work or rest with a quiet mind. [11]

Other relatives and neighbours noticed Charlie behaving oddly too. He would walk away in the middle of a conversation, wander aimlessly round the cabin after dark or constantly shift his position when outside to avoid any touch of direct sunlight. One night, Fannie awoke in the small hours to discover the bed next to her was empty and found Charlie kneeling alone in the middle of a harvested cornfield, where he seemed to be alternating between prayer and fits of uncontrollable sobbing. It was only when she eventually persuaded him to stand up and come back inside that she saw he'd brought his shotgun with him.

Charlie had always had a temper and sometimes taken it out on his family – a problem that only worsened after the mattock incident. Arthur was the only one of the boys old enough to help with the farm's heavy work, but Charlie often found fault with what he'd done and would cane him with a switch in retribution. Arthur endured this until May 1929, when he at last rebelled. The family photo taken just six months later shows that Arthur – or "Buck" as the family called him – was already an inch taller than Charlie by this time. Although only 16, he looks like a powerful young man in his early 20s, so when his confrontation with Charlie finally came, its outcome was never in doubt. Told to stand still for a beating, he faced his father down and refused.

Beulah Robbins, a friend of Arthur's, spoke to Trudy Smith about this incident many years later. "Buck told me he said to his father that day, 'You'll never be man enough to whip me again'," she recalled. "He said he broke the whip his father had cut. Buck said his father just looked at him and backed off. He said Charlie never tried to whip him again."

Some accounts maintain that Arthur took to sleeping in his clothes from that day onward so he could be ready to defend the rest of the family if Charlie should launch into one of his violent fits overnight. He knew he was the only one with the physical strength to control him and seems to have begun feeling that responsibility very deeply. In August 1929, Mary Lou was born, completing the Lawsons' now nine-strong family and giving Arthur yet another helpless soul to worry over.

There was a six-inch fall of snow in Walnut Cove on Christmas Eve 1929 and the ground was still thickly covered next day. Rabbit tracks were plainly visible all through the woods surrounding the Lawsons' farm and many of their neighbours came out that morning with their guns to bag a rabbit for the pot. All morning, Fannie and Marie heard shots ringing out from the trees as they prepared the family's festive meal.

Marie had made a cake for the occasion, coating it in white frosting and dotting its whole surface with raisins to decorate it. She placed it squarely in the middle of the kitchen table where she hoped neither Raymond nor James's probing fingers would be able to reach it, then turned her thoughts to the date she had that evening. She and her boyfriend, a local lad called Charlie Wade Hampton, were planning to attend the Christmas play at Germanton's Palmyra Church. Arthur would be going along too – perhaps to act as chaperone – but even so Marie wanted to look her best. She set out a bowl of water to wash her hair and placed her curlers in front of the fire to heat them up. Meanwhile, Fannie was splitting her time between the stove and the crib containing little Mary Lou.

As this work continued in the cabin, Charlie, Arthur and a few men from the nearby farms were outside, amusing themselves with a spot of casual target practice. They took it in turns to fire at a selection of old cans and bottles, joshing and teasing each other with every hit or miss scored. Charlie seemed in good spirits. Cooking smells began drifting their way from the Lawsons' cabin door at around 11.30 and that set everyone thinking about lunch. One by one, the men started drifting off towards their own cabins and the hefty Christmas meal awaiting them there. Soon, only Charlie, Arthur and Marion's son Sanders were left.

"Charlie mentioned that they would need more ammunition in order to go rabbit hunting that afternoon," Trudy Smith writes in *White Christmas Bloody Christmas*. "He suggested that [Arthur and Sanders] walk to Germanton to buy more shells. Charlie walked to the house and the boys started out for Germanton by way of the railroad tracks." It was common enough for stores to remain open on Christmas Day at that time and Arthur evidently felt confident he'd find somewhere to buy the shells. What he didn't know was that Charlie had lied about his own supply. [12]

About an hour after Arthur and Sanders left, Fannie glanced at the clock on her mantelpiece and saw it was almost 1 p.m. She'd arranged for Carrie and Maybell to visit their Uncle Elijah's family for Christmas lunch, so she called the two little girls over, buttoned them up into their winter coats and hustled them out the door to make the short walk over there alone. Marie was still busy with her hair, James and Raymond were playing happily on the cabin floor and Mary Lou seemed content in her crib. Fannie allowed herself to relax for the first time that day. Maybe Christmas was going to be all right after all.

Carrie and Maybell's route to Uncle Elijah's house took them along the old stage coach road running the length of the Lawsons' farm. Trudging through the snow, they passed the family's wood pile and the tobacco pack house Charlie had been draining when the mattock struck his skull, then followed the road's rightward turn towards the first of Charlie's two barns. This barn stood only a few hundred yards from the cabin they'd just left and – like all the farm's other big buildings – it faced directly on to the stage coach road. As they rounded the road's sharp curve, the girls could see the barn looming up on their right beneath a slate-grey December sky. Carrie was then 12 years old and Maybell just 7.

Charlie was already waiting for them. He'd concealed himself behind the north-west corner of the barn with a 12-gauge doubled-barrel shotgun and a 25-20 rifle – both popular guns for small game hunting among the local farmers. Hearing his daughters' excited chatter as they approached, he pressed himself back against the barn wall to be sure he wasn't seen, took a tighter grip on his shotgun and waited for them to pass. As soon as they'd done so, he took a bead on the centre of Carrie's back and shot. As she fell, he fired the second barrel, this time directly into Maybell's back and she went down too.

Switching to his rifle, Charlie approached the two girls to check his work. Maybell was perfectly still, but he could see Carrie was still breathing, so he fired a single rifle bullet into her head. Then he took a plank of scrap wood from the side of the barn and bludgeoned the two little girls' heads with it till the end of the wood was dripping with blood. Content now that they could be feeling no further pain, he picked each girl up in turn, carried them inside the barn and laid them out side-by-side. He slipped a stone under each of their heads to serve as a pillow, crossed their arms on their chests and gently drew their eyelids closed, then latched the barn door shut behind him and started back for the house.

Fannie was standing out on the cabin's porch when she saw him approach, holding Mary Lou to her chest with her right hand against the baby's back and its head resting on her shoulder. Charlie got to within a few paces of his wife, then raised the shotgun again and fired it directly into Fannie's chest. He left the baby crying there as he threw open the cabin door. Marie, who'd spun around to face the door at this sudden noise, took the second barrel's load at close range. The two little boys – James was 4 and Raymond only 2 – were screaming now and Raymond was frantically scrabbling his way behind the cabin's stove.

Charlie felled James with a blow to the head from his shotgun's stock, then used its barrel to try and lever the stove far enough from the wall to get at Raymond. All this achieved was to bend the gun's left barrel out of shape, but Charlie managed to reach Raymond anyway. He dragged him out, battered his skull in with the ruined gun's stock and then did the same for James. All that remained now was to kill the baby. Charlie returned to the porch, grabbed the wailing Mary Lou from a pool of her mother's blood and returned the child to its crib. Then he bludgeoned her to death with the same shotgun stock he'd used to kill James and Raymond.

He dragged Fannie inside, closed the cabin door and satisfied himself that she and all four children were dead. Then he climbed the narrow staircase to the cabin's attic room where the children had slept. He collected four pillows, brought them back downstairs with him and gently placed one beneath everyone but Mary Lou's head. Just as he had with Carrie and Maybell, he also closed everybody's eyes and crossed their arms on their chests in a position of quiet repose.

Exhausted at all he'd done in the past frenetic half hour, Charlie sat for a moment on the bed he'd shared with Fannie there in the cabin's main room and surveyed his work. Raymond lay in a pool of blood near the stove, his mother against the edge of the crib containing Mary Lou's mangled remains. Marie and James were laid out side by side beneath the cabin window, their crisp white pillows now turning scarlet. Carrie and Maybell still lay in the barn. Charlie sighed. "Almost done," he thought. "Almost done".

Elijah Lawson, one of Charlie's brothers, and his two sons Claude and Carroll spent their Christmas morning rabbit hunting just south of the Lawson farm. Claude killed a rabbit of his own which he carried proudly attached to his belt. By 2 p.m. all their ammunition was gone. Knowing their route back home across the railway tracks would take them close to Charlie and Fannie Lawson's cabin, Elijah suggested they stop by there and wish everyone a merry Christmas. When they got within sight of the cabin, Claude ran on ahead and bounded on to the porch, ready to give everyone inside an excited Christmas greeting.

"He threw open the door with the words in his throat, but they got no further," the *Danbury Reporter's* Glenna Hicks wrote after interviewing Claude in 1977. "In the front room were the bodies of his Aunt Fannie, his cousins Marie, James, Raymond and Mary Lou. He doesn't remember the position of the bodies. He just remembers the blood. [...]

He remembers stepping back from the door. He doesn't know if he left it open or closed it quickly to make it all go away."

Either Claude or his father must have slammed the door, because Elijah's own view of the carnage came through the cabin window. Some accounts say he heard a noise from the cabin's attic room, others that he glimpsed an indistinct face at its upstairs window, but either way, his first thought was that the killer might still be inside. With no shells left for their own guns, he knew he and the boys would be helpless to defend themselves.

Elijah called Claude and Carroll to his side and hurried them back to the family's own cabin, where he told the boys to stay put while he raised the alarm at all the houses in the area. Some families there had a telephone by this time, which helped the word spread more quickly. Soon, farmers from all around were snatching up their own shotguns and converging on the Lawson cabin to see what had happened there and whether there was anything they could do to help. Sheriff John Taylor and Dr Helsabeck, who served as the area's coroner, were summoned too.

The first arrivals saw immediately from the blood-stained snow that someone had been shot outside the cabin and dragged in through its front door. But it was the remains they found inside that froze everyone in their tracks. "The bodies of Marie and James were lying with their heads near the bureau," the *W-SJ* reported. "Raymond's body, in a pool of blood, was to the right, the mother's body at the foot of the cradle, in which were the horribly mangled remains of the baby. [...] There was a big puddle of blood directly in front of the fireplace and in this blood were several combs similar to those used by women to hold their hair." [13]

Photographs of the blood-caked room confirm this description. Even with the bodies removed, it's a horrifying sight: a dark semi-circle of splattered blood coating the bare floorboards round the fireplace like a hearth-side rug; Marie and James' gore-stained pillows propped against the bureau; a sodden red blanket at the head of Mary Lou's crib. The bed beside the fireplace shows a red stain too, this one a relic from the moment Charlie had spent resting there when the killing was complete. "That was as bloody a place as you would ever look at in your life," one eyewitness told Smith. "There was blood all over the place. I mean blood everywhere! I haven't forgotten a bit of it."

Taylor organised the men into a search party to find Carrie, Maybell and Charlie himself. Elijah's suspicions about the attic room made them wonder if these three had also been killed and perhaps laid out just as carefully upstairs as the bodies they'd already found. But what if the killer himself was up there too? The only access to the attic was a narrow enclosed staircase, which would make anyone climbing those stairs a sitting duck for a gunman waiting above. Deputy Sheriff Robert Walker and a local doctor named Bynum gingerly climbed the stairs with their own guns at the ready, but found nothing in the attic except a few bloody footprints Charlie had left behind. Searching the cabin downstairs, others in the party discovered Charlie's rifle and both his shotguns were missing.

The first to find Carrie and Maybell's bodies was Steven Hampton, whose own place was one of those closest to the Lawsons' cabin. "Blood in a roadway nearby indicated that they had been shot there and the bodies taken into the tobacco barn," the *T-CS* reported. Searching around the area, Charlie's neighbours found a trampled spot of snow where he'd waited in ambush for the two girls and the discarded plank of wood with its end soaked in fresh blood. Carrie's pretty little blue hat, now crushed and blood-stained, was found near her body on the barn floor. [14]

Now only Charlie was missing. Someone in the search party spotted tracks in the snow leading from the tobacco barn where they'd just found Carrie and Maybell towards the trees and the creek beyond. They could see from the size of the tracks that they'd been made by an adult man and from the length of his stride that he'd been running full-pelt. Cautiously, they followed these tracks into the first thicket of trees, across an open field and into the woods once again. It was there, at a little after 4 p.m., that they found Charlie's dead body slumped against a dogwood tree some 300 yards from the barn. He had a gaping wound in his chest and his single-barrel shotgun had fallen to the ground beside him. The snow surrounding the tree was trampled flat, showing he'd paced round again and again in a tight circle before finally sitting down, jamming the shotgun's barrel against his own chest and pushing the trigger home. His two faithful dogs, Sam and Queen, sat patiently by their master's side.

Four men picked up Charlie's body, taking a limb each and lugged it back to the farm's main buildings. His suicide confirmed what some of his neighbours must surely have already begun to suspect – Charlie Lawson had snapped at last and slaughtered his entire family. The coroner's jury convened by Dr Helsabeck agreed. Searching the dead man's pockets, Taylor found several bills of sale recording deals Charlie had recently struck with tobacco buyers in the area, two with his own pencilled handwriting on the back. One note read "Trouble will cause" and the second "Blame no-one but..." Everyone assumed the missing word was "me".

Also in Charlie's pockets, Taylor found a letter to Fannie from the local maternity bureau and $58 in cash. That sum would be worth over $800 today and the tobacco paperwork showed his business was doing pretty well. Whatever problems had led to Charlie's breakdown, poverty did not seem to be among them. "His corn-crib was well-filled, he had good stock and the outbuildings were far better in proportion than the three-room log house," the *W-SJ* pointed out. "Large trees about the place make it an especially pretty place for a home and one neighbour remarked that Mr Lawson had hoped to build a large modern home there in the near future."

Arthur was still in Germanton when Marie's boyfriend Charlie Wade Hampton found him there and told him all eight of his family were dead. He was bundled into a car and brought directly to the farm, where Marion and Elijah's families comforted the stunned teenager as best they could. "I don't know why he did it," Arthur sobbed to one wire service reporter at the scene. "I guess it's just like they say – he must have suddenly gone crazy." [15]

There were no formal crime scene arrangements in those days and no official police clean-up crews either, so it was left to Charlie's neighbours to help Sheriff Taylor deal with the aftermath of the massacre. Women from the cabins nearby brought their own bedsheets to give the bodies a decent covering. The men began to organise a group of volunteers to expand the Lawson grave at Browder's cemetery into the 8ft by 15ft pit they knew would be needed to take eight new corpses.

The snow of the past few days had made the steep road leading to Charlie's hilltop cabin impassable for cars, so all the remains had to be carried down to the waiting hearses by hand. Boley Tuttle, the owner of a Walnut Cove hardware store, took up Mary Lou's tiny half-pulped body in his arms and bore it gently down the hill. "It was just awful," he told Smith many years later. "I barely made it to the hearse."

The bodies were taken to Madison, about 13 miles north east of Walnut Cove, where an embalming firm called T. Butler Knight and a funeral parlour called Yelton's were waiting to deal with them. As the hearses pulled away, Charlie's neighbours set about the grim task of clearing the blood he'd left behind. Their job was made all the harder by the number of people now flocking to the cabin just to see what had happened there. "Nobody did crime scene tape and all that kind of stuff back then," Boyles reminded me. "There were people wandering around inside and outside the house and that never should have been."

Hill Hampton was one of those trying to help with the clean-up. "They tried to keep people away, but they kept on coming," he told the *King Times-News*. "I was trying to use a coal shovel to scoop up the blood on the floor. Then I dumped it in an old tin wash tub." The washtub, which Hampton and his neighbour Sherman Voss had found in the Lawsons' front yard, was then used to carry the blood outside. Out of decency, they dug a shallow grave there and poured the blood into that before covering it again with earth. Meanwhile, a less sensitive visitor was busy funnelling Fannie's blood from the cabin's porch into the little souvenir jar Smith's fan would mention six decades later. [16]

Dr Helsabeck was already waiting in Madison when the Lawsons' bodies arrived and worked through the night there to complete his formal examination. By a remarkable stroke of luck, Sheriff Taylor's brother, a newly-qualified pathologist at Baltimore's Johns Hopkins Hospital, happened to be visiting the family in Walnut Cove that Christmas. His name was James Spottiswood Taylor and he volunteered to help Helsabeck carry out the autopsies. These, combined with what Helsabeck had already seen at the farm, allowed the two men to establish the exact cause of death in each case.

This is what Helsabeck wrote on each of the death certificates:

Carrie: "25-20 Rifle gun shot wound in head. Homicide."
Maybell: "12-gauge shot gun wound in left back penetrating lung. Homicide."
Fannie: "12-gauge shotgun wound in chest. Homicidal."
Marie: "Shot gun wound in chest. Homicide."
Raymond: "Fractured skull. Homicide."
James: "Fractured skull. Homicide."
Mary Lou: "Fractured skull. Homicidal."
Charlie: "12-gauge Shot gun wound in chest. Suicidal." [17]

Slowly, it was becoming possible to reconstruct what had happened. An early theory that Carrie and Maybell died while fleeing the carnage at the house was discounted when someone pointed out that they'd hardly have bothered to put their winter coats on first. It's unlikely Charlie would have had time to kill the five other members of the family and still overtake the two little girls before they reached the nearby barn, so that means that Carrie and Maybell must have been his first victims. The evidence of the disturbed snow by the barn, the bloodstains near its entrance and the discarded plank tell the rest of their story. Anyone hearing those first two shots – Charlie's own family included – would have shrugged them off as more noise from rabbit hunting in the adjacent woods.

The blood stains on the porch tell us one member of the family was killed out there and the smeared trail Charlie left behind when dragging that body inside led directly to Fannie's corpse. The shotgun pellet wounds which the two doctors found on the outside of Fannie's wrist are significant too. "There are scars of the load on her wrist, which would indicate that at the time she received the fatal wound she had her wrist across her body as if holding a baby," the *SR&L* pointed out. "And, too, the coroner pointed out, the baby had a considerable amount of blood on it which did not come from its own wee body." It follows that Charlie killed Fannie on the porch before snatching up Mary Lou and disposing of the baby in its own crib. [18]

Arthur testified that the clock on the cabin's mantelpiece had been working perfectly when he'd left just before noon that day, but Taylor and his men found it stopped dead at 1.25 p.m. It showed no sign of damage and started again very easily when someone adjusted it for a moment. The most likely explanation is that the sudden loud noise of a shotgun blast in the cabin's enclosed room had jolted the clock's delicate mechanism to a halt. The only shot fired inside the cabin was the one which killed Marie, which gives us both a plausible time of death for her and a window of about half an hour in which all the killings most likely took place.

The death certificates tell us everything else we need to know about Marie and James' death and we have enough evidence from the scene to fill in any gaps regarding Raymond. Eye witnesses who visited the cabin that night saw a pool of blood beneath the stove where Raymond's body was found and reporters spotted splinters from the ruined double-barrelled shotgun's stock on the cabin floor next morning. Combine that with the damage to the shotgun's barrel, and it's clear Raymond, James and Mary Lou must have been the last to die. They were least equipped to flee or fight back when they saw what was going on and so could safely be left to wait till Fannie and Marie were disposed of.

We know from the tracks leading into the woods that Charlie fled there from the barn rather than from the house. My guess is that he grabbed his spare shotgun, a single barrel Volunteer model, as soon as Mary Lou was dead, but then heard Elijah and his two boys approaching the cabin. I think he really was hiding in the attic there as they took in the carnage below, perhaps ready to shoot them too if they'd dared climb the stairs.

As soon as Elijah, Claude and Carroll left, Charlie seems to have dashed over to the barn for one last look at Carrie and Maybell, before fleeing into the woods with his Volunteer shot gun and begun pacing round the tree as he worked up the nerve to take his own life. The coroner's jury confirmed it was the single-gauge shotgun which killed him.

Helsabeck was well-aware of Charlie's 1928 accident with the mattock and would already have heard the gossip suggesting this accident must be what had ultimately led to his killing spree. Keen to investigate this possibility, Helsabeck and Spottiswood concluded their overnight work by removing Charlie's brain to study it. "The theory that a sharp blow on the head, supposed to have been sustained by Lawson about a year ago, caused him to commit the deed has been discounted by Dr Taylor and me," Helsabeck announced next morning. "We find no trace of a blow to the brain." In other words, painful as the mattock's blow was, its impact stopped at Charlie's skull and had not damaged the brain inside.

But Helsabeck had another finding to report too. "The convolutions on the top part of the brain near the middle vary from those on either side," he told reporters. Interpreting this for its readers, the *SR&L* said Charlie's brain showed "an unusual spot in the centre which is not filled out in proportion to the rest". *The New York Times* said Helsabeck's examination had "revealed a low-grade degenerative process in the middle of the brain", albeit one caused by disease rather than injury. It was agreed that Spottiswood should take the brain back to Johns Hopkins with him where the hospital's own experts could study it in more detail. [19]

On 9 January 1930, the *SR&L* reported that Johns Hopkins' work on Charlie's brain was already underway. "The examination will be as complete as it is possible to make it," the paper said. "Valuable data upon the nature of the insanity which attacked Lawson may be forthcoming as a result of the tests, it was said at the Hopkins hospital." Four weeks later, it added that Johns Hopkins' report on the brain was "expected most any day and is awaited with intense interest".

And that's where the trail goes cold. If a report was ever delivered to North Carolina's authorities, they would presumably have made it public and it's impossible to imagine the papers would not have thought it worth covering. And yet there's no mention of such a report in any press database I've been able to check. None of the many writers who studied the Lawson case before me have ever managed to trace the report either.

Andy Harrison, a Johns Hopkins archivist who checked the hospital's records for me, confirmed Spottiswood remained working as a pathologist there until June 1932, but could find no trace of any work the hospital had done on Charlie Lawson's brain. The *SR&L's* information, which seems to have come directly from the hospital itself, suggests some sort of investigation was at least begun, but we know no more than that. Either the examination was abandoned before any report emerged, or all copies and traces of its preparation have been lost. Standard practice in the 1930s was for all the hospital's anatomical waste to go into the incinerator, so that's probably where Charlie's brain ended up.

The Lawson family massacre made front-page news in at least 19 different states on the morning after the killings. Wire services like the Associated Press ensured the story appeared from New York to California and from the Canadian border to the Gulf of Mexico. "The radio supplemented or preceded the newspapers and broadcast the news into every nook and corner of the nation," the *Danbury Reporter* said in a tutting editorial. "There is a peculiarly morbid interest in contemplating this terrible affair." [20]

Naturally, the coverage was heaviest of all in Charlie's home state. By 27 December, both the *Twin-City Sentinel* and the *Winston-Salem Journal* were illustrating their stories with a copy of the family portrait Charlie had so thoughtfully provided a few days before. Immediately above the portrait, the *W-SJ* carried the crime scene picture I've already described, showing the family's living room painted with blood.

The sheer weight of press coverage brought a huge influx of curiosity-seekers to watch the Lawsons' funeral. Charlie had been a member of a local fraternal organisation called the Junior Order of United American Mechanics and their local chapter helped Arthur and his uncles to organise the family's funeral. There was to be no formal church service, but simply a few words from the pastors at Browder's cemetery and burial in the mass grave Charlie's neighbours had already prepared there. The ceremony was scheduled to begin at noon on 27 December.

A cortege of six hearses drew up outside Yelton's funeral home in Madison at about 10 that morning and began loading the bodies. Mary Lou was sharing her mother's coffin, so there were seven caskets in all. Yelton's had been hard-pressed to handle so many bodies in such a short time so, despite the fact that the family had wanted white coffins for everyone, a light grey one had to be substituted in Charlie's case. Someone found a piano stool and a small table to supplement Yelton's five purpose-made coffin stands for the viewing planned at Browder's. Lacking a seventh hearse, they transported two-year-old Raymond's tiny casket to the cemetery by private car.

A press photo taken across the street from Yelton's that morning shows the six hearses double-parked in Madison's West Murphy Street, each with an undertaker standing respectfully by its open rear door. The sidewalk is packed with watching men for the length of an entire block, a few of whom have brought their young sons along, but there's no more than half a dozen women in the entire crowd. Only the undertakers are bare-headed, with the grown men all sporting trilbies and every boy in a flat cap. Everyone is obediently staring at the camera, just as the photographer must have told them to do. They're all in winter overcoats, there's still a little snow visible on the background trees and the road looks wet and muddy.

As the hearses prepared to pull out, Browder's cemetery was already packed with rubber-necking tourists. "Long before the hour of the service, people began to arrive by the hundreds," the *T-CS* reported. "Automobiles crowded the highways and traffic moved slowly. Hundreds parked their cars several miles up the road and walked to the little graveyard." Soon the surrounding woods were packed to bursting too. Reporters circulating in the crowd found visitors there from as far away as Raleigh, 115 miles to the east. The papers' consensus was that as many as 5,000 people were gathered there at the crowd's height, with as many again passing through either earlier or later in the day. Many visitors took this opportunity to have a nose round the Lawsons' cabin too. [21]

The quarter-mile dirt road leading from the highway into the cemetery was too wet for cars and pretty soon the highway was next to impassable too. Its width and durability had never been designed with this level of traffic in mind and things were made all the worse by the mud melting snow had left behind. ""A number of cars became mired down and help had to be given to get them out," the *SR&L* said. Small wonder the Madison cortege was an hour late arriving.

The hearses got as close to the cemetery as they could, then men from Charlie's fraternal order shouldered the coffins to carry them the rest of the way. Sheriff Taylor, who'd already recruited a handful of locals to keep a small area next to the grave clear of spectators, set about making a path through the crowd for the pallbearers to pass. The seven coffins were laid out like a row of Russian dolls, tapering down from Charlie's full-size casket at one end to Raymond's tiny one at the other. Charlie's family had been members of the Primitive Baptist Church, whose elders Watt Tuttle and Boss Brown conducted a short ceremony at the graveside. "We all know that this family was respected," Brown said. "We know they were companionable. But why this thing has occurred, I do not know."

Their sermons complete, Tuttle and Brown announced the coffins would be opened so anyone wishing to bid the Lawsons a last goodbye could do so face to face. Seeing the bodies again was too much for Arthur and Marion, who both collapsed in grief and had to be helped to recover themselves before the viewing could continue. Arthur's distress was made all the worse by his conviction that, if only he hadn't fallen for Charlie's ruse in dispatching him to Germanton, he might have been able to overpower his father before the killing had even begun. "They say he was just a complete basket case at the funeral because he blamed himself," Boyles told me. "If you look at the family picture, Arthur's taller than Charlie and he's probably got 35lbs on him. He said, 'If I'd been there, it never would have happened. I could have taken control of the situation'."

As friends tried to console Arthur and Marion, a line formed on each side of the coffins and people started slowly filing by. The backs of the two lines were constantly replenished by new arrivals and it was fully three hours before everyone had passed. As the afternoon light began to fade, the coffins were sealed once again and lowered one-by-one into their shared grave. As before, they were arranged in declining order of size, with Charlie's casket buried at the northern end of the grave, followed by the one containing Fannie and Mary Lou. Then came Marie, Carrie, Maybell, James and Raymond in that order. For them, and for all the mourners gathered at the graveside, it was time to go home.

"That's a portable embalming table from the 1920s," Richard Miller told me. "If you fold it up it looks like a suitcase. Those are real funeral parlour chairs from 1910. That piece right there was part of a casket that was in the building." [22]

It was April 2015 and we were standing on the upper floor of Madison Dry Goods, which now occupies the building where the Lawsons' bodies were embalmed. Miller, who bought the building in 1998, was showing me the Lawson family room he's set up there for curious visitors to inspect. A framed front page from the *Winston-Salem Journal's* 27 December 1929 edition hung beside the room's door, its eight-column headline and three large pictures blaring out news of the massacre. A second, interior, page from the same issue was framed beneath, this one showing scenes from the crowded funeral. The room's entrance was blocked by a waist-level gate to prevent people wandering in unsupervised and its shadowy interior was lit only by a single candle, its flame tinted red by the coloured glass container.

As I peered inside, I could see bare brick walls, a couple of vintage bottles which had once contained embalming fluid and a copy of the Lawsons' family portrait on a small stand behind the table. There was a dime store painting of Christ propped behind the Lawsons' portrait and a bunch of dried grasses hanging from the wall above. A small speaker in the far corner played Katharine Whalen's version of the Lawsons ballad on a permanent loop: scratchy fiddle, mandolin and reedy vocals.

"I made this room to represent the funeral home that was here," Miller explained. "I have a lot of information on the Lawsons, because they were embalmed in this building – that's a very important part of the building's history. The funeral home that was here was T. Butler Knight. At that time, they were funeral embalmers and directors. Yelton funerals, they transported the bodies and buried them. Yelton was right down the street, just about four, five doors down."

Crossing to the building's old rope-operated freight elevator, Miller opened its wooden slatted door and let me stare down the shaft to its entrance on West Murphy Street. When the Lawson bodies arrived in Madison from Walnut Cove on the night of the killings, they'd been delivered directly to this building and laid out in their makeshift shrouds on the sidewalk outside. Knight's men had then loaded them into the elevator for their trip to the embalming room behind us for work to begin. "They brought them here first," Miller confirmed. "When I first came here, somebody actually showed me a picture of the Lawsons wrapped in sheets, laid in front of the door of the elevator. I didn't know what the significance of the building was back then, or I'd have a copy of that picture today."

We know the Lawsons' autopsies were carried out at one of the two Madison funeral homes and if they were delivered first to Knight's, then its logical to assume the autopsies were done there too. Why would you carry eight corpses all the way up to Yelton's for autopsy when they'd just have to be lugged back to Knight's for the embalming work to start a few hours later?

Miller led me away from the elevator, past the building's central stairwell and into the old embalming rooms at its rear. The empty space we crossed to get there was used to store half a dozen old Christmas trees, one with its fairy lights still burning. I thought of the snow outside the Lawson cabin and Claude bounding up its steps to give everyone inside a merry festive greeting. Miller pointed out a smooth patch on the floorboards, worn down by the hundreds of grieving relatives who'd once shuffled past their loved ones' open coffins in Knight's viewing room. "Lot of ghosts here," he muttered. "Lot of ghosts."

The Lawson exhibit, which he set up in 2006, has become one of Miller's more popular attractions. People from around Madison like it for the local connections, but the thousand-odd visitors a year who come also include people from just about every state in the union and at least eight foreign countries. Perhaps the strangest visitor he's had was the Virginia lady who wanted to take her interest in the Lawsons beyond Madison Dry Goods to Miller's own house. "My dining table at home is an embalming table," he told me. "She wanted to come up and lay on it but I wouldn't let her do that."

Miller's thinking of adding a second room recreating the Lawsons' kitchen (complete with a fresh-baked raisin cake on display), plus a plaque on the front of the building pointing out its significance. By and large, he said, Madison's residents support his efforts. "Some of the family members don't like the publicity off it, but most everybody was glad we were going to have a place like this," he said. "I had one girl come to me, about 19 years old. She said, 'Those are relatives of mine and I'm very disappointed you'd be so disrespectful'. I said, 'I'm not being disrespectful. That's part of the history of the building and that's just what happened'. After I talked to her she was OK."

I asked how he'd first heard of the Lawson case. "I moved to North Carolina in 1973 and lived in Stokes County for several years" he replied. "My ex-wife was born in Stokes County and she used to sing the Charlie Lawson ballad to our kids – a lot of people over there do! I got more fascinated when I found this building I'd bought was the place where they embalmed them."

Moving outside, he showed me the spot where his elevator's door opened on to the road and the length of sidewalk where the Lawsons' eight corpses had been laid. He pointed down the street to Yelton's old block, now occupied by a boarded-up building with a sign reading "Baker Family Feed & Seed".

I walked up there, stationed myself across the street and fumbled through my pockets for the photo of the waiting cortege which I've already described. It took little effort to superimpose it on where I was standing now. The pattern of the windows in the centre shop's frontage, the unusually pale brickwork on the corner shoe shop and the glimpse of South Market Street beyond all made it clear I was standing exactly where the 1929 photographer had done. In my mind's eye, the white Toyota pickup parked opposite morphed into six old-fashioned hearses and the deserted sidewalk filled with a crowd of men in Humphrey Bogart hats.

My companion on the Madison trip was Lisa O'Donnell, a Winston-Salem journalist I'd roped into my quest before leaving London. She shared my interest in North Carolina's long history of murder ballads and had agreed to act as my guide and chauffeur on a day-long excursion to Madison and Germanton. Bidding our farewells to Miller, we climbed back into Lisa's car and set off in my ghostly hearses' wake towards Browder's Family Cemetery.

Our route, like theirs so many years before, would take us close to where the massacre took place, but we knew there was little point in visiting that site now. The cabin was torn down decades ago and, although its planks were recycled to build a covered bridge on the property, everyone in town told us the current owners did all they could to discourage visitors. The prevailing gossip was that they'd been unaware of the farm's dark history when they bought it and none too amused when they discovered its local notoriety. Boyles told me the cabin was bulldozed in the mid-eighties and that his own trip there a few years later revealed only a hole where the Lawsons' old well had been and a pile of bricks from their demolished chimney.

Lisa and I cast a wistful glance towards the farm as we passed its turn-off, but decided to drive on. A mile or so later, we found the dirt track leading to Browder's cemetery, its entrance marked by a feeding buzzard who'd spotted a tasty bit of carrion by the edge of Brook Cove Road. We could hardly have asked for a more fitting symbol of our trip.

At the end of the dirt track, we found a small, oval graveyard containing about 50 headstones. The graves were surrounded by a narrow road which began and ended at the access track we'd just used, its inner edge marked by a single length of chain strung between concrete posts. Beyond the road, we could see only trees. Another car pulled in immediately behind us, but the driver stayed just long enough to replace some faded flowers on his own relative's grave before leaving again. Then we had the place to ourselves.

The Lawsons' plot is by far the cemetery's biggest, occupying a long, thin rectangle set parallel to the surrounding road. Its boundary is marked out with kerbstones, punctuated along their front row by a series of brick-sized stones each carrying one of the family's Christian names. The headstone itself is set in the centre of the plot's long back border, looking out directly towards the graveyard's central area. It's made from three hefty blocks, carrying nine names in all – including that of William, the child Fannie lost to pneumonia in 1920. The central block's the biggest of the three, topping out at about chest height for me and contains the names and dates for Charlie, Fannie and Mary Lou. These are flanked by two smaller blocks, one for the boys (James, Raymond and William), the other for the girls (Marie, Carrie and Maybell).

All three blocks are decorated with carved tulips along their upper edge and the Junior Order of United American Mechanics – which I think probably paid for the stone – has added its own coat of arms directly above Charlie's name. At the bottom of the central block, there's a verse from Maxwell Cornelius's 1891 hymn "Sometime We'll Understand" which Marion chose from Yelton's book of suggested epitaphs:

Not now, but in the coming years,
It will be in a better land,
We'll read the meaning of our tears,
And then, sometime, we'll understand.

On the day we visited, the sky was a washed-out grey, the trees were bare and the close-cropped patchy grass worn away to bare earth. The sole splash of colour came from the bright artificial flowers decorating many of the gravestones around us. The bunch of red, yellow and lilac flowers at the base of the Lawsons' stone were so vibrant they clearly hadn't been there long. A foot or so behind his family's grave, I found

Arthur's lonely plot, where he was consigned after crashing his truck in 1945. Several members of Fannie's family, the Manrings, lie clustered round the Lawsons' plot too.

Once again, I had an old press photo I wanted to look at *in situ*. This one, taken at graveside on the day of the funeral, showed the Lawsons' closest family and friends crowded round their seven caskets. It's an all-male gathering and behind the figures at Charlie's end of the coffin row, I could see a group of half a dozen men perched atop the dirt from the excavated grave. I remembered a passage from Smith's book quoting one of the men who'd been present that day, saying Sheriff Taylor had asked him and his friends to station themselves there to help control the crowd.

The woods all around me would have been full of gawpers on that day in 1929 – you can catch a glimpse of them at the back of the photo – but for the intimate group gathered round the coffins, this was a very different matter. As with the Madison shot, the photographer has ensured everyone is looking at the camera, but here they're all respectfully bare-headed, grim-faced and sad. To these men, the Lawsons were real people, not merely names from the newspaper and that fact shows in every face.

The most haunting figure of all is the man standing by the foot of Maybell's coffin. In a crowd where everyone else is dressed in Sunday-best suits, he's still wearing his farmer's dungarees. His jet-black hair is in disarray, there's two or three days' worth of stubble on his chin and he regards us with the same thousand-yard stare Don McCullin would capture in his Vietnam War portraits. My first thought was that this must be Arthur Lawson, but it takes only a quick comparison with the lad in Charlie's family picture to see that's not so. Whoever he is, his face conveys every ounce of the horrified shock his community was feeling that day. The massacre was then just two days old and still very raw.

With the funeral behind him, Charlie's brother Marion started turning his mind to financial matters. Arthur was in line to inherit the farm, but that was a mixed blessing because it meant inheriting Charlie's remaining mortgage payments on the land too.

Arthur was still only 16, so he could hardly be expected to run the place and that meant another source of income had to be found.

Marion thought again of the huge crowds who had flocked in to watch the funeral. As many as 90 carloads of strangers a day were still turning up at the cabin to poke around there and there was no sign that interest was going to fade anytime soon. Most of the Lawsons' property was still just as they'd left it in the cabin and hence vulnerable to theft from anyone who fancied grabbing a souvenir before they left. Although Charlie and Fannie's relatives did their best to keep a watch on the place, they had their own farms to run, so that was never going to be a long-term solution. Some of Charlie's neighbours took exception to the "ghouls" visiting the cabin and there are newspaper reports of outsiders being attacked for that reason. The most serious of these involved a man called Lloyd Ends, who needed three stitches in his arm after being slashed with a knife one night while peering in through the cabin's kitchen window.

After consulting with his friends, Marion decided the answer to all these problems was to put a secure fence round the property and charge visitors 25 cents a time to take organised tours. The cash raised could go to Arthur and with luck there'd be enough left over to meet the mortgage payments and ensure the farm remained in the Lawson family too. Arthur agreed to the scheme and Marion started drawing up plans for the work needed. Fannie's family was appalled at this idea, as were some of Charlie's other brothers, and they did all they could to talk Marion out of it. But he insisted that the cabin and the tobacco barn must be securely fenced-off and commercialised. "I don't think he could have avoided it," the local historian Chad Tucker told Hodges. "People would have probably started stealing stuff right off the property."

By 15 January 1930, Marion and his workers had completed a tall chicken wire fence round the farms' key sites and had everything in place for the tours to begin. One woman quoted in *The Meaning Of Our Tears* recalls that Christmas Eve's snow had not yet melted when the first paying visitors arrived. "The charge of 25 cents [...] has not deterred the morbid and the curious," the *SR&L* reported. "Visitors are there daily, sometimes as many as 100 people making the pilgrimage. On a recent Sunday before the home was roped off and locked up, it is said that at least 500 people visited the scene of carnage."

Marion recruited friends and family to staff the cabin tours, supplementing the ticket income by supplying refreshments and organising a pack of five souvenir photographs visitors could buy before they left. I've also seen a number of leaflets which seem to have been printed up for sale either at the cabin itself or at the tent exhibition Marion took to various county shows. Often, these would include a long narrative poem telling the story of the massacre, such as Wesley Wall's "The Lawson Tragedy" or Elbert Puckett "The Song Of The Lawson Family Murders". Neither of these works would win any prizes for their merits on the page, but Puckett's verses acquit themselves rather better in performance. The singer Lauren Myers gives an attractive a capella rendition of his song over the closing credits of Hodges' documentary.

Wall's poem carries a copyright date of 1930, but even he was beaten to the punch by a *Yadkin Ripple* reader called Edith Willard, whose verses the paper reproduced in its 23 January edition that year. She calls her poem "The Lawson Family In Rhyme" and the *Ripple* liked it enough to splash it on the front page, but once again it's the work's topicality rather than its literary skill which provides the appeal. Fortunately, there was a much better song already in the works.

Walter Smith, born in 1895, was the son of a Virginia farmer. As a young man, he worked in sawmills and cotton mills, boxing a little in his spare time and always dabbling in music. It was his time in the ring which gave him the "Kid" nickname he'd carry for the rest of his life. Smith's talents as a singer won him a place in the loose collective of Virginia and North Carolina musicians which formed round the influential banjo player Charlie Poole in the 1920s. That's how he came to meet Poole's fiddle player Posey Rorer and his guitarist Norman Woodlief.

Rorer's time with Poole in his popular string band The North Carolina Ramblers had given the fiddler some useful contacts with the record companies of the day, but by 1929 neither he nor Woodlief were working with Poole any more. Rorer, who could see Smith showed a lot of promise, invited him to join the duo at a Gennett Records session in

March 1929. They got round the fact that both Rorer and Woodlief were contractually bound to rival labels by crediting the Gennett session's releases to Smith alone – quite a break for someone who'd never stepped into a recording studio before. The tracks the three men laid down that day included "The Bald-Headed End Of A Broom", which would later become a minor hillbilly standard.

Smith returned to the life of a touring musician in North Carolina and Virginia, where he saw several newspaper stories about the Lawson massacre and decided to write a song about it. He called his verses "The Murder Of The Lawson Family" and they go like this:

> It was on last Christmas evening,
> A snow was on the ground,
> Near his home in North Carolina,
> Where this murderer, he was found,
>
> His name was Charlie Lawson,
> And he had a loving wife,
> But we'll never know what caused him,
> To take his family's life,
>
> They say he killed his wife at first,
> And the little ones did cry,
> "Please Papa, won't you spare our lives?
> For it is so hard to die,"
>
> But the raging man could not be stopped,
> He would not heed their call,
> And kept on firing fatal shots,
> Until he killed them all,
>
> And when the sad, sad news was heard,
> It was a great surprise,
> He killed six children and his wife,
> And then he closed their eyes,

And now farewell kind friends at home,
I'll see you all no more,
Into my breast I'll fire one shot,
Then my troubles will be o'er,

They did not carry him to jail,
No lawyers did he pay,
He will have his trial in another world,
On the final judgement day,

They all were buried in a crowded grave,
While the angels watched above,
"Come home, come home, my little ones,
To a land of peace and love." [4]

Aside from that one slip claiming Fannie died first – a mistake many of the early newspaper reports made too – that's a commendably accurate and succinct account of what really did happen. Smith also does a good job of mimicking the form of the traditional ballads he'd learned while playing in North Carolina and Virginia, which is why so many people today innocently assume his song must be in the public domain.

The only touch which could be said to betray a professional's hand is that very neat "Lawson / caused him" rhyme in verse two. The a/b/c/b scheme doesn't even require a rhyme there, but Smith's able to give as a very natural-sounding one anyway. The fact that he does so with such precision is an added bonus. I also think the penultimate verse's "No lawyers did he pay" line is a nice touch. I mean, at least that's *some* consolation, right guys?

The final event mentioned in the song is the Lawsons' burial, which took place on 27 December, and my guess is Smith probably wrote it in the two or three days following that. He liked the song enough to perform it for Rorer, who took it to Columbia Records in New York and explained what a massive story this was in North Carolina and the surrounding states. They were convinced enough to give Smith and Rorer a March 1930 recording session to put the song on disc. Rorer recruited the banjo player Buster Carter and the guitarist Lewis McDaniels to join

261

him and Smith in a new band they called The Carolina Buddies, and off to New York they went.

"The Murder Of The Lawson Family" was by far the most popular track they cut at that Columbia session and the company quickly issued it as the "A" side of its own 78rpm disc. It's a commendably restrained performance, with McDaniel's steadily plonking guitar carrying most of the musical weight. Rorer was by far the biggest name in the band, but he limits his fiddle contributions to a brief introduction sketching out the tune's theme and a touch of decoration as each verse concludes. Carter's banjo has little to do either, but his tenor vocals join with Smith's to fill out the sound and add a ghostly moan to key lines. Even with the limitations of 1930's recording technology, everyone involved was evidently determined to ensure the story came across with utter clarity – and that's the disc's real strength.

"When the record came out, everybody that had a wind-up talking machine had a copy," the owner of a Mount Airy radio station told the *W-SJ* in 1985. "One of my school buddies could recite the words by heart." Anyone without a gramophone of their own could hear the record on the radio or at one of the many North Carolina restaurants and shops which played it for their customers' entertainment. [23]

Part of the song's power, as Donald Nelson's essay points out, lies in the matter-of-fact way the band chooses to tell its bloody tale. "The song is presented in the straightforward manner of the mountain ballads, the performers knowing among themselves that the story was sufficient to draw the proper emotion from the audience without injected impetus," he writes. Alvin, who released his own cover version in 2000, agrees. "It's told kind of deadpan," he said. "You have this incredibly violent story that's told, like [he inserted a shrug into his voice] 'Yeah and here's another one'."

Alvin and his brother Phil, who'd later join him in forming The Blasters, discovered the song when out on a record-hunting trip at the end of the 1960s. "I was about 13, 14 years old and my older brother and I were little record collector guys," he told me. "The name on the 78, just the title, caught my eye. 'Murder? A whole family murdered? What?' We were predominantly looking for blues records, but that caught my eye. I picked it up for a quarter somewhere, took it home and listened to it and it was, like 'Wow!'

"The singers were called The Carolina Buddies. I didn't know much about them, but I always was kind of fascinated by the song. It was always in my mind, 'Well, maybe someday we'll record it'. So when I was working on that album [*Public Domain*], that was one of the first five or six songs I chose."

I mentioned to Alvin that I'd been surprised when I'd gone back to the *Public Domain* album earlier that week to discover he'd had the full band backing him on "Murder Of The Lawson Family". True, most of the band don't enter until verse three, but I'd remembered the track very strongly as a solo performance with just Alvin's rich voice and his acoustic guitar throughout. "It might be that you got sucked into the words – which was the idea," he said when I confessed this. As with The Carolina Buddies before him, he'd had the good sense to recognise that this ballad is primarily a story song and ensure the musical backing remains in service to that. In Alvin's case, that means carefully-placed percussion and bass, a melancholy accordion's quiet drone and a pinch of mandolin to sweeten the broth. But he had another card up his sleeve too.

"When we recorded it, I knew I didn't want to do it musically like The Carolina Buddies did it, because I was going to do another song on the record, 'Engine 143' fairly straight with the 1-4-5 chords over and over again," he said. "I decided if I was going to do 'Murder Of The Lawson Family', I'd have to make the accompanying music a little more melancholy and dramatic, so I took the melody from 'In The Willow Garden'. The lyrics fit perfectly inside that melody."

"Engine 143" is a disaster song rather than a murder one, but it does end with the train engineer's death in a terrible crash. In fact, almost all the 15 songs on *Public Domain* deal in dark subjects of one kind or another. "A Short Life Of Trouble" and "East Virginia Blues" are both songs of heartbreak, "What Did The Deep Sea Say" tackles the indifference of nature in drowning an innocent sailor and "Don't Let Your Deal Go Down" contains a threat of suicide. "Mama, Ain't Long For Day" touches on both illness and depression, "Texas Rangers" describes the loss of 300 comrades in battle and "Railroad Bill" demands violent revenge against a local bad man. "Delia", like "Lawson Family" itself, is a full-on murder ballad.

It's important to understand that Alvin did not fill the album with these particular songs for any gratuitous reason. He's convinced they played a valuable therapeutic role for the people who first performed and listened to them.

"These songs served a purpose for their community," he told me. "I've always referred to folk music and ballads in particular, as poor people and working people's psychiatry. You have these events – a murder or a train wreck or a ship sinking – and then the balladeer comes in to be the shrink: 'Here's what happened. Here: let's make sense of this'. So you have these ballads that functioned both as a community mourning the murder of somebody and then trying to make sense of it. This was how people soothed their minds in the past, how they explained the world and its injustices and its mercies to themselves."

Even today, dark songs like those on *Public Domain* can serve the same function – as Alvin discovered for himself in the weeks leading up to the record's sessions. "I was doing the album as my father was dying and I was turning to these songs in a strange way for comfort," he told me. "I was hiking every day before I went to the hospital – I would drive out to the hills and just get lost for a little while. While I was hiking, I found myself singing these old songs in my head. In a weird way they helped me get through all that. They were something to hold on to."

As interest in the Lawson cabin started falling away, Marion first changed the tours from daily to weekly affairs and then dropped them altogether. The consensus seems to be that they ended around 1935. I've seen reports both that Arthur eventually received about $31,000 from the tours' income and that the bank ended up foreclosing on Charlie's mortgage anyway. If both those things are true, then presumably the issue was not how much money Marion and Arthur were able to get to the bank, but how quickly they were able to raise it.

Marion quit farming to start a construction business and Arthur went to work for him there. In May 1945, Arthur was driving home after a night's drinking when he crashed his truck into an excavation on the highway near Walnut Cove and died. "Lawson apparently failed to see the barricade which blocked the passage across the pavement where the repairs were underway," the *Danbury Reporter* explained. He was just 31 years old. [24]

By the 1960s, the cabin was falling into disrepair, but still notorious enough to attract a fair number of visitors. Photographs from that era show the fireplace with visitors' graffiti covering every inch of its surface. "Even the old pack house had names and addresses carved in it," Marion's daughter-in-law told Smith. "Those addresses were from all over. It was an amazing thing to see."

A steady trickle of bands covered The Carolina Buddies' song throughout the fifties and sixties, including The Stanley Brothers (1956), The Country Gentlemen (1959), Mac Wiseman (1966) and Doc Watson (1967), but then it dropped off most listeners' radar. It stayed that way for 30 years, appearing again on fresh recordings only when the new century arrived. Among the best of the recent covers, we have Dave Alvin's (2000), The Violet Rays' (2007) and Vandaveer's (2013). Some of these versions are very good, but even the best of them have never managed to dislodge the 1930 original as this tale's single most essential telling.

Once we start looking for alternatives to Walter Smith's composition, the pickings get very thin. Way back in 1930, Donald Thompson, who'd just quit his job as fiddle player with The Carolina Night Hawks, wrote a Lawsons song called "A Family Murder In Carolina", but sadly it never seems to have been recorded. Although the lyrics survive, they're not a patch on Smith's. We get an enjoyable 53 seconds of White Knuckle Trucker's 2006 Lawsons song "Blood From The Ground" in Hodges' DVD extras, but I'm damned if I can find the full track anywhere. I've already mentioned Lauren Myers' version of Puckett's "Song Of The Lawson Family Murders" – also on the DVD – and that leaves just one other song to consider. It's not really a Lawsons song at all, but I'd argue it belongs here all the same.

One popular interpretation of the Lawsons ballad has always been that Charlie must have killed his family to save them from the starvation which many small farmers of that era faced. Smith's song comes from the era of the dustbowl and the Great Depression, after all, so this is a natural enough assumption for casual listeners to make. "He killed his family not because he hated them, but because he loved them," one Virginia woman told song collectors in 1985. "He thought they was going to starve to death." [25]

I often wonder if that view of the Lawson case inspired the young Bob Dylan to write his own 1962 song "The Ballad Of Hollis Brown", in which a hard-pressed South Dakota farmer shoots his own wife, his five children and himself for precisely the reason that woman describes. Knowing Alvin had toured with Dylan, I put this idea to him and asked if he thought Bob might have had the Lawson ballad in mind. "I think he probably did," Alvin replied. "People say that, in the early days, he'd sit down in Dave Van Ronk's house or Tom Paxton's house and just study the old records. 'Let me see those old 78s, let me hear those old albums,' you know. So yeah, I would imagine 'Murder Of The Lawson Family' crossed his path at some time."

For me, "Hollis Brown" will always be a Lawsons song in all but name. Its highlight is a wonderfully cinematic moment between verses eight and nine when Brown's shotgun leaps from its perch on the wall to his hands without him having any idea how it got there. It's a chilling evocation of the killer's fractured mind at that moment, and it's always Charlie Lawson I think of when those lines are sung. A verse later, everyone's dead.

As the 1980s drew to a close, the theories about why Charlie killed his family remained as scattershot as ever. Despite the fact that the two doctors' post-mortem found no sign of an injury to his brain, many people clung to the idea that the mattock incident must somehow have driven him insane. Noting that the killings coincided with the beginning of the Great Depression, others leapt to the conclusion that Charlie's farm must have gone bust – but that idea's not supported by the evidence either. We know from the paperwork found on his body that Charlie's own business was actually doing rather well in December 1929. Ruined financiers may have been leaping from every skyscraper on Wall Street, but what was that to him? He, like his Stokes County neighbours, had no stock market investments to lose.

The daftest theories of the lot insist that Charlie wasn't the killer at all. Some prefer to finger Jesse McNeal, the black worker who served time for stabbing Charlie back in 1918. But people telling the story that way usually claim the warehouse fight took place no more than a year before the Lawson massacre. Now that we know the real date was ten years earlier, the McNeal theory becomes easier to dismiss than ever. Even if we assume he was still alive on Christmas Day 1929 – which is by no means certain – it strains credulity to imagine him silently nursing a grudge for over ten years before taking such extreme revenge.

The other suspect put forward is the legendary bank robber John Dillinger. In this scenario, we're assured that Charlie and his entire family were wiped out in a mob hit performed by Dillinger himself. Quite why he would have wanted to switch from robber to hit man at this point in his career, let alone why he'd have targeted the Lawsons, is never explained. There's also the awkward fact that, on the day the Lawsons were killed, Dillinger was 700 miles away serving a nine-year term at Indiana State Penitentiary. He didn't get out till May 1933.

These efforts to drag Dillinger into the Lawson story seem to spring from a persistent rumour that he visited the family's cabin during its days as a tourist attraction and left either a signature in the visitors' book (assuming the cabin had such a thing) or a mocking note on some local lawman's door.

In *The Meaning Of Our Tears*, Trudy Smith relates a version of this tale which pins down Dillinger's visit to 17 December 1933 and says he left his note on the door of Stokes County deputy sheriff Hill Hampton. It's true that Dillinger was back on the run by then, travelling south from Chicago towards Florida by car, and that he sometimes used to amuse himself by posing for pictures with unsuspecting policemen. But the tale remains a very unlikely one.

Dary Matera's painstaking biography of the gangster reveals Dillinger woke up on the morning of 17 December 1933 in a Nashville hotel and ended that day in Jacksonville, Florida. In order to visit the Lawsons' cabin on the way, he'd have had to detour 445 miles east and increase his total distance covered that day from just under 600 miles to over 900. Add the fact that this would have been in a 1933 car long before the interstates were built, and I think we can dismiss the Dillinger-as-visitor story too. Maria Hodges, the chief researcher on *A Christmas Family Tragedy*, wrote in 2007 that she'd found a Stokes County highway patrolman who also happened to be called John Dillinger, and concluded Hampton's note actually came from him. If so, then I dare say that's where the whole Dillinger connection began. [26, 27]

All the discussion of Charlie's motives took a dramatic new turn when Bruce Jones and Trudy Smith published *White Christmas Bloody Christmas* in 1990. The book secured a scoop from Charlie's niece Stella Boles, who came forward with some brand new information just before it went to press. Stella, born in 1915, was Marion Lawson's daughter, so she'd had a front row seat for everything that went on in the family after the murders. She confirmed some dark Stokes County rumours the book's authors had already been investigating.

These began with an anonymous informant's recollections of touring the Lawsons' cabin with her parents in July 1930, when they were shown around by a man who matched the description of Charlie's neighbour and relative Sam Hill. They asked him why he thought Charlie had done it and were shocked by the reply he gave. "The old man told them that Charlie Lawson had found out that his daughter Marie was pregnant," Jones and Smith write. "He also told them that Charlie Lawson himself had been the father of the baby. The old man had gone on to say that Charlie Lawson had warned his daughter that, if she told her mother or anyone else about the pregnancy, that 'there would be some killing done'." The book goes on to explain that, according to Hill's account that day, Fannie became aware of her daughter's condition and kept badgering her to name the father. Eventually, Marie cracked and told her mother it was Charlie's baby – the very thing he'd warned her never to do.

When Stella Boles came forward, she described overhearing a meeting of all the Lawson women on 27 December 1929, when she was just 14 years old. Ida and Nina Lawson, who had each married one of Charlie's brothers, were among the group. Years later, the adult Stella questioned her Aunt Nina about what was said that day. Nina told her that Fannie had discovered the incest in her family shortly before Christmas Day 1929 and had confided in Ida and Nina as she agonised over what to do. "Stella's Aunt Nina told her of all these things and asked her not to repeat it," *White Christmas Bloody Christmas* says. "It was such a scandalous thing to have happened and the murders had been more than enough for the family to endure." It was not until 60 years later that Stella felt free to speak up.

When Smith published her second Lawson family book in 2006, she was able to add some supporting evidence from Ella May Johnson, who she describes as Marie's best friend. Ella May said Marie had slept over at the Johnsons' house "a week or two before Christmas [1929]" and confided she was pregnant by her own father as the two girls talked that night. She also seems to be the first person Marie ever told about Charlie's "going to be some killing done" remark – and perhaps played a part in spreading it further afield. Confronted with these accounts in the DVD documentary, two or three elderly Walnut Cove residents admitted they too had heard rumours Marie was pregnant when she died.

If so, she clearly wasn't very far along. The family portrait, which was taken at about the same time as her sleepover with Ella Mae, shows Marie's belly quite clearly and you certainly wouldn't guess she was pregnant from that. Perhaps that also explains why neither Helsabeck nor Spottiswood seem to have noticed any sign Marie was pregnant during her autopsy. It's certainly possible that shame over such a horrible misdeed helped to spark Charlie's killing spree and I'm sure any family of that era would have guarded such a secret very carefully, but the fact is that we'll never know for sure.

I was mulling all this over when I came across the transcript of a 2012 BBC radio programme discussing crimes like Charlie Lawson's. The modern term for such atrocities is "family annihilation" and one of the experts interviewed was Dr Kevin Murray, a consultant forensic psychiatrist at Broadmoor, the high-security mental hospital where many of Britain's most dangerous killers are kept. His description of what leads to family annihilation started with a man who'd hit his wife, but seems equally applicable to one who'd just impregnated his daughter:

> The idea that that person would be able to survive and accuse them of what they've done, I think is simply intolerable and so the partner – typically the woman – must be killed. And then, if there are children, the idea that the children should survive and the man should face the children and they would know what he has done to their mother is similarly intolerable. And then the man turns the rage on himself. [28]

Combine that analysis with Stella Boles' testimony and perhaps we're as close to understanding Charlie Lawson's actions as we'll ever get: he simply couldn't bear the thought of facing Marie and Fannie's accusing stares. As Smith's song reminds us, he killed six children and his wife – "and then he closed their eyes".

Family favourites: 10 great versions of Charlie's story.

"The Murder Of The Lawson Family", by The Carolina Buddies (1930). The original and still arguably the best. As the list below demonstrates, Walter Smith's composition is now so firmly embedded in the tradition that it's known by at least four different titles. Song collectors were still presenting it as a forgotten mountain ballad as recently as 1985.

"The Story Of The Lawson Family", by The Stanley Brothers (1956). Recorded in a relaxed after-hours session at Larry Ehrlich's Virginia radio studio, Ralph and Carter's voices twine together here to gorgeous effect. It's a gently mournful version, full of slow, careful guitar and keening, harmonised vocals. Ralph Mayo's fiddle solo ain't too shabby either.

"Ballad Of Hollis Brown", by Bob Dylan (1962). Dylan's farmer kills himself and his family to save them from ruin and starvation. With no employment, rats in his flour, a sick mare, a dried-up well and his pasture turning black, Brown decides family annihilation is the only answer. None of the details match Charlie Lawson's plight, but the thrust and atmosphere of the song are so close I always think of it as a Lawsons ballad under the skin.

"The Ballad Of The Lawson Family", by Mac Wiseman (1966). Opening with an explosive burst of fiddle, this version remains bizarrely cheerful throughout. There's a sunny tone to Wiseman's voice in every line and the arrangement's a jaunty, foot-tapping affair. Even when Charlie's kids beg him not to kill them, they sound like they haven't a care in the world.

"The Lawson Family Murder", by Doc & Merle Watson (1967). Both men turn in some great picking on this *Ballads From Deep Gap* selection. By cutting Smith's final verse, they end the song not on the promise of the children's redemption but the prospect of Charlie's punishment in Hell.

"Murder Of The Lawson Family", by Dave Alvin (2000). Alvin borrows the melody from "Down In The Willow Garden" here, and his rich vocals make it a great rendition. He reverses the Watsons' approach, repeating the "peace and love" couplet to stress there's some hope at the song's conclusion. The band fills out the sound nicely, but is never so intrusive as to distract us from the unfolding story.

"The Song Of The Lawson Family Murders", by Lauren Myers (2006). Based on Elbert Puckett's 1935 poem, this a capella rendition can be found playing over the closing credits of *A Christmas Family Tragedy*. It's an object lesson in how even the least promising verses can be salvaged by a great performance.

"Blood From The Ground", by White Knuckle Trucker (2006). Another track from the DVD, this one by one of North Carolina's own bands. It's sparse, echoey and noir-ish, using just a solo voice and acoustic guitar. Why did Charlie do it? "Sometimes Jesus just ain't looking down," the band's Scottie Bruner explains.

"The Lawson Family Murder", by Sports Fishing USA (2013). Supplementing Smith's lyrics with a few verses of their own and adding a brand new tune, this Ohio band transforms the song into a crowd-pleasing rocker. It's the honky-tonkish piano breaks weaving in and out of the mix that make it for me.

"The Murder Of The Lawson Family", by Vandaveer (2013). Mark Heidinger and Rose Guerin's full-bodied harmony vocals lead the way on this enjoyable version. Dobro player J. Tom Hnatow adds a touch of blues with his excellent solo just after Charlie's suicide. It's also good to see such a recent version retaining the topicality of Smith's opening line: "It was on *last* Christmas evening".

Sources & Endnotes

1: Stagger Lee

[1] *Newspaper Days*, by Theodore Dreiser (University of Pennsylvania Press, 1922).

[2] Lyrics: Trad / Public Domain.

[3] Reproduced in George Eberhart's chapter of *A Question Of Manhood: A Reader In US Black Men's History (volume 2)*, ed. Earnestine Jenkins & Darlene Clark Hine (Indiana University Press, 2001.)

[4] *Stagolee Shot Billy*, by Cecil Brown (Harvard University Press, 2003).

[5] *Frankie & Johnny*, by John Huston (Benjamin Blom, 1968).

[6] Excerpt from notes taken at Billy Lyons' inquest. Reproduced in (4) above.

[7] *St Louis Globe-Democrat*, 27 December 1895.

[8] *Memphis Down In Dixie*, by Shields McIlwaine (E. P. Dutton, 1948).

[9] *St Louis Globe-Democrat*, issues of 26 June 1896 and 14 July 1896 respectively.

[10] Collected in *American Ballads And Folk Songs*, by John & Alan Lomax (Macmillan, 1934).

[11] Quoted in *Deep Down In The Jungle: Negro Narrative Folklore From The Streets of Philadelphia*, by Roger Abrahams (Folklore Associates, 1964).

[12] Collected in *A Treasury Of American Folklore*, by B. A. Botkin (Bonanza, 1983).

[13] *Fort Wayne Journal-Gazette*, 2 October 1918.

[14] *St Louis Globe-Democrat*, 28 December 1895.

[15] *St Louis Star-Sayings*, 29 December 1895. In (3) above Eberhart gives the killer's name as William Brown, but I can't explain this discrepancy.

[16] *The Misapprehension Of The Coon Image*, by R. Fiore, published in *The Comics Journal*, February 2003.

[17] *Kansas City Kansas Globe*, 3 December 1908.

[18] *A Blues Life*, by Henry Townsend (University of Illinois Press, 1999).

[19] Collected in *The Life: The Lore and Folk Poetry of the Black Hustler*, by Dennis Wepman, Ronald Newman & Murray Binderman (University of Pennsylvania Press, 1976).

[20] Author's interview with Mick Harvey, April 2015.

[21] *Nuthin' But A "g" Thang*, by Eithne Quinn (Columbia University Press, 2005).

[22] Quoted in *Mystery Train: Images Of America In Rock 'n' Roll Music*, by Greil Marcus (Faber & Faber, 1975).

[23] *NME*, 17 December 1994.

[24] *Mojo*, January 1996.

2: Frankie & Johnny

[1] *Frankie & Johnny*, by John Huston (Benjamin Blom, 1968).

[2] *Lakeland Ledger*, 29 May 1975. Some sources say Frankie's testimony here was given at Britt's inquest hearing, others that it's taken from one of her actions against the Hollywood studios. All agree on the wording, however.

[3] *The Real Story Of "Frankie & Johnny"*, by Dudley McClure (published in *Daring Detective Tabloid*, June 1935).

[4] *We Did Them Wrong: The Ballad Of Frankie & Albert*, by Cecil Brown (published in *The Rose & The Briar*, ed. Sean Wilentz & Greil Marcus, W. W. Norton & Co, 2005).

[5] "Frankie And Johnny or You'll Miss Me In The Days To Come", by Leighton Bros. & Ren Shields (Tell Taylor, 1912).

[6] These lyrics appear in the Vaughan Williams Memorial Library's online database.

[7] Reproduced in Huston's book – see (1) above.

[8] *Immortalia*, by A Gentleman About Town (Parthena Press, 1969).

[9] *Lubbock Avalanche-Journal*, 15 February 1942.

[10] *Salt Lake Tribune*, 7 May 1933.

[11] *Harrisburg Telegraph*, 2 March 1935.

[12] *Lubbock Morning Advertiser*, 7 March 1935.

[13] *Oregon Statesman*, 19 October 1939. The paper took a cheap shot at

Frankie in this quote by using phonetic spelling to mock the way she spoke ("figger", "dollah", "pitcher" etc). I've restored the standard spelling here.

[14] *Daily Capital Journal*, 21 October 1939.

[15] *Ottawa Journal*, 18 February 1942.

[16] *Decatur Daily Review*, 21 October, 1939.

[17] *Ottawa Journal*, 25 February 1942.

[18] Figures sourced from *Movie Icons: Mae West*, edited by Paul Duncan (Taschen, 2008).

[19] *Medford Mail Tribune*, 9 January 1952.

[20] Author's interview with Anna Domino, January 2015.

[21] Lyrics: Trad/Domino. Reproduced with Domino's kind permission.

3: Knoxville Girl

[1] Lyrics: Trad / Public Domain.

[2] Willie is a generic name used in many old British ballads, including some of "Knoxville Girl's" source songs. In transferring that name to the American version, the folk process has often given "Knoxville Girl" a very neat triple-syllable internal rhyme: "Oh *Willie dear,* don't *kill me here* / I'm unprepared to die". The Louvins narrowly miss this opportunity by opting for "Willard" instead, but other singers have taken full advantage of it.

[3] *Diaries & Letters Of Philip Henry 1631-1696*, by Philip Henry (Trench & Co, 1882). Many modern transcripts of Henry's diary wrongly date this entry as 20 February 1684, but that's because they've forgotten England had not yet adopted the Gregorian calendar. The Julian calendar, which England clung to until 1752, started each new year on 25 March rather than 1 January, so under that system 1684 had not yet begun when Henry made the crucial entry. This is important, because it establishes his diary entry matches the year given in the Westbury Parish register for Anne's burial and Ichabod's baptism.

[4] *The Pepys Ballads Vol III*, ed. Hyder Edward Rollins (Harvard University Press, 1930).

[5] *American Balladry From British Broadsides*, by G. M. Laws (University of Texas Press, 1957).

[6] "The Bloody Miller", printed by P. Brooksby in Pye Corner, London, and collected in (4) above.

[7] "The Berkshire Tragedy or The Wittham Miller", printer unknown. Transcribed from a copy held by the Bodleian Library, Oxford.

[8] *A Dictionary Of Superstitions*, ed. Iona Opie & Moira Tatem (Oxford University Press, 1989).

[9] *The Cassell Dictionary Of Folklore*, ed. David Pickering (Cassell, 1999).

[10] *The Diary Of Samuel Pepys: Volume VIII*, ed. R. C. Latham & W. Matthews (Harper Collins, 2010).

[11] *The Island Queens*, by John Banks (Augustan Reprint Society, 1995).

[12] "The Lexington Miller", printer unknown. Reprinted in (5) above.

[13] *History Of McDonald County, Missouri*, by Judge J. A. Sturges (publisher unknown, 1897).

[14] "The Noel Girl", collected in *Ozark Folksongs Vol IV*, ed. Vance Randolph (University of Missouri Press, 1980).

[15] "Flora Dean", collected in *English Folk Songs From The Southern Appalachians*, ed. Cecil Sharp & Maud Karpeles (Oxford University Press, 1960).

[16] *Root Hog Or Die*, by Nathan Salsburg (https:\\roothogordie.wordpress.com/posts, 2008).

[17] Author's correspondence with Ruth Gerson, June 2009.

[18] Author's interviews with Ralph Stanley and Ralph Stanley II, February 2015.

4: The Lonesome Death Of Hattie Carroll

[1] *The Afro-American*, 6 July 1963.

[2] *Broadside 48*, July 1964.

[3] *Little Sandy Review*, Summer 1963 issue. Quoted in Heylin (see 23 below).

[4] *Time*, 22 February 1963.

[5] *The Afro-American*, 29 June 1963.

[6] *The Afro-American*, 23 March 1963.

[7] Message board post (www.mudcat.org. 23 February 2006).

[8] *The Afro-American*, 14 December 1963. Pine Street Police Station was responsible for Baltimore PD's Western District – the same area of

the city Jimmy McNulty and his colleagues on *The Wire* would find themselves policing 40 years later.

9   *The Afro-American*, 16 February 1963.

10   *The Baltimore Sun*, 10 February 1963.

11   *The Afro-American*, 23 February 1963.

12   www.findagrave.com.

13   US Dept. Of Veterans' Affairs (www.cem.va.gov).

14   *The Afro-American*, 16 March 1963 and 23 March 1963.

15   *Broadside* 20-23, February and March 1963.

16   Author's correspondence with Calla Smorodin, May 2011.

17   Reproduced in *Broadside* 23, March 1963. I've seen the original clipping attributed to *The Baltimore Sun*, but it's nowhere to be found in that paper's archives. All my own efforts to trace its source have failed.

18   *New York Times*, 28 June 1963.

19   *The Afro-American*, 7 September 1963.

20   *A Regular Old Southern Maryland Boy*, by Peter Carlson (*Washington Post* magazine, 4 August 1991).

21   *The Afro-American*, 26 October 1963.

22   *Down The Highway: The Life Of Bob Dylan*, by Howard Sounes (Doubleday 2001).

23   *Revolution In The Air*, by Clinton Heylin (Constable & Robinson, 2009).

24   Author's interview with Billy Bragg, January 2015.

25   *A Lonesome Death*, by David Simon, published in *The New Yorker*, 26 January 2009.

26   *Dylan's Visions Of Sin*, by Christopher Ricks (Canongate Books, 2011).

27   *Chronicles: Volume One*, by Bob Dylan (Simon & Schuster, 2004).

28   *Bob Dylan: Behind The Shades*, by Clinton Heylin (Penguin Books, 2000).

29   Message board post (www.mudcat.org, 21 May 2009).

30   *Washington Post*, 7 June 1991 and 17 August 1992.

31   *Washington Post*, 7 September 1991.

32   *Washington Post*, 4 January 1992.

33   Lyrics © Billy Bragg. Reproduced with his kind permission

34   Author's interview with Angela Correa, March 2015.

5: Tom Dooley

[1] *Invisible Republic: Bob Dylan's Basement Tapes*, by Greil Marcus (Henry Holt & Co, 1997).

[2] *Hit Singles: Top 20 Charts From 1954 To The Present Day*, ed. Dave McAleer (Carlton Books, 2003).

[3] *Brother, Can You Spare A Rhyme*, by Spencer Leigh (Spencer Leigh Ltd, 2000).

[4] *Folk Song USA*, by John and Alan Lomax (Duell, Sloan & Pierce, 1946).

[5] *Tom Dooley: The Eternal Triangle*, by Rufus Gardner (Rufus Gardner, 1960).

[6] *Lift Up Your Head, Tom Dooley*, by John Foster West (Down Home Press, 1993).

[7] Taken from an 1866 summary of key witnesses' evidence at Dula's Statesville trial. This summary was prepared by Judge Buxton and his court clerk C. L. Summers.

[8] *The New York Herald*, 2 May 1868.

[9] *The Story Of The Ballad Of Tom Dooley*, by James Rucker (Appalachian Heritage, Winter 2008 edition. Published by University of North Carolina Press).

[10] Isbell's newspaper columns were collected into a book called *The World Of My Childhood* (*Lenoir News-Topic*, 1955).

[11] "The Murder Of Laura Foster", by Captain Thomas Land.

[12] *Death In North Carolina's Piedmont*, by Frances H. Casstevens (The History Press, 2006).

[13] *The Daily Dispatch*, 26 October 1866.

[14] *The Frank C. Brown Collection Of North Carolina Folklore*, ed. Frank Brown (Duke University Press, 1952). Sutton names the original tune as "Run Nigger Run, The Patty Roller's After You". A "Patty Roller" (corruption of "patroller") was one of the white vigilantes who pursued runaway slaves.

[15] Unidentified newspaper article, reproduced in (5) above.

[16] *The Statesville American*, November 5, 1868.

[17] *The Viking Book Of Folk Ballads Of The English-Speaking World*, edited by Albert Friedman (Viking Press, 1956).

[18] *The Songs Of Doc Watson*, by Doc Watson (Oak Publications, 1971).

[19] *The Legend Of Tom Dula*, www.unctv.org

[20] Author's interview with Bob Shane, February 2015.

[21] Author's interview with Jon Langford, February 2015.

[22] Lyrics © Angela Correa, reproduced with her kind permission.

[23] Author's interview with Angela Correa, March 2015.

[24] Lyrics © Jerry Lankford , reproduced with his kind permission

6: Pretty Polly

[1] Original transcript held by the Cecil Sharp Manuscript Collection.

[2] Author's interview with Rennie Sparks, January 2015. Sparks wrote her own essay on "Pretty Polly" in *The Rose & The Briar*, edited by Sean Wilentz & Greil Marcus (W. W. Norton, 2005).

[3] Lyrics; Trad/Public domain.

[4] Letter from Thomas Williams, quoted on www.williams.gen.nz

[5] Roxburghe Collection, British Library.

[6] "The Gosport Tragedy", chapbook version, printed by George Caldwell in 1808.

[7] Lyrics: Trad/Bodner. Reproduced with Bodner's kind permission.

[8] Copies of this ballad – also known as "The Sailor's Tragedy" – were in print as early as 1770, but it may be much older than that. The version I've quoted here was collected in Newfoundland by Helen Creighton.

[9] Professor Fowler's essay, titled *The Gosport Tragedy: Story Of A Ballad*, appears in *Southern Folklore Quarterly* vol 43, pages 157–196.

[10] Hook's log of the Bedford (ADM 51/132) and the ship's paybook are both available for study at the UK's National Archive in Kew.

[11] These losses in the Baltic were reported in *The Weekly Journal* of 15 October, 1726.

[12] Author's correspondence with Jennifer Wraight, December 2011.

[13] In his 2010 essay *Scurvy: The Sailor's Nightmare*, Grant Sebastian Nell describes the final stage of scurvy as "a terrible fever which left men raving and ranting before they died".

[14] Unfortunately, the Bedford's records can't tell us whether any other members of the carpenter's gang died on the Baltic voyage. Everyone below a certain rank is marked simply as either an able ("Ab") or an

ordinary ("Ord") seaman, with no indication of what their particular job might be.

[15] *The British Seaman, 1200-1860*, by Christopher Lloyd (Collins, 1968).

[16] Original sheet held by the Bodleian Library.

[17] Original sheet held by the Library of Congress.

[18] *The Cambridge Guide To American Theatre*, ed. Don Wilmeth & Tice Miller (Cambridge University Press, 2007).

[19] *Unprintable Ozark Folk Songs And Folklore Vol 1*, by Vance Randolph (University of Arkansas Press, 1992).

[20] Quoted on www.mudcat.org from an unidentified collection of Sharp's North Carolina songs.

[21] *Banjo Women In West Virginia And Eastern Kentucky*, by Susan A. Eacker (www.marshall.edu).

[22] Author's interviews with Crispin Gray and Katie Jane Garside, January 2012.

[23] Author's interview with Kristin Hersh, January 2012.

[24] Message board post (www.mudcat.org, 17 September 2001).

[25] Author's interview with Jake Speed, January 2012.

[26] Lyrics © Fred Burns. Reproduced with his kind permission.

7: Poor Ellen Smith

[1] Author's interview with Fam Brownlee, April 2015.

[2] *Western Sentinel*, 14 September 1893.

[3] Lyrics: Trad/Public Domain.

[4] *Western Sentinel*, 29 June 1893.

[5] *Union Republican*, 29 June 1893.

[6] *Union Republican*, 8 February 1894.

[7] *Western Sentinel*, 17 August 1893.

[8] *Western Sentinel*, 25 March, 1886.

[9] *Twin-City Daily Sentinel*, 21 July 1892.

[10] *People's Press*, 25 June 1891.

[11] *Union Republican*, 28 July 1892.

[12] *Frank Proffitt Sings Folk Songs* (Folkways Records, 1962).

[13] *Union Republican*, 4 August 1892.

[14] *Twin-City Daily Sentinel*, 4 August 1892.

[15] *Western Sentinel*, 27 October 1892.

[16] Author's interview with Laura Cantrell, March 2015.

[17] *Banjo Women In West Virginia And Eastern Kentucky*, by Susan A. Eacker (www.marshall.edu).

[18] "Ellen Smith", collected by Olive Dame Campbell in Pike County, KY, in 1911. Source: Vaughan Williams Memorial Library.

[19] In this usage, "country" simply means "the area round here".

[20] Author's correspondence with Laura Cantrell, May 2015.

[21] *Western Sentinel*, 7 December 1893.

[22] *Western Sentinel*, 8 February 1894.

[23] *Union Republican*, 11 January 1894.

[24] *Western Sentinel*, 25 January 1894.

[25] *Western Sentinel*, 4 January 1894.

[26] *Winston-Salem Journal*, 20 April, 1975.

[27] *Swinging Into Eternity*, by Fam Brownlee. (https://northcarolinaroom.wordpress.com).

[28] *Banjo Tunes & Songs*, by Pete Steele (Folkways Records, 1958).

[29] Author's interview with Randy Furches, June 2015.

[30] Lyrics © Randy Furches. Reproduced with his kind permission.

8: *Murder Of The Lawson Family*

[1] *The Meaning Of Our Tears*, by Trudy J. Smith (DTS Group, 2006).

[2] *A Christmas Family Tragedy: Legends Of The 1929 Lawson Family Murders*, directed by Matt Hodges (Break of Dawn Productions, 2007).

[3] Author's interview with Dave Alvin, June 2015.

[4] "The Murder Of The Lawson Family". Words & Music by Kid Smith. © Peer International Corp, USA. Reproduced by arrangement.

[5] *Winston-Salem Journal*, 28 December 1929.

[6] *Statesville Record & Landmark*, 3 February 1930.

[7] Author's interview with Patrick Boyles, April 2015.

[8] *Charlotte Observer*, 22 November 1918.

[9] *Twin-City Sentinel*, 5 December 1918.

[10] *The Lawson Family Murder*, by Donald Lee Nelson (*JEMF Quarterly*, University of California, 1973).

[11] *Danbury Reporter*, 18 August 1977.

[12] *White Christmas Bloody Christmas*, by M. Bruce Jones with Trudy J. Smith (UpWords, 1990).

[13] *Winston-Salem Journal*, 27 December 1929.

[14] *Twin-City Sentinel*, 26 December 1929.

[15] *Daily Journal-Gazette*, 26 December 1929.

[16] *King Times-News*, 7 October 1987.

[17] Death certificates supplied by Patrick Boyles.

[18] *Statesville Record & Landmark*, 30 December 1929.

[19] *New York Times*, 27 December 1929.

[20] *Danbury Reporter*, 1 January 1930.

[21] *Twin-City Sentinel*, 27 December 1929.

[22] Author's interview with Richard Miller, April 2015.

[23] *Winston-Salem Journal*, 9 October 1985.

[24] *Danbury Reporter*, 10 May 1945.

[25] Interview with Margarie Quinlin, recorded by song collector Kip Lornell in 1985. (Digital Library of Appalachia: http://dla.acaweb.org).

[26] *Dillinger*, by Dary Matera (Carroll & Graf, 2004).

[27] Charlie Lawson Family Murders message board (http://maria333.proboards.com).

[28] Dr Murray was speaking on BBC Radio 4's *File On 4*. The episode, called *Family Annihilation*, aired on 6 March 2012.

Index

About The Author

Paul Slade is a London journalist. His work's appeared in *The Guardian*, *The Independent*, *The Telegraph*, *The Times*, *Mojo*, *fRoots*, *Time Out*, *Sight & Sound*, *The Idler* and many other publications. He's also made a handful of documentaries for BBC Radio 4, covering subjects such as the craze for innuendo-laden blues lyrics in 1920s America and the history of rap battling. His www.PlanetSlade.com essay on Reg Smythe's *Andy Capp* was ranked one of the ten best articles of 2012 by Longform.org. This is his first book.

For more of my writing, please visit:
www.PlanetSlade.com

The latest material there includes this book's bonus "DVD Extras" section, giving more comments from all the musicians interviewed here, plus a handful of sidebar stories which got squeezed out for reasons of space. Just click the "U2D Bonus" link in my site's blue menu box. Here's what you'll find:

1. Songs
Billy Bragg, Laura Cantrell, Dave Alvin, Rennie Sparks and other leading musicians continue our discussion of their favourite murder ballads. These comments from the book's interviews are the "leftovers" I couldn't bear to waste.

2. Comments
How did you discover murder ballads? Why do we love them so? I asked my interviewees far too many questions for all their answers to fit in the book. These are some of the replies that got squeezed out.

3. Digressions
Other stuff came up too. Includes Jon Langford on putting together *The Executioner's Last Songs* project, Mick Harvey on The Bad Seeds' studio habits and Dave Alvin on killer bees.

4. Postscripts
Every chapter's research uncovered sidebar stories I had no space to include in the book. Meet Charlie Lawson's killer cousin, see how Winston's sheriff was attacked for failing to catch Ellen Smith's killer and join me on a trip to Tom Dula's grave.

5. Playlists.
I've put together a one-hour Spotify playlist for every chapter in this book, each one carefully selecting the most interesting recordings of its song down the decades. To hear these, just go to https://player.spotify.com/browse and search for "U2D" in the Playlists section. If you're not already a Spotify user, you may have to open an account with the site first, but you'll still be able to stream all the music free.